D1614085

The Self in
Social Theory

C. FRED ALFORD

The Self in Social Theory

A Psychoanalytic Account of Its Construction in Plato, Hobbes, Locke, Rawls, and Rousseau

Yale University Press

New Haven and London

Published with assistance from the foundation
established in memory of William McKean Brown.

Designed by April Leidig-Higgins.
Set in Electra type by G & S Typesetters, Inc., Austin, Texas.
Printed in the United States of America by Book Crafters, Inc.,
Chelsea, Michigan.

Library of Congress Cataloging-in-Publication Data
Alford, C. Fred.
      The self in social theory : a psychoanalytic account of its
   construction in Plato, Hobbes, Locke, Rawls, and Rousseau /
   C. Fred Alford.
          p.   cm.
   Includes bibliographical references and index.
      ISBN 0-300-04922-6
      1. Self (Philosophy)—History.   2. Social sciences—Phi-
   losophy—History.   3. Social sciences and psychoanalysis.
   4. Psychoanalysis and philosophy.   5. Self psychology.
   I. Title.
   BD450.A459   1991
   126'.09—dc20   90-39887
                                                         CIP

The paper in this book meets the guidelines for permanence and
durability of the Committee on Production Guidelines for Book
Longevity of the Council on Library Resources.

10   9   8   7   6   5   4   3   2   1

Contents

Preface

Authors praise the self, blame the self, deconstruct the self, and say it isn't there. The self is the locus of all value, the source of a rapacious individualism that is destroying Western society, and little more than the mirror of its culture. All this and more has been claimed about the self in recent works. Yet few who have claimed any of these things have made a systematic study of the entity they are writing about. Perhaps this is because the self seems not so much an entity as an idea. Or rather, the logical consequence of other ideas about freedom, responsibility, the good society, and so forth. This book seeks to go at the issue from the other direction, so to speak. From authors' assumptions about freedom, responsibility, and so forth I seek to make explicit their concepts of the self. Along the way I occasionally write about the real self, more to incite those who assume that such an entity could not exist than because I assume that it absolutely must. (Actually, this debate has more to do with how one defines *real* than anything else, as any philosopher of science could tell you.)

Although I value a particular construction of the self, my primary concern is not to defend it against all others. It is rather to render explicit the implicit, often inchoate, assumptions about the self held by Plato, Hobbes, Locke, Rawls, and Rousseau. These authors, like all who write on this topic, make trade-offs between the value of the self and other values, such as social peace. They are willing, in other words, to weaken, split, and shatter the integrity of the self, in order to render it more tractable or more ideal. There is probably no alternative. A society of integral, ideal selves is not possible . . . and perhaps not even desirable. Nevertheless, how one bends the self to suit other goals and the degree to which one does so are important. This issue, however, cannot be addressed—indeed, cannot even be raised—unless one possesses a developed concept of the self in the first place. My goal is to raise this issue and so render the self more than the dependent variable in this or that social theory. In so doing I am, of course, defending a particular view of the self. It is, however, a commodious view, with ample room for nonliberal, nonindividualistic conceptions, as shown in chapter 9, particularly.

vii

Alfonso Damico, Ronald Terchek, and James Glass all read portions of this manuscript. Damico raised some substantial objections to the Locke chapter, particularly. I have kept them in mind but have probably not addressed all of them successfully. Terchek made a number of helpful comments, all of which reveal his understanding and appreciation (though perhaps not his agreement) of what I am trying to do. That is always a pleasure for an author. Glass, who knows truths about the self that most authors, including myself, barely glimpse, made a number of helpful suggestions regarding the organization of the manuscript. Charles Butterworth helped with several technical points regarding the interpretation of Rousseau, but he has not read the manuscript. Elaine Feder Alford helped with the section on sociological views of the self. Through three books, my editors at Yale, Gladys Topkis and Jeanne Ferris, have been a pleasure to work with.

The Self in
Social Theory

The self is human nature
insofar as we can know it as
a subject of humane study.

CHAPTER ONE

Metaphysical
Selves, Real Selves

Several years ago, *Social Research* devoted a special issue to Reflections on the Self. In his introduction to the issue, James Walkup suggests that a concern with the self and its value is the only remaining tenet of the Western tradition still able to command general assent.[1] Recent political theory seems to affirm this claim. Communitarians such as Michael Sandel criticize liberals such as John Rawls for holding an insubstantial concept of the self, one that "makes the individual inviolable only by making him invisible."[2] Yet the terms of the debate have changed. Whereas once liberals were accused of holding faulty empirical views about the self, reducing it to a "possessive individualist" and the like, today liberals and their critics generally proceed at an abstract metaphysical plane. Accusing Rawls of holding an abstract, metaphysical view of the self, Sandel responds with a different but equally abstract and metaphysical view.[3] To controvert this tendency in recent political theory to value the self only as an abstract theoretical entity, a postulate in social theory, is the purpose of this book.

Associated with the metaphysical focus on the self is a tendency toward dualism: that the self is either a socially constituted entity or a self-constituting one but never both. Thus, as Amy Gutmann points out, Sandel criticizes Rawls for betraying "incompatible commitments" by combining into one theory both "intersubjective and individualistic images."[4] As though the most obvious and compelling thing about the self were not that it is both. A source of this dualism lies in the metaphysical character of the debate, the way it has less and less to do with real selves, more and more with metaphysical and philosophical derivations of the self from universal principles. This tendency toward abstraction is reinforced by recent developments in philosophy both on the Continent and in North America. In the same issue of *Social Research* in which Walkup posits the self as a source of value, Amelie Oksenberg Rorty argues that the self does not exist. It is a rhetorical construct, employed to make philosophical, legal, and political claims by attributing certain rights, duties, and so forth to particular beings but having no significance beyond this.[5] Continental deconstructionists of the self, such as Jacques Lacan, carry this argument further, asserting not only that the self does not exist but that what we take to be the self is actually a symptom of our inability to accept our own inauthenticity.

In the next chapter I devote considerable attention, much of it favorable, to Lacan. I do not seek to establish the value of the self by an act of wild self-assertion that in the end can only corroborate the thesis of Lacan, Foucault, and others: that when the self is not deceiving itself, it is but an assertion of the will to power. My purpose is not to deconstruct the self but to reconstruct it. Drawing upon the work of Heinz Kohut and Jacques Lacan, I develop a psychoanalytic perspective on the self which in subsequent chapters I apply to accounts of the self found in Plato, Hobbes, Locke, Rawls, and Rousseau. All but Plato are state of nature theorists, and the state of nature they are concerned with is human nature: thus the epigraph at the beginning of this chapter. Most important, these theorists build their accounts on real, empirical (not necessarily true, of course), often troubling assumptions about the self. In demonstrating this I hope to counteract the recent tendency to see the self strictly as an abstract metaphysical entity, if not a fraud.

This same point can be expressed in a slightly different fashion. The methodology or concepts that we use to explain the self are not separate from how we value it. Conceptualizing the self as an abstract metaphysical entity leads to a way of thinking that in the end values not the self but the abstract principles from which it is derived. Amelie Rorty's argument is the epitome of such a view, but it is also found, it will be shown, in Sandel. Conversely, focusing upon actual, real selves fosters (though it does not logically require) an appreciation of the self for its own sake as a center of value, not a derivation from "higher" values. This is so even when an empirical approach requires that we recognize some unpleasant aspects of the self. Psychoanalytic deconstructionists, such as Lacan, transform the unconscious into a type of text, arguing that it is not the case that the self uses language; rather, language uses the self. My approach is in some ways the opposite. My reading of texts about the self will seek to uncover claims about real selves. This will require the development of a psychoanalytic theory of reading, one of the tasks of the next chapter.

Who Needs a Theory of the Self?

The position of many social theorists regarding the self seems to be something like the following. Of course, the self exists, and it is valuable. But for every claim about the self, it seems that an opposite and equal claim can be made. Furthermore, there seems no way to test various claims about the self, just as there is virtually no way to test human nature. Fortunately, detailed knowledge about the self is unnecessary. A rudimentary knowledge or model of the self, coupled with our fairly extensive knowledge of institutions, will usually suffice.[6] That it is usually groups rather than individuals that we wish to explain only reinforces these considerations. There is no group self but only group behavior. That the economic model of people based on a simplified, stimulus-response view of the self, generates sophisticated predictions regarding the outcome of various interactions among producers, consumers, and so forth may be cited in support of this claim. Nor is the economic model the only workable simplified model. Models of strategic man (Thomas Schelling), bureaucratic man (Max Weber), and so forth have all been fruitful.[7] More subtle and complex models may be interesting, but they are not necessary to do real social science.

A few paragraphs cannot assuage these concerns. The totality of this book may. Here I can only refer again to the epigraph at the head of this chapter. Political theorists have always been concerned with human nature and from two directions. For classic authors, such as Plato, the core questions are the nature of the good man and how politics can support and foster him. For moderns, the question is often reversed. How can society be organized so as to control the worst aspects of human nature and so allow people to live in peace? Today many theorists regard such questions as a little naive, as though human nature actually exists. And perhaps it does not, at least not in any fixed sense. This does not mean, however, that it is pointless to address those attributes of human nature with which these authors were concerned: desire, hubris, fear, ambition, lust, greed, envy, hatred, rage, aggression—and even love; feelings of emptiness, meaninglessness, and purpose. To write of the self is to write of the constellations, or patterns, within which these passions, emotions, needs, and fears are held. The self may change dramatically over time and across cultures, which means that the ways in which these attributes are patterned will vary. That these attributes *are* patterned is what is meant by the self. And in the end who would argue that the way in which they are organized is either irrelevant to political theory or a mere sidebar to the real action?

Why philosophers should feel the need to conceptualize an entity called the self is easy to understand. Hume conceived of the self as a strictly relational entity in order to explain how disjoint experiences of discrete sensations, feelings, and images could be rendered meaningful. His answer was the "bundle concept of the self," in which it is the self, using categories such as resemblance, succession, and causation, that provides the hidden thread holding discrete experience together: "There are some philosophers who imagine we are every moment intimately conscious of what we call our SELF . . . . But setting aside some metaphysicians of this kind, I may venture to affirm . . . [that the self is] nothing but a bundle or collection of different perceptions."[8] Kant's objection is famous: if events are as "loose and separate" as Hume supposed, then not only would we be deprived of any insight into the connections of things but we would have no unitary consciousness at all. To explain the unity of perception requires the assumption of a transcendental subject who can connect experience according to particular universal laws: "Therefore the original and necessary consciousness of the identity of oneself is at the same time a consciousness of an equally necessary unity of the synthesis of all phenomena according to . . . rules, which render them not only necessarily reproducible, but assign to their intuition an object."[9]

Today, of course, it is generally held that Kant moved too quickly from the correct assumption that the unity of consciousness requires rules of connection (which may be identified with the self) to the false conclusion that these must be transcendental reality-constitutive rules rather than actual empirical ones, such as those discovered by Piaget. Although their concerns were epistemological and metaphysical rather than psychological and political, the issues raised by Hume and Kant continue to frame most discussions of the self. They frame my discussion, too (my position falls somewhere in between), in which I argue that we can define the self as the way in which we organize, or bundle, our passions, particularly those that concern how we use others to support our sense of self.

In conceptualizing the self, I make no fundamental distinctions among self, ego, I, me, the person, the subject, or the individual. To be sure, sometimes it will be useful to contrast different senses of the self, senses captured by these terms. Lacan's distinction between ego and subject is especially fruitful. Such distinctions are not, however, theoretically fundamental; they do not structure the analysis. Consequently, arguments such as whether

.Freud's ego is tantamount to the self, or whether the self is a representation in the ego or an alternative to it, will play only a small role in the analysis. The self is the individual, the subject, and the object of psychology and social theory. Yet he or she is not merely this. In the everyday sense of the term, at least in the Western world, *self* connotes not merely "the permanent subject of successive and varying states of consciousness" but self-direction and self-control.[10] A psychoanalytic view of the self cannot leave this sense of the term too far behind either (i.e., it should not ignore it, though it may challenge it), even as it may, as in the case of Lacan, show such experiences of the self as defense or bad faith.

These considerations lead me to reject or qualify a number of views of the self popular in academic literature, particularly psychoanalysis and sociology. Rejected is any view of the self as a little person in the machine, sometimes used to explain a particular action because it does or does not meet the needs of the "inner self." Such explanations tend to be tautological. For similar reasons I reject the view of Otto Kernberg who, though he is not an ego psychologist, like many who are, views the self as an internal representation, an internal image with various dimensions such as self as reflection of parents' ideals, self as carrier of narcissistic grandiosity, and so forth. I reject this view not because it is false, for clearly something like it is the case, but because of the way it separates self from ego, which presumably *has* this representation. Consequently, this view too tends to lead to a tautological explanation along the lines of "He did not do it because it contradicted his self-image."

By formulating these rejections as assertions, I am glossing over some important distinctions—such as that between self as representation, self as idea, and self as an internal image or inner picture of the individual. It is these distinctions that distinguish the positions of the early Heinz Kohut, Roy Schafer, Edith Jacobson, and Otto Kernberg, psychoanalysts concerned with the self. Although I will take up several of these distinctions later, they are not central to my argument. Thus, though some distinctions are simply specious, others are important but not directly relevant. That a particular distinction is not taken up does not automatically consign it to the first category.

The Social Self

More relevant is the sociological view of the self, the social self. At the heart of the concept of the social self is the ability to see oneself as one sees others, to become an object to oneself much as other persons are objects to us. It is this ability that "is the core of the concept of the self," according to the sociologist George McCall. Of course, this view of the social self is not unique to sociologists. It unites otherwise very different views of the self, such as those of Adam Smith and David Hume, and even the Kantian duality of self as the knower and the known, subject and object of consciousness. What the American philosopher-sociologists added, says McCall, was the idea that the central means through which a person sees himself is the reactions of others. This social self Cooley called the "reflected or looking-glass self." It has, according to Cooley, three parts: (1) how we imagine we appear to the other; (2) how we imagine the other judges us; and (3) pride or mortification as a consequence of number 2. Cooley goes on to argue, however, that the looking-glass metaphor does not really capture the second element. Our imagination regarding the judgment of others is a more active, constructive process than that suggested by a looking glass.[11]

The sociologist Robert Park better captures the second element, with the metaphor of living in each other's minds. What makes human conduct unique, in this view, is that it is oriented toward the reactions of others. "It is in this social conflict, in which every individual lives more or less in the mind of every other individual, that human nature and the individual may acquire their most characteristic and human traits."[12] To this view Erving Goffman has added an important emphasis. His dramaturgical model, an exaggerated version of the looking-glass self, stresses the great conventionalizing influence of such a self, constantly regulating itself to the expectations of others and dependent for its very existence on their responses.[13]

Such a view is not simply false; indeed, it finds significant echoes in the work of Kohut and Lacan. Nor is this view deficient because it ignores depth psychology. Were it possible to explain everything important without reference to depth psychology, then depth psychology would be unnecessary. The sociological view is incomplete because it has great difficulty explaining the individual, the exception. It can explain, for example, why most obey the authorities but not (at least not in a nontrivial way) why Luther, Ghandi, or Sharansky opposed them. For this we require, at a minimum, something like Erik Erikson's concept of individual identity, which represents the convergence of the psychological development of the self with the social position of the individual. As Theodore Mischel puts it, "there is no point to stretching the concept of 'social identity' to cover not only tinker and tailor but also 'compassionate person,' because the distinction . . . is not a distinction that can be explicated in terms of social roles," at least not without making social roles trivial.[14] Similarly, though there are probably many marriages that can be adequately explained in terms of the social roles of "husband" and "wife," to the degree this is the case we must say that the relationship lacks intimacy, depth, personality. Since we want to explain both the deepest sources of intimacy and resistance to authority as well as the way in which both may be corrupted by social expectations, we require more than an explanation of the social self. At the same time we cannot leave the social self behind, in part because it helps explain the corruption of intimacy and autonomy.

On Human Agency

In his classic "What Is Human Agency?" Charles Taylor distinguishes between the strong and the weak evaluator. For the weak evaluator, the function of the self is to weigh desires and evaluate how they might best be met, taking into account the intensity of desire, that desires may conflict, that they may have undesirable consequences, and so forth. Such an individual, says Taylor, is fully rational and a complete self. Nevertheless, he continues, the person lacks depth. What gives the self depth is its willingness and ability to evaluate the quality of its desires, an evaluation that employs categories such as higher and lower, noble and base, courageous and cowardly, integrated and fragmented. Taylor's argument is important because it explicitly links rational reflection, what Taylor calls second-order evaluation, and the concept of the self. "I have been exploring," he says, "some aspects of a self or human agent, following the key notion that a crucial feature of human agency is the capacity for second-order desires or evaluation of desires . . . . Our identity is therefore defined by certain evaluations which are inseparable from ourselves as agents. Shorn of these we would cease to be ourselves."[15]

Others too have written about the decline of the second-order evaluator, generally in terms of the decline of a culture that can support a distinction between higher and lower desires, higher and lower expressions of the self. This is the theme of Alasdair MacIntyre's study of the decline of the "narrative self," as he calls it, in *After Virtue*. Allan Bloom's brief remarks, in a chapter called "The Self" in *The Closing of the American Mind*, are aimed in a similar direction.[16] The virtue of these two works is that they appreciate how the depth of the self depends in good measure on the depth of the cultural resources available to it. Their drawback is that they risk equating the self with its culture. In this respect their position is similar to that of Michael Oakeshott. As John Passmore puts it in a review of *The Voice of Liberal Learning: Michael Oakeshott on Education*, "For Oakeshott, of course, understanding the self is understanding a culture; there is no separate entity, 'the self,' to be explored by introspection."[17]

Taylor's piece is fruitful because he connects self and culture without reducing one to the other. (As will be shown later, Taylor does not do this quite so well in his recent book *Sources of the Self.*) He thus appreciates that organized introspection and empathy—that is, psychoanalysis—might be helpful in understanding their relationship. One reason Taylor is able to reach this conclusion is that he appreciates that not all psychoanalysis is Freudian or concerned with the vicissitudes of the drives. Rather, Taylor turns to Heinz Kohut's self psychology, arguing that the ability of the self to make second-order evaluations depends upon those aspects of the self analyzed by Kohut, such as its ability to integrate its ambitions and ideals. This will in turn depend in part upon the cultural resources the self has to draw upon. There is a connection between the self, the way it reasons and evaluates, and its culture. But this is only a connection, not an identity. A psychoanalysis that focuses upon the self can help us understand some of these connections. Taylor concludes his essay this way:

> Thus I believe that there are links between the rather groping remarks about identity in this paper and the much more fully developed notion of a "cohesive self" that Kohut and Ernest Wolf have introduced. These links would greatly repay further exploration. They are made all the closer in that Kohut and Wolf are not working with a drive or psychic "force" view of motivation. . . . The prospect of psychoanalytic theory which could give an adequate account of the genesis of full human responsibility, without recourse to such global and reified mechanisms as the super-ego, and with a truly plausible account of the shared subjectivity from which the mature cohesive self must emerge, is a very exciting prospect indeed.[18]

It is toward this prospect that this book is aimed. But in contrast to Taylor (and also to Kohut), the approach taken here places more emphasis on the way fear and desire divide the self against itself. The self is never as whole, never as coherent, never quite as much master of itself, as Taylor and Kohut sometimes suggest. Not only are our second-order evaluations frequently rationalizations of desire rather than evaluations of them, but there is a fluidity and instability to the self, even in the best of circumstances, that gives rise to the experience of a lack in the self, what Jacques Lacan calls a lack (*manque*) in human subjectivity. It is for this reason that I employ Lacan in chapter 2 to decenter Kohut—that is, to overcome a certain philosophical utopianism in Kohut's account of the autonomy and cohesion of the normal, healthy self.

Since Michael Sandel and Charles Taylor are the subjects of so much mutual admiration, it may be surprising that it is Sandel's *Liberalism and the Limits of Justice* that best exemplifies the way of thinking about the self that I set out to criticize. But this is really the point. Taylor takes the first and most important step, recognizing that if we are to do political philosophy intelligently, we must write about the self. Sandel writes about the self, and Taylor concludes that "this is political philosophy on the level it should be written, confronting our moral beliefs with our best understanding of human nature."[19] My goal is to take the next step. Applying the self psychology of Kohut to theorists who wrote of actual selves shows why abstract, philosophical, metaphysical discussions of the self—particularly when one writes as if one is discussing real selves, "human nature"—risks devaluing the self in the name of protecting it.

Sandel's book is organized around his criticism of Rawls's *A Theory of Justice*. Although a very different interpretation of Rawls will be offered in chapter 7, it cannot be denied that many of Sandel's criticisms hit home. The very idea of a subject (Sandel treats this term as synonymous with the self) prior to its values, goals, desires, talents, and possessions seems not so much suspect as unimaginable. What is clear, as Sandel suggests, is that such a self has more to do with solving a philosophical problem—how to establish the priority of right over the good—than it does with grounding a theory of justice in the needs of real individuals. Rawls's thin concept of the self, designed to protect the self from the contingencies of its environment, calls "into question the dignity and autonomy this liberalism seeks above all to secure."[20] A self shorn of its interests, ends, talents, goals, and relationships with others, even if it could be imagined, is a self that seems hardly worth protecting. Moreover, Rawls's ideal community does not sufficiently penetrate the selves of its members to generate the type of fellow-feeling and individual sacrifice that equality and mutuality require. Only when individuals define themselves in terms of the good they share with others are they willing to make the necessary sacrifices to keep such a community going. In a word, individuals tend toward self-interest. But if they live in a community in which the boundary of the self is extended so as to include the good of others, then self-interest will be broadened, too.

Not only are many of Sandel's criticisms trenchant, but several of his otherwise puzzling comments regarding the psychological limits of individualism actually make a good deal of sense from a psychoanalytic point of view. Thus Sandel argues that in certain moral circumstances "the relevant description of the self may embrace more than a single, individual human being."[21] Conversely, he argues that sometimes it makes sense to talk of multiple selves inhabiting a single human being, as when conflicting desires seem to divide the self or when a conversion experience leads us to talk in terms of "the self I once was" and "the self I am now." Norman O. Brown, quoting the analyst R. E. Money-Kyrle, puts it this way: "The existence of the 'let's pretend' boundary does not prevent the continuance of the real traffic across it. . . . 'There is a continual unconscious wandering of other personalities into ourselves.' Every person, then, is many persons; a multitude made into one person."[22] Whatever the inadequacies of Sandel's account, they do not stem from his view of the self as penetrated by other selves, constituted by them and constituting other selves in turn. These insights are the stuff of depth psychology.

The problem is that Sandel does not use these psychological insights to construct a concept of the self, employing this theory to explore the interaction of self and others. Instead, he abandons attempts to conceptualize the self at this point (even though the terms *self* and *subject* continue to appear), using insights like these to justify his treatment of the self as in effect no more than an instance of its community. In fact, these insights support only the weaker (and actually far more interesting) claim that the self is not self-constituting—it is formed in constant interaction with its community. There is thus no midpoint in Sandel's discussion of the self, no sense that the self might best be conceived of as an active entity, profoundly influenced by its community, but not a mere reflection, outgrowth, or extension of this community either. It is this lack of a midpoint—which means, in effect, that Sandel conceptualizes the self as a reflection of its environment rather than a subject in interaction with it—that leads him, almost without pause, to switch from writing about a socially constituted self to "a constitutive conception of community." One could argue, of course, that the concept of a community that constitutes the selves of its members is but the counterpart of the socially constituted self. Sandel, however, treats it not as counterpart but as equivalent.[23] They are the same thing; there is no difference between them. Self is community writ small.

Perhaps the best evidence for this claim is the way in which Sandel's discussion of the self deviates from Taylor's. Sandel argues that the Rawlsian self cannot be a strong evaluator in Taylor's sense, but only a simple weigher.[24] But neither can the self that Sandel writes of, unless, that is, one is willing to identify the evaluation of the community with the individual's evaluation, which seems to miss the point. More important, none of the terms or their cognates that Taylor uses to characterize the person, the human subject, plays any role in Sandel's account. For Taylor, the self "creates" significance, "reflects" on its desires, "judges" itself and others, and "chooses" well or foolishly—active verbs that find no place in Sandel's account of the constituted self.[25] Even the less active experience of feeling oneself to be a historical person, located at the nexus where past and future meet—what MacIntyre calls a "narrative self"—is unrepresented in Sandel's work. To be sure, Sandel identifies the dangers associated with what he euphemistically calls the "radically situated self" that risks "drowning in a sea of circumstance."[26] But identifying the dangers is no substitute for doing something about them, taking them up in some way, which Sandel does not do. For the Rawlsian self so abstract that it becomes invisible, Sandel substitutes a self that is not so much abstract as contentless. Or rather, its content becomes identical with the values, goals, and beliefs of its community.

The reader sympathetic to Sandel might argue that this criticism takes his work out of context. Sandel emphasizes the constitutive community only because Rawls and other liberals so emphasize the inviolable-invisible self. Perhaps. But it is worth noting that not once in *Liberalism and the Limits of Justice* does Sandel characterize the self in terms of its actions or emotions. Stephen Toulmin points out that in common, everyday use, the term *self* usually refers to some aspect of autonomy, choice, or freedom.[27] Certainly this is reflected in the definition of *self* from the *Oxford English Dictionary* mentioned earlier. Sandel might have begun with this everyday concept, challenging and revising it along the way, showing how it is both right and wrong, revealing and concealing, much as some Marxists criticize ideology. Not only does Sandel not do this; he does not really characterize the self at all other than as being constituted by the community. The self is always an object, never an active subject. In reality, of course, it is both. The reason is evidently not because Sandel believes that the self has no attributes, no constitutive powers of its own, but rather that though he writes of the self, he is actually interested in solving a problem in social and political theory: showing that Rawls's theory of justice "depends ultimately for its coherence on precisely the intersubjective dimension he officially rejects" (i.e., treating assets as common property makes sense only if we regard the self as something held in common, too).[28] In this solution the self is not a phenomenon to be studied. It is more akin to a strictly formal assumption, or an arbitrary constant, necessary for the solution of a theoretical problem but having no importance or existence outside this problem context.

Charles Taylor suggests that one reason academic accounts of the self are frequently so removed from common experience is that the academic is not really concerned with understanding or explaining the self at all. He or she is instead concerned with explaining something else—for example, social inequality. The concept of the self adopted by the academic is chosen strictly with this goal in mind: not what concept best captures the manifold experiences of the self but what concept best allows us to predict or derive something else, perhaps an esteemed value such as community.[29] One might argue that if this is what Sandel is doing, then all he need do is acknowledge it in an introductory paragraph. The problem is not Sandel's practice but simply his confusion of "scientific" concepts of the self with experiential ones.

Much of this book will be directed toward demonstrating why such a clarification would be insufficient. The basic argument is this. If our accounts of the self are not directed toward real selves, then not only do we fail to understand the self, but we no longer know or understand what it is we value. It is quite possible, as the politics of countless nations reveal, to esteem abstract metaphysical ideals of the self (the worker, the citizen, the soldier, the all-American boy) while ignoring the interests of real selves. To be sure, even the real self is an abstraction, the "person as rhetorical category," as Amelie Rorty has it. Today, more than ever before, we are reminded of this by various intellectual movements, such as deconstruction on the Continent and analytical philosophy in the United States. Nevertheless, there are differences in the degree of abstraction. Some concepts and representations come closer to reality than others. In this claim the doctrine of intertextuality is rejected, which in its extreme form holds that texts are only about other texts, never about the world (the world as wall-to-wall text is how Edward Said puts it).[30] In fact, the great enemy of the ideal of mediated presence (in this context, the idea that some concepts come closer to reality than others) is unmediated presence: that if our concepts cannot capture reality perfectly and completely, then one is as good as another. It is from this perspective that I will argue that we can learn from Lacan about the self without accepting his conclusions.

It is a puzzle. Why would Sandel criticize Rawls for holding an abstract metaphysical view of the self and then oppose to this self a socially constituted self that is equally, if not more, abstract? To be sure, Sandel is not alone in this regard. As Amy Gutmann suggests, much of the communitarian criticism of liberalism in recent years has been aimed at the metaphysical assumptions about the self held by liberals such as Rawls (I assume for the time being that Rawls is a liberal). Against these metaphysical assumptions, these critics invoke *other* metaphysical assumptions. Among these critics Gutmann includes Alasdair MacIntyre, Benjamin Barber (*Strong Democracy*), and Roberto Unger (*Knowledge and Politics*).[31] To be sure, the metaphysical proclivities of these authors vary considerably. Barber is quite down to earth, whereas Unger writes like a nineteenth-century Continental idealist for whom "everything false in the [liberal] doctrine results from its disregard of the mode of union between self and world."[32] Nevertheless, this turn toward conceptualizing the self in terms most abstract can hardly be denied. This will become clearer in subsequent chapters, where I will argue that Plato, Hobbes, Locke, Rousseau, and even Rawls write about the self in quite different, far more substantial, terms. Can it be that the metaphysical character of the Rawlsian self, at least as these critics see it, has so structured the debate that even when critics disagree with particular metaphysical assumptions, they accept that this is the proper level of analysis?

This does not seem a complete explanation, and another possibility suggests itself. At least some of these authors, such as Sandel, seem to believe that it is by not privileging the self in our *theories* that we quell its possessive, individualistic tendencies in *practice*. If we do not write about the self qua self, then maybe it will go away. Conversely, those who put the self at the center of their theories contribute to the imperialism of the self in practice. Political individualism is inseparable from the analytic study of the individual. One is reminded of Freud's comments in *Totem and Taboo* on the narcissism of primitive thought, in which it is believed that thought influences reality just as readily as action does.[33] Of course, thought does influence reality. Marx writing in the British Museum is a classic example. Nevertheless, there does seem to be an element of denial among those who appear to write about the self but do not. It is as though they have said to themselves "We dare not look that entity in the eye whose acquisitive imperialism we are trying to overcome, lest we be overwhelmed by its greed and aggressiveness."

Rather, we must approach it indirectly (like Medusa, who could be safely glimpsed only in reflection) from the top down, via a veil of abstractions, in order to try to contain it. It is the great achievement of Plato, Hobbes, Locke, Rawls, and Rousseau that each faced this problem directly. Each looked the self in the face, blinked once or twice, and went on to confront its fearful, desirous, domineering nature, designing institutions and psychologies to contain it. They were not always right, of course, but they did not retreat into abstractions, at least not without first confronting the self.

The Narrative Self

Is Alasdair MacIntyre the theorist who fills in the gaps in Sandel's account of the self? He comes close, but a gap remains. For MacIntyre, reason is not an independent function. Whether an argument is rationally convincing or not depends on what values or attitudes the individual has internalized as part of himself. In a sense, MacIntyre does for reason what Sandel does for community, showing how reason also depends upon the antecedent commitments of the self. As Thomas Nagel says in a review of MacIntyre's *Whose Justice? Which Rationality?* what appeals to MacIntyre about traditions

> is that they give their members something more basic than arguments and justifications to ground their moral convictions in; they actually create persons whose nature is such that certain things count without question as reasons, justifications and criticisms for them—they generate the dispositions of thought and character on which reasoning of that kind depends; and thus provide a confidence in the results which reason alone is powerless to bestow.[34]

Instead of pure reason, what is needed is a "self whose unity resides in the unity of a narrative which links birth to death as narrative beginning to middle to end."[35] Such a narrative is supplied by tradition. It is tradition, internalized, that allows us to be responsible, accountable selves who can see a meaning in life. Traditions tell us what the human good is, how to seek it, as well as providing standards of success and failure. This is what gives a life narrative unity.

MacIntyre's account has the great virtue of demystifying the self. It is not some ineffable entity but straightforward things moderns have nonetheless almost forgotten: a sense of one's place in history, even it is just a tiny place, one link toward the end of the Great Chain of Being; a sense of purpose and accountability; standards for success and failure; and so forth. The disadvantage of MacIntyre's account is that like Sandel, MacIntyre identifies the self with tradition and community so thoroughly that nothing is left over. Once again the self is community writ small. Thus, in response to the question of how we should approach difficult moral choices, MacIntyre answers in *Whose Justice? Which Rationality?* "that will depend upon who you are and how you understand yourself."[36] As MacIntyre makes clear, *this* question is answered when one figures out which tradition one belongs to. Period.

Yet, as Emily Gill points out, *After Virtue* and some other works by MacIntyre seem to appreciate the complexity of this issue. For though the self's identity is indeed constituted by its membership in the community, this, says MacIntyre, "does not entail that the self has to accept the moral limitations of the particularity of those forms of community. . . . It is in moving forward from such particularity that the search for the good, for the universal consists. Yet particularity can never be simply left behind or obliterated."[37] Constituted by the community, never able to escape it, the self nevertheless is able to challenge its community. It may do so by drawing upon the resources of another tradition or upon competing strands of its own. But the question is never, insists MacIntyre, "what code ought I as rational person to adopt? but rather How ought *we* as members of this particular community, sharing these particular beliefs, inheriting this particular moral tradition or traditions, to resolve this issue?"[38]

It is through conflicts such as this, suggests MacIntyre, that the self makes itself, defines itself, confronting conflicts, even tragic ones, learning more clearly about its goals and purposes.[39] Conversely, a key problem with liberal society is that its absence of a coherent hierarchy of values means that the self can escape conflicts by "compartmentalizing its attitudes." Not required to face its conflicts and thus unable to "organize its menu," as Lacan puts it, the liberal self is characterized by what MacIntyre calls "schism and conflict within the self. . . . Lacan . . . remind[s] us that this issue of the unity and division of the self, how it is to be characterized and how, if at all, it is to be dealt with in practical life, arises for all the traditions which have been discussed and not only for liberalism. Nonetheless, it *is* a problem for liberalism."[40] Presumably it is a *greater* problem for liberalism, but on this decisive point MacIntyre waffles. It is an important point, of course, for if liberalism is no more split than other traditions, this suggests that the splits stem from within; they are not a mere reflection of the culture, as MacIntyre

generally treats them. In any case, MacIntyre argues that the self under liberalism is unable to construct a narrative unity out of its life, as the culture is
too fragmented to provide the materials. It is this phenomenon that is mir-
rored by the liberal self's separation of its values into separate watertight com-
partments. In *Narcissism: Socrates, the Frankfurt School, and Psychoanalytic
Theory*, I have shown the similarity between this self and the self that Christopher Lasch writes of in *The Culture of Narcissism*.[41]

MacIntyre's account is an improvement over Sandel's, for MacIntyre
leaves room for an active self, whom Taylor calls a second-order evaluator,
capable of challenging the tradition it is situated in, albeit always from within
the constraints of tradition. None of my criticisms of MacIntyre is aimed at
this last point: that selves are constituted by traditions and never leave them,
except to join other constitutive traditions. Indeed, this point is one of
the clear cases in which metaphysics, epistemology, and the psychology of
the self intersect: as the self is not self-constituting, neither are its knowledge
claims. Nevertheless, to recognize this does not answer all the things we
should like to know. For example, why is it that some selves are better able to
stand back from (not outside) their traditions than others? And why is it that
some traditions, more readily than others, foster selves that are able to stand
back? Presumably the answer has in good measure to do with the *interaction*
of self and tradition, and this requires a fuller account of the self. One is
reminded of Mischel's criticism of role theory noted above. What one wants
to explain is not merely that people are constituted by traditions but why
some are able to challenge these traditions and how far back they are able to
step from them in order to do so. This is not merely a metaphysical or epistemological issue. It is also a psychological one. MacIntyre explains at an
epistemological level what it takes to challenge a tradition, but he does not
come close to explaining why some selves challenge traditions and others do
not, and what it takes to foster such selves. Yet it seems that this is precisely
what we want to know in order to build a good society. MacIntyre's is not just
a metaphysical account of the self, but it tends to confuse metaphysical selves
with real ones.

In the last analysis, MacIntyre's remains a mirror-model of the self: the self
is the reflection of its traditions. Unlike Sandel, MacIntyre explains *why*
such a self need not drown in its tradition, but the explanation proceeds almost completely at the level of traditions themselves—for example, the complexity of traditions fosters immanent critique. It is as though traditions were
the real actors and selves merely their carriers. The narrative unity of the self

is more about the unity of narratives than the unity of the self. MacIntyre has a more subtle and sophisticated view of traditions and communities than does Sandel, but not always a more subtle and sophisticated view of the self (although occasionally he does, as when he refers to the self's tendency to split when faced with difficult choices and, conversely, observes that personal growth occurs when difficult choices are faced). Yet in the end even MacIntyre's psychological theses seem aimed at the psychoanalysis of traditions, the assumption being that the unity of the self is a direct reflection of the unity of its tradition. In the next chapter I will emphasize the *activity* of splitting, the way in which it is not merely a *response* to a fragmented tradition but a way of coping with the intensity of our hopes and fears. We split traditions; they do not just split us. And when traditions do split us, they do not just split us into pieces. There are patterns to these splits, resulting from the internal dynamics of the self in interaction with its environment, that produce particular types of selves, which in turn create particular types of worlds. It is such modal selves that this book is about.

The Great Divide and the Price of Self-Control

For MacIntyre, as for so many other theorists, the great divide in political philosophy is between Plato and Aristotle on the one hand, and moderns on the other, a divide that loosely corresponds to the distinction between Taylor's second- and first-order evaluators. For Plato and Aristotle, it is the purpose of tradition, as validated by reason, to educate and direct the passions and desires toward their proper aim. Moderns, on the other hand, treat the passions and desires as given; reason is but the instrument of desire. As Hume put it, "Reason is, and ought only to be the slave of the passions and can never pretend to any other office than to serve and obey them."[42]

Against this argument, defenders of liberalism frequently respond that modernity is not of one piece. Liberal traditionalism, as it has been called, holds that "liberal culture can find within itself the resources to accomplish the restraint on selfish passions that they [liberal traditionalists] agree is necessary for a viable polity. Instead of looking to a specifically political force 'out of themselves' to perform this task, they hope that liberal society can morally habituate its citizens in ways sufficient to the demands of self-government."[43] To be sure, controlling selfishness via the internalization of norms of self-control (the superego in place of the superstate, as it has been expressed) is not the same thing as subjecting passion and desire to reason. Liberal traditionalism is no refutation of the great divide. But this is really my point. Given that Plato and moderns such as Locke hold that the good society requires self-control, how does each transform the self in order to achieve it? Is the self sacrificed—or strengthened—in order to achieve this inner control? This is the key question addressed throughout the following chapters. We know what happens to reason as we move from Plato and Aristotle to the moderns: it becomes less ambitious, more concerned with security and order than truth and the goodness of the psyche. But what happens to the self? Is its path similar, a downward spiral? After all, it is the self who reasons.

My thesis, in a nutshell, is that the history of the self does not follow a similar downward path. The self fares worse in some accounts, such as Hobbes's, but in others it fares better or at least as well. Plato's great contribution is to have put the self (psyche) and its desires at the center, making the care of the self the focus of philosophy and politics. It is his focus that is of permanent value, not his solution, which is to sacrifice self-consciousness for self-knowledge. One reason for beginning with Plato, then, is to challenge the widely held belief, asserted most dramatically by Bloom in *The Closing of the American Mind*, that most of our current problems stem from the failure to return to the classical concept of the psyche and its correlate, objective reason. The solutions of Hobbes, Locke, Rawls, and Rousseau are filled with problems, but they are not solved as easily as that. Does this mean that Plato's solution is inferior to that of several moderns? Not really. Every theorist considered either divides the self against itself in some way, as Plato does, or, in the case of Rousseau, denies the difference and otherness inherent in the existence of other wills, rendering the self whole only by denying others. Plato is the most brilliant theorist ever to confront the self. That he could not solve its problems—protecting its integrity while making it safe for society and itself—says as much about the intractability of the problem posed by the self for political theory as anything else.

All the authors I discuss, even Locke, are concerned with passions, not just interests, to use Albert O. Hirschman's distinction. It is this that makes them worthy of study as theorists of the self. My primary interest is how a strand of liberal traditionalism, represented by Locke and Rawls, confronts the insights into the self of Plato and Hobbes. Liberal traditionalism in effect blends the insights of Plato and Hobbes into an eclectic (but not for this reason false) account of the self and its relationship to society. This account splits the self against itself in various ways in order to make the self safe for society and from itself. In so doing, it sacrifices much of the autonomy it sets out to protect. Plato, in this regard, is no exception; rather, he is the originator of this strategy. He is the greatest psyche-ologist of them all, but his answer is the problem, not the solution. If Plato divides the self against itself, Hobbes unifies it, but only by reducing the self to its lowest common denominator. It is on elements of both solutions that Locke and Rawls draw. Rousseau is the shadowy presence, the silent witness (at least until the next to last chapter), holding out the promise that the self need not be divided against itself in order to be both social and whole. That is why I consider him last. In the end, however, Rousseau's epiphany on the road to Vincennes finds little resonance in my account. People may indeed be born good, but to keep them that way Rousseau must deny their humanity.

John Stuart Mill is not considered for the same reason that Aristotle is not. Mill might seem appropriate, for he puts the self first, valuing political participation not for its own sake but for the way it enriches private life, the cultivation of the self. Nevertheless, Mill, like Aristotle, though never substituting interest for passion, tends to rationalize the passions, downplaying the demanding, demonic desires of the self, making them on the whole safer. Even Mill's preference for pagan self-assertion over Christian self-denial remains tepid, as Nancy Rosenblum suggests.[44] Or as Martha Nussbaum puts it regarding Aristotle, we find in his work "an almost complete lack of attention to the erotic relationships that Plato defended. . . . Platonic *eros* seeks wholeness; [Aristotelian] *philia* embraces the half."[45] Since it is the demanding, erotic, needy, desiring aspects of the self that make it such a problem, Plato's account is superior for my purposes, as it begins at the beginning.

The Self-Psychological Basis

In the next chapter I develop a theory of the self and then apply it in the following chapters. But to put it this way is a little misleading. By *theory* is meant merely a model of the self, or rather two models: those of Heinz Kohut and of Jacques Lacan. The models are different, to say the least, so that I devote much attention to demonstrating that they are commensurable, which, of course, does not mean identical. It makes sense to employ Lacan's account of the self to decenter Kohut's, showing the self to be less whole and integrated than Kohut's idealistic account sometimes suggests. If the term *theory* is used loosely, *application* is used even more loosely. By *application* is meant not the assignment of theoretical principles to particular cases but simply aspects of self psychology that seem fruitful in particular cases. Here is the difference, I hope, between formula and wisdom, a wisdom that takes the texts as seriously as it does the principles of self psychology. How I apply these principles depends upon the text. Sometimes I use Kohut's model, sometimes Lacan's, but generally I employ a mixture of the two. Occasionally, however, neither model is applied: self psychology fades into the background, becoming merely the source of informing ideas, things to keep in mind.

The relatively loose connection between psychoanalytic models of the self and the texts studied means that the impatient reader could skip the next chapter and still make considerable sense of the argument. Doing so would be a mistake, however. The key problem with so many accounts of the self is that they render the self the dependent variable—the last thing to be explained, formulated to fit the theorist's favorite concepts but in effect having no reality independent of these concepts. This is why a theory of this independent reality, the self, is so important, and hence why the next chapter is.

The account of the self I develop there emphasizes Kohut's account of the selfobject transference, as he calls it: the way in which the self uses other selves and objects to support itself, to maintain its sense of being a self. This account can be fruitful for two reasons. First, it generates a phenomenological account of the self, one that stays fairly close to experience, depending less upon abstract, theoretical forces, such as libido, than do many psychoanalytic theories. Second, it lends itself to the psychoanalytic reading of texts about the self. It makes free association less important and analysis of how the self uses other selves, as well as institutions, symbols, and ideas, to support itself more important.

Psychoanalytic theories of reading have become more influential in recent years, the result of the influence of Lacan and others who see the unconscious—indeed, the entire world—as a text. One of my concerns is to develop an alternative psychoanalytic approach to texts about the self, one that leads not to its deconstruction but to its reconstruction on a more realistic basis. This methodological interest is not, however, entirely separate from my substantive one. A methodology that respects the self is a great help in developing an account that does, even though they are not identical.

By now it may have occurred to the reader to ask the question: but isn't the self really a historical concept? I have alluded to this question in various ways throughout this chapter. To many it must be the fundamental question—and challenge: can one really understand the self without understanding in great detail the historical development of the concept? Isn't this what Michel Foucault and all those concerned with the archaeology of knowledge have taught us? Certainly this was the direction that Foucault was headed in his last works, especially "Technologies of the Self." Written shortly before his death, this essay was an outline of a research program that was to have studied the historically different ways in which people have understood what it is to be a self and to transform oneself.[46] Charles Taylor makes a related argument, noting that the inwardness of the self, understood as the notion that the authentic self lies within, is a strictly modern idea.[47] To assume, he says, that because Plato's Socrates is concerned with the "taking care of the self" (*epimelesthai sautou*) he had such an inner-oriented entity in mind is to be anachronistic, unhistorical. But in my two chapters on Plato, I argue to the contrary, or rather, that inner- and outer-oriented concepts of the self (a distinction captured by Leo Strauss with the terms *self-consciousness* and *self-knowledge*) are in competition and conflict throughout Plato's work. In a similar fashion, I point in chapter 6 to Christopher Foxe's argument that Locke's concept of the self in his *Essay* was not merely a systematization of conventional thinking on the topic. Instead, it posed a fundamental challenge to the Christian tradition in which it is God who grants identity. It is possible, of course, that my arguments are mistaken, but they will not be mistaken because the historical context is ignored.

There is another and even more fundamental reason that the objection regarding the historicity of the self does not apply to my project—because it is already factored into the approach, so to speak. To study an author's concept of the self by examining the selfobject transference allows for historical variation. Indeed, this is the point of this approach: to appreciate what an author is saying about the self by approaching his concept of the self naively, as an unknown, something to be revealed by how he uses selfobjects, not by the imposition of this or that theory. Indeed, it may well be that my approach is more sensitive to historical context, as it does not assume that the historical self is determined by this or that experience or concept—for example, it does not assume that the self in the capitalist era must always be a possessive individualist. Rather, it renders an author's concept of the self a problem to be solved by a sensitive reading of his texts. In the language of an older philosophical tradition, one might characterize my approach with the term *verstehen*, in which the goal is to think oneself into the concept of the self held by a given author (to be sharply distinguished from the actual self of the author) in order to better understand it. The selfobject transference, from this perspective, is the medium of sympathetic interpretation, just as it is for the analyst.

In his recent *Sources of the Self*, Charles Taylor sees Locke as a theorist who epitomizes inwardness, understood as an ideal of autonomous, rational self-control. I, on the other hand, see Locke as attempting to weaken the self so as to make it profoundly dependent upon the good opinions of others. What accounts for these different assessments (my assessment of Plato also differs from Taylor's)? Only a quick answer (all too quick: Taylor's is in many respects a magnificent book) can be given here. Taylor devotes too much attention to the *sources* of the self and too little to the self. Thus, he analyzes Locke's stress on freedom, independence, and responsibility, but not the assumptions that Locke makes about the entity that is the locus of these values: the self. The consequence is what is in effect a mirror-model of the self. The difference with most mirror-models is that the image in the mirror, the different traditions that make up the modern identity, is richer in Taylor's account than almost any other. Yet, as Taylor appreciates, the question remains open whether the modern self can take advantage of these sources. Whether it can depends as much upon the self as its sources. Or rather, it depends upon their interaction.

At the end of his book, Taylor wonders if a commitment to beneficence and justice can be sustained in the absence of a belief in external sources of goodness, such as a loving god. His "hunch," he says, is that it cannot. "High standards need strong sources," and neither guilt nor self-satisfaction are strong enough. Taylor does not, however, pursue this point, arguing that it would require another book. In her review of *Sources of the Self*, Martha Nussbaum responds with some "hunches" of her own, citing Melanie Klein and Richard Wollheim to the effect that benevolence (what Klein calls reparation) may have sufficiently strong roots in the self so as to need no external reinforcement.[48] To be sure, this is an area in which proof seems impossible. Nevertheless, there exist more than hunches. There exist arguments and theories. Most of Freud's *Civilization and Its Discontents*, for example, concerns why the injunction to "love thy neighbor" is virtually impossible to fulfill (basically because love is a scarce resource). Freud is not necessarily correct, of course, but this is not the point. The point is that if one is to understand the human world, one must understand not merely the sources of the self but the role that these sources play in the psychic economy. In order to do this one must have a fairly sophisticated model of the psyche. Taylor makes assumptions about how the self uses its sources, as all social theorists must. Because he does not do so in a programmatic manner, however, he ends up often writing as if the self were equivalent to its sources, even when he knows it's not.

Taylor's concluding speculations about the need for external sources of goodness is one of the few places where these sources meet an explicit model of the self. Taylor argues that (1) political extremism may be a response to a meaningless life, not just poor material conditions; (2) "meaninglessness is frequently accompanied by a sense of guilt," though he does not state why; (3) thus, many young people respond to ideologies of polarization by projecting guilty impulses (apparently the guilt-producing impulses, such as rage) outward and fighting them there and so creating "a sense of purity by lining up in implacable opposition to the forces of darkness." The problem, Taylor suggests, is that even universal accounts of external sources of goodness, such as Christian *agape*, may lose their universalism when adopted by selves afflicted with meaninglessness, so that they become just one more weapon (and one more psychological defense) against an implacable opposition.[49] Here, it seems, is where genuine social analysis must begin: with the study of the interaction between ideational sources and the needs of the self. Unfortunately, it is where Taylor's book (as well as most works in political theory and the history of ideas) ends. This becomes even more problematic if psychoanalytic theorists such as Lacan are correct: not just some young people but almost all people are confronted by a grave sense of meaninglessness and so tend to use political ideologies and theories as defenses against the lack (manque) in themselves. Is this a thesis that we can really afford to ignore? Yet to analyze the sources of the self independently of the self, as though their analytic separability had anything to do with the way self and ideas combine in the real world, is to do just this.

CHAPTER TWO

Man is born broken. He lives by
mending. The grace of God is
glue.—Eugene O'Neill,
quoted by Heinz Kohut,
The Restoration of the Self

A Psychoanalytic
Account of the Self

The ego is structured exactly like
a symptom. Interior to the
subject, it is only a privileged
symptom. It is the human
symptom par excellence, it is
the mental malady of man.
—Jacques Lacan,
Le séminaire, vol. 1

Kohut as Decentered
by Lacan

Heinz Kohut is a little like John Locke—both deeply conservative men who found themselves promoting a revolution. Kohut, past president of the American Psychoanalytic Association, developed a new psychoanalytic theory, called self psychology, that in effect abandons the major premises of Freud's account: drive theory; the centrality of the oedipal conflict in emotional disturbance; and the structural theory of the mind (ego, superego, and id). Yet Kohut devotes considerable energy to demonstrating that his model is compatible with, or at least complementary to, Freud's. Kohut's self psychology has become enormously influential; the new orthodoxy in American psychiatry, it has been called. The strategy of accommodation with Freud presumably accounts for some of his popularity, allowing analysts to embrace Kohut without rejecting Freud.[1]

The Selfobject Transferences

Kohut began his reformulation of psychoanalysis with a new theory of narcissism. To many he is still best known as a theorist of narcissism. The impetus for this new psychoanalytic theory, he says, was his experience of a new type of transference, which he originally called a narcissistic transference and later came to call a selfobject transference. In psychoanalysis, the transference refers to the analysand's emotional reaction to the analyst as though he were not merely the analyst but important people from the analysand's past, such as mother and father, whom he both loves and hates. Long-repressed emotional reactions to significant others are "transferred" to the analyst. As such, the transference involves the displacement of affect from one relationship to another, in which the analyst comes to contain or represent the idea of another.[2] The transference may be positive or negative, depending upon whether it recapitulates affectionate or hostile feelings. Although some have held that a psychoanalytic cure brings about the end of the transference, Kohut holds that what changes is only the quality of the transference. We are involved in transference relations not just with analysts but with friends, spouses, colleagues, and children from birth to death. The transference is the universal medium of relationships.

Kohut came to believe that he saw something else going on in the transference. He was being emotionally regarded by his patients not merely as an archaic mother and father figure but as part of the patient's self (what Kohut came to call a selfobject), as though he were an alienated aspect of the patient's own self. Sometimes he was treated as though he contained all that the analysand hoped and wished to be, the avatar of his or her deepest ideals. Conversely, sometimes he was treated as though he had no value at all. Kohut came to call this the idealizing selfobject transference, one that may also contain its opposite, when the analyst is denied all value. Kohut discovered another transference, which he came to call the mirroring selfobject transference. This transference was operative, he said, when the analyst was treated not as a person in his own right but strictly as a mirror for the analysand's ambition and grandiosity. It was as though the analyst's only purpose was to confirm the greatness and perfection of the analysand. When this confirmation did not immediately occur, Kohut often observed a great deal of rage in the patient, a rage that seemed to say, in effect, "When you do not mirror me, empathizing with my every emotion, I feel as if my self is about to fall apart. This scares me to death, and I feel enraged at you. I feel enraged at your lack of response, as well as your own self-contained wholeness, which I envy and want to destroy, as it makes me feel even less whole." Kohut calls this narcissistic rage, rage at another who refuses or is unable to be a perfectly responsive selfobject. Otherwise expressed, it is rage at another who fails to adequately perform (from the analysand's perspective) his function as selfobject: an object whose purpose is to merge with the self of the analysand and support it, confirming its narcissistic ideals.

The relationship of both transferences to narcissism is apparent. One is the counterpart of the other. In the idealizing selfobject transference the analysand locates all her ambitions and ideals in the selfobject, with which she seeks to merge and so share in its perfection. In the mirroring selfobject transference the analysand locates all that is worthwhile and good in herself, demanding of others only that they confirm this. Kohut does not argue that selfobject transferences are immature or pathological. They are at the center of emotional life virtually from birth to death. What changes is not that we use selfobjects but how we use them. Do we seek to merge completely with our ideal selfobject so that nothing is left of the self? Or do we learn to choose and use those idealizable selfobjects that support our chosen projects? Do we require constant mirroring of particular others to feel whole and coherent, or can we wait for this mirroring and accept only that which corresponds with our ideals? Ernest Wolf calls this the "developmental line of selfobject relations." The key point is that selfobject transferences in adults are normal, not pathological. What is pathological is the persistence of selfobject transferences in which the object is not recognized as whole, its all good or all bad aspects being split off and treated as the object per se. Also pathological is when the transference becomes a total merger.

Though Kohut distinguishes between narcissistic and idealizing selfobject transferences, they are really counterparts with a common core. Both lines of development have in common their origin in the ideal of perfection, understood as primitive narcissistic equilibrium, perfect harmony between self and world.[3] This perfection is not yet split into perfect beauty, morality, strength, and goodness. It is still a whole, what Kohut calls an omniwhole, characterized by the equation of perfection and omnipotence. As he says, "Both self-esteem and what later becomes our system of ideals come from the same root . . . often referred to as primary narcissism." Later Kohut would devote more energy to an attempt to distinguish them theoretically.[4] In some respects this is unfortunate, as it is really their close link that is so fruitful, focusing our attention not on the content of the ambition or ideal but on the role it plays in the psychic economy: is it a mature or an immature actor? From this perspective, ideals are best seen as *objectified ambitions*, and the important question concerns not their common origin but the degree to which the idealized ambition is serving as a narcissistic prop or is overly contaminated with *primitive* ambition, so that power and goodness become one. Rather than seeing the issue as ambitions versus ideals, it might be more useful to distinguish subject- and object-bound narcissism, a formulation Kohut employed in an early work.[5] In the case of object-bound narcissism, the question is whether the idealized object can be valued in terms other than those that enhance the subject's power and perfection. Can the object set limits on the subject?

Kohut's structural model of the self, the bipolar self, is a formalization of these transference relationships.[6] This is important, for it supports the claim that Kohut stays close to experience. The bipolar self is not the imposition of a structural model on analytic experience; rather, it is an explication of this experience. Diagrammatically it may be expressed like this:

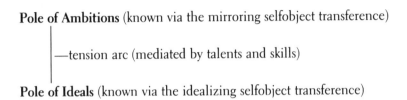

Pole of Ambitions (known via the mirroring selfobject transference)

—tension arc (mediated by talents and skills)

Pole of Ideals (known via the idealizing selfobject transference)

The self, says Kohut, is this entire structure: the two poles, mediated by the tension arc, which connects our ambitions with our ideals by means of talents, skills, and abilities. Otherwise expressed, the self is concerned with how our skills and abilities connect who we *want* to be with who and what we think we *should* be. Implicit in such a definition is that the self is an initiator with continuity in time and space. The self is a project in which we use our talents and skills, over time, to come closer to who we want to be, as defined by how we believe we should be.[7] It is easy to see why Taylor would find Kohut attractive.

In Kohut's account, analysis cures through "transmuting internalization," in which the empathic response of the analyst helps the analysand to internalize this response as part of himself.[8] This is what occurs in the transference. The analyst's response need not be perfect, Kohut quickly adds. Were it perfect, the analysand would be encouraged to remain in a state of narcissistic equilibrium, never needing to take over this selfobject function for himself. Empathy need be only partial, but generally on target—optimally frustrating, Kohut calls it. Originally an external selfobject, the analyst ideally becomes an internal selfobject: an integrated part of the analysand's own psychic structure (for Kohut, psychic structure *is* the internalization of functions previously performed by selfobjects), so that the analysand is able to do for himself what he previously depended upon external selfobjects to do.[9] This, though, is always a question of degree. We never fully internalize the selfobject function.

The Developmental Line

Development, says Ernest Wolf, one of Kohut's collaborators, is characterized not by the abandonment of the need for selfobjects but by a transformation of them. In maturity, we do not depend upon a particular person; we
find appropriate support from a number of persons. We can also use cultural
symbols and beliefs as alternatives to persons. For example, an imprisoned
draft resister may turn to religious beliefs or symbols of his cultural values as
selfobjects. For the mature self, says Wolf, a variety of relationships and symbols "take over much of the function of the originally highly personal, concrete, and focused relation to the archaic selfobjects of childhood."[10] Jay
Greenberg and Stephen Mitchell argue that the developmental line (a term
whose linear, progressive connotations are inescapable) trivializes Kohut's
claim that "autonomy is impossible," as we depend on selfobjects from birth
to death.[11] Kohut and his followers are again exaggerating the uniqueness of
their perspective: the narcissism of small differences, Freud called it. I would
put it somewhat differently. The developmental line trivializes Kohut's insight into the constant connection between archaic and mature selfobject
transferences. The line is not so much false as simplistic. Consider, for example, how individuals may have immature, archaic relations to national
symbols, such as the flag. The abstract character of a selfobject is no guarantee of its maturity. Conversely, the fungibility of persons is no sign of maturity, a point Kohut recognizes when he states that the ability to readily substitute persons or symbols is a sign of shallow, narcissistic relations, in which
the reality of the other is unimportant.[12] Is it a sign of maturity if we can
easily substitute one spouse or lover for another?

Not substitutability but the degree to which the other is appreciated as a
complex whole, so that her selfobject function does not require the denial of
her reality as another person, is a better standard of maturity. This means, for
example, that the mirroring selfobject is valued for herself, not just the self-
psychological function she performs. Narcissism and object love, while perhaps following separate developmental lines, as Kohut argues, are "inter-
twined" in the perception of the other as both mirror and object in her own
right.[13] One reason it hurts so much to lose a loved one is because that person
is a unique, irreplaceable other, not merely the interchangeable performer of
a psychological function. Wolf continues that "by the time the adult has
reached old age, he may often have achieved a selfobject relation with the

wider world of mankind and beyond. Mature selflessness is really the expansion of the self and its selfobjects to take in the whole world."[14]

Wolf's statement exemplifies the most problematic tendency in self psychology taken to its extreme. The tendency is to deny the otherness of the other, to achieve autonomy only by absorbing the other. Transmuting internalization becomes transmuting absorption, and what is supposed to be a statement of maturity is actually the quintessential narcissistic fantasy: the entire world as selfobject—as extension of oneself. In fact, the insight that the entire world need *not* be a selfobject in order to make life worthwhile better captures the essence of maturity.

Some, such as Greenberg and Mitchell, have argued that this problematic tendency stems from the origins of Kohut's scheme in a theory of narcissism.[15] A valid theory of narcissism, Kohut's self psychology must transform all of psychological life into an instance of narcissism in order to explain it. Perhaps this is part of the problem. Another part, however, may be that Kohut is performing an inherently difficult balancing act, acknowledging the limits of autonomy while appreciating the fact that many people experience themselves as autonomous centers of initiative. Is this experience an illusion, a defense? No, but it always rests, albeit mediately, upon the ability to use others as selfobjects via the phenomenon that Kohut calls transmuting internalization.

Transmuting internalization, it is apparent, is not a benign act but an aggressive one, a point insufficiently emphasized by Kohut. It involves consuming the other, using him up, metabolizing him, so that the other becomes part of myself. To put it this way is, of course, a metaphor, as the other is not actually consumed. Rather, he is actually ignored, except as a source of support for the self. The unique otherness of the other, except insofar as it can be appropriated, is rejected—not acknowledged. To be sure, Kohut stresses that narcissism is not an alternative to object love. Rather, they ideally develop in tandem, as noted above. Nevertheless, Kohut pays almost no theoretical attention to object love, devoting virtually all his attention to the selfobject transferences, which are narcissistic by definition. Kohut's neglect of the object qua object is a de facto rather than de jure decision, but for this reason no less real. And no less aggressive either. To deny the otherness of the other means that the other is conceptualized and valued strictly in terms of how he serves my ends. That the object has ends of his own is quite irrelevant. It is ultimately upon such aggression that Kohut rests the autonomy of the self: absorbing the other, rejecting any otherness that is left, as though it were a foreign body. The question is whether this unacknowledged aggression, expressed in the denial of otherness, makes Kohut's account an instance of "wild self-assertion," as Theodor Adorno calls it—that is, an act of the ego against other subjects in order to defend against its own subjectivity. The answer is yes and no; to pursue this point further it will be necessary first to study Lacan.

Narcissistic rage is aggression in response to threats to the grandiose self and the omnipotent object. Kohut did not originate the concept, but his "Thoughts on Narcissism and Narcissistic Rage" is probably the single most influential work on the topic.[16] The more the grandiose self is unintegrated, walled off from the mature self by a vertical split (discussed more fully below), the more the individual will respond with narcissistic rage when her fantasies of perfection and omnipotence are challenged by reality. The key characteristic of narcissistic rage is its cold, calculating, relentless, unforgiving character. Quite the opposite of wild, regressive, explosive, uncontrolled anger, which often overwhelms the ego, narcissistic rage puts the ego in the service of avenging narcissistic humiliation. Its source, Kohut argues, is an unconscious experience of the entire world as an extension of one's own self, its only purpose being to confirm one's perfection and grandiosity. Narcissistic rage denies separation and otherness, rather, it is activated when separateness and otherness impinge on narcissistic grandiosity. This is why it is so relentless and unforgiving, being aimed not at real persons but at a world that fails to cooperate with one's fantasies.[17]

Like most emotional illness, Kohut continues, narcissistic rage is best conceptualized on a continuum

> that reaches from such trivial occurrences as a fleeting annoyance when someone fails to reciprocate our greeting or does not respond to our joke to such ominous derangements as the furor of the catatonic and the grudges of the paranoic. Following Freud's example, however, I shall use the term *"a potiori"* and refer to all the points in the spectrum as narcissistic rage . . . which not only form a continuum but, with all their differences, are essentially related to each other.[18]

They are essentially related (as all are a reaction to narcissistic injury) to loss of self-esteem, with the threat to the cohesion of the self that this may pose, if only for a moment. Rich in some respects, troublesome in others (do we really want to claim that the momentary annoyance felt when someone fails to say hello is "essentially related" to the monomania of Captain Ahab?), this conception of narcissistic rage makes it difficult to identify its more moderate expressions, those falling in the middle of the continuum. The very rationality with which narcissistic rage may be pursued will frequently disguise it as tough-minded realism, rational self-interest, maintaining an appearance of toughness in order to enhance deterrence, and so forth. This will be particularly the case when narcissistic rage is institutionalized in those institutions of organized reason, bureaucracies. There are no magic keys to identifying narcissistic rage, so it will be important to look closely at every rationalization of aggression, suspecting that it might well be rationalization in the psychoanalytic sense as well: good reasons but not the real reason. The real reason may be narcissistic rage.[19]

Splitting

Splitting is a puzzling concept and not merely in Kohut's work but throughout psychoanalysis. The puzzle begins with Freud's not entirely clear distinction between repression and splitting. Repression, in classical analysis, refers to the ego's removal from consciousness of an unwanted impulse and any derivatives thereof, such as memories. Ego and id are thus opposed; this is what repression means. Freud never developed a correspondingly sophisticated concept of splitting.[20] In one of his late works, however, "Splitting of the Ego in the Process of Defense" (1940), Freud wrote about how the ego itself could hold two conscious, contradictory beliefs at the same time: for example, that women have a penis and that women don't have a penis.[21] This is not repression, but a division of the ego, so that the parts holding the conflicting beliefs never touch. What Kohut calls a vertical split in the self seems similar to what Freud called splitting of the ego, whereas by a horizontal split Kohut is referring to a repression barrier.

   Tolpin argues that the difference between Kohut and an otherwise diverse group of psychoanalytic theorists, such as Melanie Klein, Karen Horney, and Harry Stack Sullivan, is that for the latter three, splitting results from the intensity of desire and the fragility of the ego. In a word, desire splits the ego. For Kohut, on the other hand, it is not desire that splits the ego but faulty empathy: the unempathically responded to part of the self goes underground—it becomes split off, where it waits to be recognized.[22] It does not, however, wait silently. The split-off part of the self frequently operates on its own, independently of the rest of the self. It is this that accounts for psychopathology: the split-off part of the self, operating independently, seeks satisfaction in archaic selfobject transferences. As in narcissistic rage, the more mature sectors end up rationalizing this pursuit rather than controlling it. Expressed structurally, the vertical split is *within* a pole of the self, in which faulty empathy leads the pole of ambitions or ideals to be divided against itself.

Kohut argues that it is the archaic, split-off parts of the self that are most heavily involved in the selfobject transference. In this account, the therapist is a merger-object. Therapy requires not the rejection of the analysand's archaic wishes but their empathic acceptance so that they may be called forth from hiding and integrated with the mature self. Less emphasized in Kohut's account is how the analyst may come to contain rejected, split-off, and projected-out parts of the analysand's self, parts filled with envy, hate, and rage. Kohut does not reject this phenomenon entirely, paying special attention to the devaluation of the analyst. Nevertheless, he seems much more comfortable as a merger-object (aren't we all?) than as a container for unwanted aspects of the self.[23] Yet a complete analysis—even of textual selves—must analyze not merely archaic desires for merger but also the rejected parts of the self, those that are driven underground and projected out. The *dustbin selfobject transference*, it might be called. Sticking strictly to Kohut's approach might cause this aspect to be downplayed. The similarity between this criticism and the more common complaint, by Otto Kernberg and others, that Kohut ignores the negative transference (hostile feelings toward the analyst) is apparent.[24]

Putting these considerations together with those in the earlier discussion on the developmental line suggests an important point not developed by Kohut. A nonintegrated selfobject can become a defense object by containing either all good or all bad aspects of the self, and thus reinforcing splitting by holding the good and bad even further apart. Furthermore, this may be readily accomplished not merely by symbolic selfobjects, such as the flag, but by abstract ones as well, such as the metaphysical self. It might be called the abstract selfobject as defense object, in which the abstraction serves to deny the mundane fly in the ointment, all those "details" that render the abstraction unrealistic, an idealization in the psychological sense: a denial of all that does not correspond to the ideal. This concept will play a particularly important role in the chapters on Plato and Rawls. We must ask ourselves when we think we observe a selfobject transference, what exactly is occurring. Is the selfobject transference being used to *reinforce* the cohesion of the self, or is it being used to *split the self* in order to mitigate internal conflict by projecting bad parts of the self into others (albeit at the cost of the long-term integrity of the self)?[25] Some analysts call this phenomenon *projective identification*.

In projective identification we make the other a holder, or container, of parts of ourselves.[26] One might argue that it is the opposite of the selfobject transference. In the selfobject transference, we use others to support our-selves; in projective identification, we put part of ourselves into others. In fact, they are not really opposites at all but different ways of looking at the same process. A condition of using another as a selfobject is to see the other as a container, or holder, of a part of oneself in the first place, albeit an alien-ated part that we may not know or acknowledge. One first puts this part of oneself in another; it is then brought back via the selfobject transference. This is implicit in the definition of the transference as a phenomenon con-cerned with the *idea* of the other. The idea, of course, originally comes not from the other but from ourselves.

Projective identification serves several functions. It may reinforce self-splitting, as in the dustbin selfobject transference. More positively, it stabi-lizes and familiarizes the other, making him or her more like us. In so doing it helps to coordinate expectations and actions. If I project part of myself into you, and you do the same with me, and it is the same part (e.g., similar ideals), then our actions can be readily coordinated. We expect the same things of each other, and these expectations are generally fulfilled, because they are the same expectations we have for ourselves. "Mutual endowment" this process is called in social psychology. This is a primary mechanism by which most groups and societies are coordinated. When projective identifi-cation is too extensive, too much of the self being projected into too many others, it can debilitate the self. But it can also enrich the self, allowing the individual to feel a part of the lives of others. It is something like this last point that Sandel is aiming at in his idealization of the socially consti-tuted self.

Sandel is not simply mistaken. What he lacks is what so many other social theorists lack, an appreciation of the subtlety and complexity of the issues involved, any sense that it is all a matter of degree. How much of what parts of the self are given up to others? How extensively? Can they be reclaimed? What remains? These are important questions, not just details. They make the difference between a totalitarian regime, an authoritarian one, a liberal regime, and a communitarian one. In short, the answers to these questions make all the difference in the world. To ignore them is not just to ignore the details. It is to ignore the self, subordinating it to one's favorite theory. The questions noted above should strike a bell, for it is questions like these that have traditionally been asked about the social contract. Who contracts with whom? What is given up, and what retained? Can the contract be rescinded? Is it worth the cost? Generally asked about individual rights, these questions apply with equal importance to the self possessing these rights. Or rather, these are not separate questions. How much we value the rights of the self depends, in large measure, on how we value the self, which is not unrelated to how we study it.

The Selfobject Transference and Reading Texts

By putting the selfobject transference at the center of psychoanalysis, Kohut makes an important point. Structural models of the mind, models that posit unseen forces such as drives, may add to the precision with which we express our theories. But they do not necessarily add anything to the depth of our understanding. Otherwise expressed, the surface, experienced in the self-object transference, is the depth. Kohut gives a good example of this point, arguing that we will misunderstand the significance of Proust's *Remembrance of Things Past* if we interpret it in terms of Freudian depth psychology.

> When he remembers his mother visiting him in the night and giving him the madeleine that he smells, the major point is not that they are screen memories covering oedipal material of being alone with mamma or wanting daddy to be dead . . . . The Proustian search can only be understood when you read—which most people don't anymore—the last volume of his novel, which explains the moment at which he decides to undertake this work, when he suddenly trips on the curbstone and slips and feels out of balance. . . . It is at that point he decided he had to write his total life history, not to figure out the past and its meanings in the unconscious but to reestablish a continuity within himself.[27]

As in an Ann Tyler novel, the surface runs deep. It *is* the depth. What we really want, most of all, is to be recognized for who we are so that we may know this ourselves. This is what the selfobject transference focuses on. This is what is deep. Furthermore, there is nothing magic about the selfobject transferences that Kohut identifies. The selfobject transference is about how we use others to support our sense of ourselves, and there are presumably myriad ways of doing so.

Putting the selfobject transference at the center of psychoanalysis has another advantage for those interested in applying psychoanalysis to texts. It makes, as Kohut points out, free association, even dreams, less important, and it is these that one often cannot find in texts (though certainly sometimes both are present).[28] The key issue is closer to the surface: how does the self that the text is about use selfobjects? One could treat the texts themselves as selfobjects, as Susan Grayson does in "Rousseau and the Text as Self."[29] I am not so ambitious. What the selfobject transference does, in my account, is allow one to draw conclusions about the self in the text not merely from what the author says about the self but also from what the author says about people, things, and ideas that are clearly selfobjects. It is, for example, from this perspective that Plato's polis, Hobbes's Leviathan, and Locke's concept of property are studied. Otherwise expressed, the focus on the selfobject transference allows one to learn about the self by reading from right to left, as it were, not merely left to right—that is, to draw conclusions about the self by looking at its selfobjects.

Jacques Lacan

In an article in *Psychoanalytic Quarterly*, Martha Evans treats Kohut's work on the mirroring selfobject transference as a continuation of Lacan's work on the mirror stage.[30] Although Kohut is no successor to Lacan (and nowhere mentions his work), both are fundamentally concerned with the way we use others to support our sense of ourselves. In this sense, at least, their projects are continuous, and shortly I will argue that they are continuous in a more fundamental sense as well.

Because of my narrow focus, I do not study extensively the aspects of Lacan's work that others have found so valuable, such as his transformation of psychoanalysis into a form of language analysis.[31] Some may hold that this omission must miss the point of Lacan's work, in which the play of his language mimics the free associations of the unconscious, and so forth, thus demonstrating the limits of rational argument. The medium is the message. On the contrary, I hold that it is Lacan's "linear" thesis—the self does not exist except as symptom—that is so valuable in his work. It is a brilliant, crushing thesis that deserves to be confronted. Too often, it seems, a focus on Lacan's stylistics is a way of avoiding this confrontation, substituting medium for message. This too is abstraction as defense.

The Mirror Stage

One of Lacan's most influential works remains his early (1936–1949) work on the mirror stage of development (*le stade du miroir*). The mirror stage runs from about six months to two years of age. At some time during this stage the young child recognizes himself (*moi*) in a mirror. ("Lipstick experiments" and the like, in which the child's nose is smeared with lipstick and he is placed before the mirror, it being presumed that if he responds with embarrassment he must recognize himself, generally support Lacan's timing of this stage.)[32] He is impressed by the wholeness of the image, the appearance of definite boundaries, form, and control seen in the mirror. Yet this wholeness is really an illusion. He is none of these things. Sometimes he even confuses his own image with the image of his mother who, in one of Lacan's versions, is holding him before the mirror.[33] Nor does the image in the mirror anticipate a future wholeness. It is not even a promissory note; he will always be less than the image in the mirror. As Bice Benvenuto and Roger Kennedy put it, "The infant's mastery is in the mirror image, outside himself, while he is not really master of his movements. Alienation is this lack of being by which his realization lies in another actual or imaginary space."[34]

Although Evans perhaps goes too far in treating the mirror stage as metaphor, it is apparent from the context of Lacan's discussion that it need not always be an actual mirror. It could just as well be what Kohut calls the mirroring response of the parents, a response that seems to confirm the child's own grandiose, narcissistic ideas of himself as whole and perfect. Sometimes, at least, his parents seem to regard him thusly, or at least to play along. It is, says Kohut, the parents' treatment of the young child as though he were a coherent self that teaches him that he is one, via "transmuting internalization," in which the appropriate parental mirroring is internalized in the child as part of himself. It is this concept, more than any other, that Lacan in effect challenges. The coherence and control of the self that one feels when looking in the mirror, or when in the presence of mirroring others, is never internalized, but always remains alienated in the other. In this sense it is an illusion (*méconnaissance*), for it can never become one's own. Put simply, for Lacan the selfobject always remains the other (*Autre*). Like Kohut, Lacan agrees that we always need selfobjects: "autonomy is impossible." But unlike Kohut, Lacan questions whether we can ever effectively use selfobjects to support ourselves. Or rather, doing so must always involve a significant element of bad faith: rather than internalizing the support of the other ("transmuting internalization"), we alienate a part of ourselves in the other. Expressed in the language of a previous section, we projectively identify with others, putting a part of ourselves in them, but are never able to reinternalize it, to get it back.

Here is the source of a fundamental lack (manque) in human existence, a lack that is never overcome, for it represents the distance between what we desire for ourselves (that is, what we desire ourselves to be) and what we are, a distance represented in the insuperable gulf between the selfobject and the self, mirror image and reality. It is this gulf, says Lacan, that gives rise to rage and desire. Lacan is thus in agreement with Kohut on several important points. Rage and desire (*désir*) are not primary biological givens. They are responses to the lack in human existence. Unlike Kohut, however, Lacan makes this lack permanent. It is an ontological condition, reflected in the distance between how we are and how we want to be: the distance between the subjective experience of being pulled every which way by our desires and the image of wholeness, power, and control that the subject sees in the mirror. In fact, Lacan seems to suggest that it is with this experience of the mirror image that rage is born: in envy of the wholeness and perfection of the image in the mirror. At base our rage and unbridled desire are rooted in the envy we feel at an image of ourselves that will always remain alienated, as well as envy of the apparent wholeness of others. Like Kohut, Lacan argues that the young child experiences the discord and distance between her ideal image of her body and her actual experience of being fragmented by desire (*corps morcelé*) as the result of a sadistic attack on her own body from the inside. It is against this sadistic attack that the child responds in kind. Here is the origin of narcissistic rage. Aggression, says Lacan, is a "correlative tension of the narcissistic structure in the coming-into-being of the subject."[35]

Given these considerations, what is the task of the analyst? For Kohut, as for much of the British school of psychoanalysis (such as W. R. B. Fairbairn, D. W. Winnicott, and Harry Guntrip), the analyst takes the place of the insufficiently empathic mother (less frequently, the insufficiently idealizable father), providing the emotional responsiveness and support for the self that the mother did not. For Kohut a key aspect of this responsiveness will be a willingness to accept the analysand's archaic and split-off grandiosity, as well as her need to merge with an ideal. Lacan, on the other hand, sees the analyst as more akin to the tough father, who in effect says to the analysand, "Grow up. You cannot overcome your lack, and if you spend your entire life trying to do so you will live an inauthentic, miserable, symptom-plagued existence. If, however, you learn to accept this lack you can experience a certain authenticity, and occasionally a certain joy. Your desires need not tear you apart, and you can learn to 'organize [your] menu.' To do this, however, you must recognize that you do not really exist as a subject, but are 'in the position of the dead.'"[36] Lacan holds that analysis may cure some dramatic symptoms of emotional distress, such as psychosis, which irrupt through holes in the symbolic order, as he puts it. Analysis may also help us lead a more authentic existence, but only in the sense that it teaches us the uselessness of the quest for authenticity and the disingenuousness of the strategies by which we avoid confronting this fact: frantic work, wild self-assertion, perpetual immersion in relationships, and so forth. One is reminded here of Freud's statement that a successful cure will consist of transforming the analysand's hysterical misery into ordinary, human happiness.

Language and the Self

We are convinced, says Lacan, "that our researches justify the epigram of the philosopher who said that speech was given to man to hide his thoughts; our view is that the essential function of the ego is very nearly [a] systematic refusal to recognize reality."[37] For Lacan, the key error of many analysts, including the later Freud (and, I would add, many philosophers) is to have confused the subject—what I have called the self—with the ego. The subject is better seen as an attribute of the unconscious, which, Lacan argues, is organized like a language: a chain of signifiers, each signifying a desire. The subject, the self, is from this perspective not so much the locus of the dynamic unconscious as it is just one more signified, one more object of desire: the desire, destined to be eternally frustrated, to be the self in the mirror. Whether he knows it or likes it, "the subject will function like a signified [i.e., as constituted by a sign, which represents desire], and will always slide under the signifier. Thus the subject is constituted as secondary in relation to the signifier [i.e., secondary to desire], while signification has a life of its own."[38] Language, the realm of the signifier, can represent this lack in being, but it can never cure it because we cannot get beyond it.

Here Kohut and Lacan differ decisively. Kohut holds that empathy can transcend the limits of language, reaching out to support the self, even to become a part of the self, in a way that bypasses language and is in the end ineffable. Lacan, while recognizing that important aspects of experience, such as joy (*jouissance*) and death, themselves transcend language, nevertheless holds that the self cannot be reached in any way except through language. Because the unconscious is structured like a language, a chain of signifiers, it can be reached and understood only through language, a fact that allows us to understand it but not, as it were, to touch it.

The same holds true for the self. For Lacan, the sense of being an active subject is not merely analogous to, but dependent on, the use of the term *I*. But just as the term *I* (known as a "shifter" in linguistics) belongs to no one and in a conversation moves around among the participants, so the sense of being a subject, a self, is not a transcendent quality. We possess it for a moment, as when in a conversation we say that "I" did this or that, and then we lose it to the next conversationalist. For Lacan, the sense of being an active self, a center of initiative, is an effect, an illusion, of language, especially the "I" (*je*). Ironically, we overcome this illusion only to the degree we are willing to lose ourselves in language, *becoming* the shifter, the "I" that appears and disappears in the mouths of various participants, having no existence beyond this. I do not use language; it uses me. "I identify myself in language, but only by losing myself in it like an object," as Lacan puts it. Authenticity is a matter of knowing and accepting this. Period.[39]

One of the most distinctive features of Lacan's writings is a consequence of his linguistic focus. He simply does not write about feelings and emotions, what most analysts hold to be the stuff of psychoanalysis. There is instead a dry, arid, intellectualistic quality to his work totally unlike that of Kohut or most other psychoanalytic writers. It is this evidently that accounts for Lacan's great popularity among literary critics and others professionally concerned with texts: in the end there is little difference between people and texts. Both are objects to be decoded, deciphered. Neither is to be apprehended at an emotional level, at which language is no longer the medium but just the vehicle by which we try to explain what we already know. Kohut's claim that psychoanalysis "is the only one among the sciences of man that explains what it has first understood" through empathy finds no resonance in Lacan.[40]

For one interested in developing a psychoanalytic theory suitable for reading texts, Lacan would seem to have much to offer. Nevertheless, I do not find this aspect of his work valuable. Its abstract, intellectual approach to psychoanalysis is itself a schizoid phenomenon, in which we gain cognitive (but only cognitive) control over desires by transforming them into sentences. In fact, Lacan's view of language is reminiscent of the delusion of the influencing machine, or as Sass puts it, "Lacan's opposition to any form of humanism is so intense that he ends up emphasizing only the automatic, deterministic aspects of language, as if language lived itself in man and the reverse were not at all true—and this *is* akin to a homogenizing mechanism."[41] Instead of transforming selves into sentences, my concern is to try to find real selves in texts about selves, using the selfobject transference as a guide, reading from right to left, from selfobjects to the self. Doing so requires the rejection of a key poststructuralist claim, that of intertextuality, which in its most extreme form argues that texts are only about other texts. Some texts are about real selves, albeit only mediately, a distinction addressed shortly.

For Lacan, the self is the symptom, the disease:

> In Lacan's view, "the ego is structured exactly like a symptom. Interior to the subject, it is only a privileged symptom. It is the human symptom par excellence, it is the mental malady of man." From such a standpoint, self psychology and action language would be but the playing-out and reification of the delusion of the mirror phase. . . . The humanistic therapies of Kohut and Schafer are, on this account, doomed to the continuing reification and petrification of this "privileged symptom."[42]

Hume states that whenever he looks inside himself, there is no self to be found. Lacan might put it like so: "If I am honest with myself, every time I think that I find myself, I realize that I have found only one more defense, one more symptom, one more layer of rationalization protecting me from the truth: that what I desire and long for above all else, my self, does not exist."

In one respect, Lacan is just taking the Freudian revolution (what Kohut calls man's second great narcissistic injury, the first being the discovery that the earth is not the center of the cosmos) further. Rather than being the master of ourselves, we are generally dominated by our desires and fears—that is, the unconscious. Freud appears to have believed that a few exceptional individuals might transcend this way of life, a possibility expressed in his famous characterization of the successful outcome of analysis as "Wo es war, soll ich werden," usually translated as "Where id was, there ego shall be." Lacan, arguing that Freud has generally been misinterpreted on this point, states that one could better read Freud's intent this way: "There where it [id] was just now, there where it was for a while, between an extinction that is still glowing and a birth that is retarded, 'I' can come into being and disappear from what I say."[43] By this Lacan seems to mean that we become authentic to the degree that we abandon the illusionary attempt at control, the attempt, bound to fail, to be more than the desiring, lacking subject. Or as Sass puts it, the point is not that the ego should replace the id but that the ego should come to exist in the realm of the id. "That is, it should shed the illusion of integral, controlled selfhood and dissolve into those associative chains normally repressed into the unconscious."[44]

Lacan claims to have returned psychoanalysis to Freud, particularly to his early work, a claim about which there is much disagreement. In one respect at least, however, Lacan seems to be correct. As John Muller points out in "Ego and Subject in Lacan," Freud's early work stressed the defensive functions of the ego. For example, the ego organizes the defenses against remembering certain experiences. This leads to more organized repression by the ego, such as the repression of various threatening possibilities and fantasies. Surely this is an adaptive function, even a coordinating function, but it seems misleading to suggest that it implies such ego functions as autonomy, self-control, and self-direction. In fact, these latter functions play a less significant role in Freud's work than in that of the ego psychologists, such as Heinz Hartmann and Erik Erikson. "In pointing this out, the Lacanians argue that the Americans have missed the ego's fictional, alienating and distorting role."[45] Lacanians thus do not fail to recognize the adaptive, coordinating functions of the ego, even granting it considerable autonomy. They remind us, however, that these functions are primarily defensive, protecting us against reality, including inner reality, not adapting us to it.

Mediated Presence?

The thoughtful reader may well be thinking at this point that "Lacan's theory does not just decenter Kohut; it swallows him whole. What remains of the self that Kohut would cure if Lacan is correct? One does not cure a symptom; at best it just goes away." Such a view is understandable but incorrect. To demonstrate this requires a discussion of presence and whether it may be partial, mediated. It also requires that the ego and subject be distinguished further. Both tasks are best approached by asking what the self would be like for Lacan were it to exist. Raymond Tallis, in *Not Saussure: A Critique of Post-*

Saussurean Literary Theory, argues that it would be a self in which there was a complete coincidence of desire and the self that desires. It would be immediately present to itself, completely transparent, like "Rilke's angel 'a perfect consciousness . . . a being in whom thought and action, insight and achievement, will and capability, the actual and ideal is one.'"[46] It is this perfect self that is the enemy of the real self. I argued in chapter 1 that a strictly metaphysical concept of the self might lead us to fail to respect real selves. Here we see an extreme instance of this phenomenon. Because the self is split, torn by desires, rarely transparent to itself, means neither that the self does not exist nor that it is never present to itself. To conclude this, says Tallis, is a giant synecdoche, in which absolute unmediated presence is confused with presence. Since the former is impossible, so is the latter.[47] It is upon this false conclusion that Lacan's work is based. He demands too much and accepts too little.

Much of Western philosophy, says Tallis, including that of Hegel, Husserl, Heidegger, and Sartre, expresses a desire for a union of absolute lucidity and undeniable substantiality, of thinglike thereness and thoughtlike transparency. Such a union would be absolute presence. But, continues Tallis, such a union of perfect knowing and being is impossible. As being or presence moves toward transparency, it becomes less substantial, an idea. As it gains substance, it becomes less transparent. "The actual cannot be both absolutely general and utterly particular." The self-presence that Lacan and others deny is an instance of this metaphysical tradition, one

> that goes even beyond Husserlian absolute presence. His [Derrida's] assertion[s] that meaning and presence are effects of language rather than existing prior to them are really reformulations of ancient worries about agency—the feeling that even in our apparently voluntary actions we are not fully the agents of what our actions mean. We are not, and cannot be, transparent to ourselves.[48]

Lacan, like Derrida, will accept as a standard of the self nothing less than an absolute coincidence of consciousness and meaning. Because he cannot get it, the self does not exist.

With these considerations as background, it makes sense to write of mediated presences, degrees of self-presence, and so forth—once, that is, we recognize that we are talking about the wholeness, transparency, unity, self-consciousness, and self-control (all aspects of presence) of real selves, not metaphysical ones. If this is so, then it makes sense to put Lacan and Kohut on a continuum. They are commensurable, talking about the same thing, even if their answers are different. Each is concerned with how the subject uses selfobjects to support his sense of self. And while they reach very different conclusions—for Lacan, the selfobject is always the other; transmuting internalization is an illusion—they are nonetheless writing about the same entity, if, that is, we interpret Lacan as a psychoanalyst of the real self, not a metaphysician of ideal selves. In reality, of course, he is both. He mixes them together. I sort them out, for much the same reason that I sort out metaphysical claims about the self in political theory from real ones.

In fact, there is even greater continuity between Lacan and Kohut than these considerations suggest. Once we deny Lacan the opportunity to switch back and forth between metaphysical and real selves, some of his most extreme claims become self-refuting (and perhaps Lacan intends as much; it would certainly fit his antiprogram), for much the same reason that absolute relativism is self-refuting. Lacan has been compared to Faust, looking into the abyss and calling out for more light. To spend a lifetime seeking the self, not finding it, but finding the courage to face this fact and report back to others, is the act of a motivated, directed, reflective human being. It is the act of one who pursues the highest of values: the truth, for its own sake, even when it hurts. Ordinarily we call such beings noble selves, perhaps tragic ones, flawed, but nonetheless real selves. To deny this seems to require, as we have just seen, a quick transposition of the argument to the metaphysical realm of absolute selves. In response it might be argued that Lacan's whole approach, seen most clearly in a writing style that has been called "precious," "obscure," and "like a tangled thicket," stands as a barrier to this conclusion.[49] Lacan's text seeks to mimic the free play of the unconscious—following trains of association rather than linear arguments—and so even in its mode of presentation it denies that it is the act of a coherent, unitary subject, suggesting instead that it is the act of a subject identical with its unconscious. But this is, of course, the point. It is intended by Lacan, an effect, a literary device. There is all the difference in the world between such a device and the spontaneous flow of the unconscious. It is the difference between self and text.

Much the same point as that made in the preceding paragraphs can be made by distinguishing more fully between the subject and the ego. The subject is the one who desires itself, who can fulfill itself only by going outside of itself, finding itself in another's desire for it. By going outside of itself in this way, however, that subject alienates itself, finding itself only in another's desire for it. The subject desires a desire, as it were, and ends up understanding itself as it imagines the object of desire conceptualizes it to be (a phenomenon Lacan analyzes in terms of the child's desire to be mother's phallus, what she presumably desires). In this sense the subject is not: the subject is the lack, manque, need, emptiness, want, negativity. The ego is the defense against this: it fills the lack, but only with defenses. It is in this regard, says Muller, that "Lacan sees [in] the working of the ego, the source of all resistance to the *subject's growth*." [50] The "subject's growth"—what a surprising phrase. How could such a nullity grow? By accepting its desires, its lack, not spending its whole life defending against them. This does not, of course, mean that the subject ceases to pursue its desires. But the subject can "organize [her] menu," distinguishing to some degree phantasm from reality and in so doing avoid seeing herself as simply the agent of another's desire. They are genuinely her desires . . . she has appropriated them. There is a self hiding here somewhere, more akin, we shall see, to Locke's self in *An Essay concerning Human Understanding*, able to appropriate its own experiences, than Hume's bundle self, the mere container of experience.

Decentering Kohut

Lacan and Kohut are not really saying the same thing in different ways; they are saying decisively different things. Nevertheless, they may be compared and contrasted. It makes sense to use Lacan to decenter Kohut because they are writing about commensurable entities, albeit hardly identical ones. If we take Lacan seriously as a theorist of real selves, as Kohut is, then in what way should we reinterpret and reformulate Kohut?

The most important point is that we emphasize and appreciate *otherness* more. The whole world, contrary to Wolf, is not a selfobject. To see it as such is not merely a theoretical conceit. It serves to defend the self against the recognition of its own incompleteness. The risk, which from a Lacanian perspective is not limited to archaic selfobject transferences, is that the self will alienate itself in the selfobject, seeing itself as the object of the selfobject's desire. This is similar to the function of selfobject as defense object analyzed previously. What Lacan adds is a fuller appreciation of how this defense alienates the subject from himself. Only by appreciating the otherness of the other do we confront our own lack, our own limits, our own splits. Doing so is a sign of personal and intellectual honesty in the face of a difficult reality, the Faustian will to truth that Lacan exemplifies. Finally, the other cannot set limits on the subject (required if ideals are to constrain ambitions) if the other is not seen as separate. Here is another reason ambitions so often masquerade as ideals. Ideals are identified with the needs of the subject, which is not the same thing as their internalization.

It is not merely for reasons of one's own authenticity that one should appreciate the other more. To see others strictly as selfobjects is to deny their unique individuality as well. In this regard Plato and Kohut are remarkably alike. Both see love relations almost entirely in terms of selfobject relations. That this involves considerable aggression against the other will be apparent in the analysis of the *Phaedrus* in chapter 4. Does this mean that all selfobject relations are aggressive ones? Yes, but so too are virtually all relationships. To live is to be aggressive. But to the degree that the selfobject relationship is tempered and integrated with an appreciation of the otherness of the other, which means that the separate developmental lines of narcissism and object love converge, this aggression need not be destructive. As with presence, aggression too is a question of degree. There is no need to become analytically paralyzed in its presence, concluding that the exploitation of others as selfobjects is always bad. It is always aggressive. Whether it is bad depends upon the balance of forces, so to speak.

A related point suggested by Lacan is that there is not enough empathy in the world to overcome the lack, the *manque*, in ourselves. Even if there were, transmuting internalization could not appropriate it. The lack stems ultimately not from the failure of insufficiently empathic others (though this is obviously important) but from the intensity of our own desire to be one, absolutely present to ourselves. On this particular issue Lacan may be right to collapse metaphysics, ontology, and psychoanalysis. The self sets and demands an impossibly high standard of oneness, of presence, in almost every aspect of life, including intellectual life. Where Lacan goes wrong is in transforming the desires of the self into the standard by which philosophy, or psychoanalysis, is to be evaluated. We do not adopt the fulfillment of the young boy's desire to possess mother as the standard of the successful resolution of the oedipal conflict. Nor should we adopt the standard of absolute presence as the criterion of the real self, even though both reflect real desires.

Lacan nonetheless comes closer to an important truth than Kohut. We *desire* the self far more than we *are* or ever will be the self. Self psychology risks inauthenticity if it is read as suggesting that therapeutic empathy can give us what we desire. On the contrary, the intensity of our desire to be one with ourselves is so great that it can never be satisfied. The lack in human existence is not just the measure of failed empathy. It is also a measure of how much we want. But, it might be asked, is not the desire for absolute presence itself an archaic, narcissistic ideal? Perhaps, though one must be careful not to use the ideal of maturity as a means to deny the contradictions of existence.

The political implications of Lacan's thought are almost unimaginable. Would he see every revolution, every protest, as an escape from the lack in oneself, a diversionary tactic? Or would he rather take an "existentialist" position? The only standard is authenticity: that the action not be an escape from the nonself, or an attempt to create self, but an expression of the self that lives in the realm of the id. It is hard to know what Lacan would hold, though probably the latter comes closer to the mark. Yet, for all Lacan's apparent skepticism about action, there is in his account of the subject more activity than Kohut's. Kohut conceptualizes the self primarily, albeit not exclusively (we are talking here strictly about tendencies), as an entity that responds to the empathy of others. The concept of a selfobject reflects this orientation insofar as it suggests that the self sees its world almost entirely in terms of where it can find support: the world as mirror of the self. Lacan's subject, on the other hand, makes, breaks, and creates worlds, anything to assure himself of his own existence, anything to avoid confronting the lack within, anything to try to overcome it. One suspects that Lacan comes closer to the mark and that this is good reason to worry.

It is from this perspective that one should consider the implications of Lacan's thought for reason. Unlike Kohut, Lacan does not make the mistake of equating reason with the adaptive functions of the ego.[51] On the contrary, he recognizes such an equation as a bad-faith attempt to escape from our own lack. As Benvenuto and Kennedy put it, "in Lacan's view, the ego's mastery of the environment is always an illusory mastery, as a result of the way it is formed at the mirror stage, and the human subject will continue throughout life to look for an imaginary 'wholeness' and 'unity.' He will want to master his environment, and feel a unified and total person."[52] A troubling possibility suggests itself. If reason is ultimately an expression of the whole self, with all its needs and fears, then what Kohut calls narcissistic rage may also be expressed in, and not merely through, reason. This is a subtle distinction, which the chapters that follow will seek to make clearer. For now the key point is that narcissistic rage at a world that fails to confirm one's "wholeness" and "unity" may be expressed not merely in the ends of reason: clearing forests, subordinating other species, waging war, and so forth. It may also be found in the activity of reasoning itself. This is seen quite readily in what the Frankfurt school of critical theory calls instrumental reason, which apprehends the entire world in terms of how it may be manipulated and controlled—that world as prey, as Theodor Adorno puts it. Since I have written three books and numerous articles on this topic, I shall not pursue it here. Nor is it necessary; other instances of reason as rage abound.

Martha Nussbaum finds it in Creon's "temper that builds cities" (*astunomous orgas*), which, she argues, "is *orge* indeed, ungovernable rage, violent anger [*Antigone*, 280,957,766; cf. 876]. Thus the ode's odd vocabulary invites us to consider that it is, precisely, anger that builds Creon's city; violent rage at our vulnerability before the world is the deep motivation for these strategies of safety. Progress begins to look very like revenge."[53] Or, as Nietzsche put it, "To imagine another, more valuable world is an expression of hatred for a world that makes one suffer: the *ressentiment* of metaphysicans is here creative."[54] Not merely instrumental reason but idealism may be an expression of narcissistic rage. It is in this context that Adorno writes of "idealism as rage" at a world too sparse to be dominated: that is, too sparse and recalcitrant to serve as mirror and desperately needed selfobject.[55] With this thought in mind I turn to Plato.

A Final Thought

One might argue that this mix of Kohut and Lacan is so eclectic, so informal, and so lacking in a principled analysis of where choices must be made that the result is a list of considerations or analytical themes, not a true theory of the self. This would be roughly correct. Though it is informed by an appreciation of the risk of mixing incommensurables, mine is indeed a list of considerations and themes that one should keep in mind when reading texts about the self from a psychoanalytic perspective. More is unnecessary for the task at hand and risks approaching these texts with a self-psychological formula, rather than a self-psychological perspective. Less is more.

Some clever fellow . . . likened
the self to a leaky jar, because
it can never be filled.
—Plato, *Gorgias*

CHAPTER THREE

The Prehistory
of the Self

The Psyche from Homer
to Plato's *Gorgias*

To treat Plato's concept of the psyche as his concept of the self is, of course, not unproblematic, for the term *psyche* has a much wider range of connotations and is generally translated into English as "soul." The German *Geist*, which suggests both spirit and self, comes closer to the mark. But German translators usually render *psyche* as *Seele* rather than *Geist* (though *Seele* too has a much broader connotation in German, more accurately reflecting the original Greek; thus, Germans write of *seelische Gesundheit*, whereas we say *mental health*). Since it is a purpose of the next two chapters to demonstrate that Plato actually possesses a fairly well developed concept of the self, I shall not defend here what is really the purpose of these chapters to justify: that it makes sense, in some contexts, to treat Plato's concept of the psyche as a concept of the self. The focus in this chapter is on the continuity between Plato's use of the term *psyche* and its use by various pre-Platonic authors. Thus, I stop at Plato's *Gorgias*, presumably an early middle dialogue, in which the continuity is most apparent. The next chapter takes up Plato's fully developed concept of the psyche, beginning with *The Republic*.

In understanding Plato's use of the term *psyche*, the linguistic context is important. Although there are other words for "soul" in ancient Greek, particularly in Homer, by the time Plato wrote, *psyche* was the only noun used to refer to the soul. Quite often, however, Plato uses the term to refer to the ordinary empirical self, occasionally shifting from the noun *psyche* to a pronoun such as *himself* (*sauton*) in a single sentence (*Protagoras*, 313a2).[1] Of course, the term *self* will be employed in my own analysis of Plato's writings about the *psyche*. Earlier Greek uses of the term will also usually be rendered as *psyche*.

Whether it makes sense to write of Plato's concept of the self will, in the end, be decided not by linguistic issues but by conceptual ones. For Leo Strauss, the classical authors sought *self-knowledge*, that is, knowledge of humanity's place in the cosmos, an order that is prior to and independent of human will. Moderns, on the other hand, usually pursue not self-knowledge but *self-consciousness*, reflection upon strictly human nature, the way in which it determines our relations to others of our kind.[2] To write of Plato's concept of the self, a Straussian might argue, is to impose a more superficial modern concept on a classical one. Such an argument would not be entirely false, but it frames the issue in terms too extreme. Self-consciousness is part of self-knowledge (they are not alternatives but complements), and one can have self-knowledge in the absence of a perfected cosmology. To be sure, to "know myself" (*gnothi sauton*) I must know how I fit into a larger scheme of things, but this can be a tradition or a way of life. Were it impossible to distinguish classical cosmology from classical teaching about the good life, then the classics would be of merely historical interest, as Alasdair MacIntyre suggests in *After Virtue*. Conversely, much of what the classics have to teach us is about self-consciousness: the nature of human beings and how this nature is best fulfilled. A psychoanalytic approach to several of Plato's dialogues is employed in this chapter and the next. The goal is neither to psychoanalyze Plato nor to reduce his teachings about self-knowledge to ones about self-consciousness. It is to appreciate better the complexity of his concept of the self.

Plato and Psychoanalysis

It is not uncommon to apply psychoanalysis to the ancient Greeks, including Plato. In *The Glory of Hera*, Slater applies Freudian analysis to the classical tragedies of the middle period in order to draw conclusions about the psychological dynamics of Greek families. George Devereux applies Freudian analysis to explain what he calls "Greek pseudo-homosexuality and the 'Greek miracle.'"[3] A number of other authors have applied psychoanalysis to the works of Plato and sometimes to Plato himself. Hans Kelsen, in his otherwise interesting essay "Platonic Love," sees Plato's interest in eros, which he interprets almost entirely in terms of pederasty, as an attempt by Plato to come to terms with his own homosexuality; Kelsen argues it was much more intense than was the norm in Athens.[4] The problems with such an argument are apparent. We have very little evidence regarding Plato's private life, what evidence we have is unreliable in any case (such as Plato's seventh letter), and we are far from sure what the homosexual norm was at Athens.

More common, fortunately, is an attempt to draw comparisons between Plato's concept of eros and Freud's. Freud himself was among the first to do so. Answering those who questioned his extension of the concept of eros to include nonsexual relations, Freud stated, "As for the 'stretching' of the concept of sexuality . . . anyone who looks down with contempt upon psychoanalysis from a superior vantage point should remember how closely the enlarged sexuality of psychoanalysis coincides with the Eros of the divine Plato."[5]

A number of critics have concurred. George Boas, for example, argues that there is only a "verbal difference" between the views of Plato and those of Freud on this subject:

> The libido, as a term for generalized desire . . . by reintegrating humanity and its strivings into the natural world . . . has revived in a new form the kernel of Diotimas' speech in the *Symposium*. Freud, along with most Platonists, would deny this. However, since love in the *Symposium* is found not only in sexual attraction but also in scientific research and philosophic meditation, there is only a verbal difference between the two philosophies.[6]

In fact, this has it precisely backward, as F. M. Cornford recognizes. Although eros, like libido, is generalized desire that can flow either upward or downward into the physical or the spiritual, there remains a decisive difference between Plato and Freud. For Plato, humanity is drawn upward, and the self-moving energy of the psyche resides in the highest, not the lowest, part.[7]

It was not until a recent work by Gerasimos Santas, *Plato and Freud: Two Theories of Love,* that the proper conclusion regarding their relationship was systematically laid out and defended. Plato and Freud, in spite of their mutual references to eros, are writing about very different things. In many respects, Plato's view of eros, and particularly its relationship to reason, is the opposite of Freud's. Plato is superimposing a rationalist metaphysics on eros rather than rooting this metaphysics in eros.[8] In his review of Santas's book, A. W. Price suggests that the real parallel between the two lies not in their concepts of eros but in Freud's structural model of the mind (ego, superego, and id) and Plato's model of the three-part psyche in *The Republic.*[9]

When psychoanalytic theory is applied to Plato, it frequently seeks to establish a parallel between Plato's categories and those of Freud's as though Plato were anticipating psychoanalysis in some way. This will not be the approach taken here. I will not argue, for example, that rather than anticipating Freud, Plato was actually anticipating Kohut or Lacan. Nor will I argue that there are important structural parallels between their works. One can apply psychoanalysis to Plato without arguing that he anticipated the same psychoanalytic theory one happens to be applying. The same holds for the other authors examined in this book. Yet it is understandable why scholars and analysts try to find psychoanalysis in Plato. It is troublesome, sometimes even disingenuous, to apply psychoanalysis to authors whose intentions were clearly not psychoanalytic. Such an interpretation of Marx might be an example. To see Plato as a virtual psychoanalyst would be one way of avoiding this difficulty.

My approach is somewhat different. Plato writes about several entities that seem to serve as selfobjects, such as his comparing the three parts of the psyche to the three classes of the ideal polis, the city in speech. To be sure, Plato is not writing of the polis as a selfobject in the same theoretical sense that Kohut might. But Plato is not merely making an analogy between the city of speech and the self either. Rather, his point is that one should internalize the order of the polis in oneself. The ideal polis, he says, "is laid up as a pattern in heaven, where he who wishes can see it and found it in his own heart" (*Republic*, 592b-c).[10] It does not seem misleading or a gross misrepresentation of Plato's intent to treat the polis as a selfobject. There are other selfobjects in his work, too, such as the "nurse of generation" in the *Timaeus*. Indeed, the point of approaching Plato via self psychology is to remain as phenomenological as possible, not reducing his account to a presumably more fundamental one, such as libido theory.

Nevertheless, it cannot be denied that even a self-psychological approach imposes a perspective that deviates from Plato's presumed intent, though perhaps not as much as some who would claim to know Plato's intent might make out. The self-psychological perspective puts the self first, in that it seeks to ascertain the consequences for the self of organizing and pursuing its ideals or ambitions in a particular way. The self-psychological perspective neither affirms nor denies the existence of an objective cosmological order. How could it? It focuses instead on the consequences to the self of believing in, and relating to, this order in a particular way. In this respect, the self-psychological approach stands somewhere between Strauss's self-consciousness and self-knowledge. Or, better put, it stands outside this continuum. Self-consciousness is concerned with the self's relationship to itself and others; self-knowledge is concerned with how the self fits into a cosmological order. The self-psychological approach asks how Plato's commitment to self-knowledge affects the self-consciousness of those he writes of. No claim is made that the self-psychological approach is more fundamental, showing the existence of a cosmological worldview to be an epiphenomenon of the needs of the self, or whatever. Rather, the claim is that Plato possessed a sophisticated concept of the self and of self-consciousness. Investigating his concept of self-knowledge, by viewing some of his objects of self-knowledge as selfobjects, can help us understand it better.

Plato's key move is to locate desire in the psyche, not the body. From this move stems two strategies for self-fulfillment, the first of which is fruitful, the second not. The first strategy is to demonstrate that if desire is of the psyche, not the body, then knowledge, truth, and beauty are better soul foods than physical pleasure, for physical pleasure never lasts, dripping out of the body as though it were a leaky jar. Otherwise expressed, what really satisfies is relationships with people who possess these attributes. This is how we temporarily, contingently, and imperfectly overcome the lack in ourselves, employing these people as selfobjects and so sharing for a moment in their beautiful qualities. Sandel, quoting Rawls, argues that the good regime can encourage this sharing, so that "the members of community 'participate in one another's nature,'" recognizing that "'the self is realized in the activities of many selves."[11] An important question to be asked is whether Plato, who knows truths about the self that Rawls and Sandel barely glimpse, actually provides much support for this ideal.

In fact, he does not. In many of his dialogues Plato takes great pains to split off these good qualities from those who possess them, appropriating the qualities and abandoning the person. In pursuing this second strategy Plato moves from an analysis of how to live well with the lack in human existence to a strategy of how it can be transcended. Evidently the lack in the self is so painful that its partial fulfillment in relationships with real persons only makes it worse, reminding us of what we are not. It must be all or nothing. Such a strategy not only sets self-consciousness in opposition to self-knowledge; it requires the obliteration of the former in service of the latter. In the language of Lacan, it is the strategy of the ego, not the subject.

Pre-Socratic Views of the Psyche

Often viewed as a schizoid, not very well integrated amalgam of desires (much like Lacan's view of the subject), the pre-Platonic self was in fact somewhat more sophisticated than this. Plato developed a new concept of the psyche, but he did not develop it out of nothing, contrary to Burnet, in "The Socratic Doctrine of the Soul."[12] E. R. Dodds gives what is by now the standard view of the self before Plato, an account that finds Plato's innovation in his transformation of the Orphic "occult" self into the rational self. Plato was forced to turn to the Orphic tradition because the Homeric tradition provided insufficient resources to draw on. It contained "no unified concept of what we call 'soul' or 'personality.'"[13] By the time Plato wrote, says Dodds (observing the puzzling fact that the meaning of the term *psyche* has not expanded much since Homer's use of it to denote a "shade"), the psyche had come to represent what Homer had called *thumos*: the living self with appetites and desires. Because such a view of the psyche was obviously not the best material for Plato to draw upon, he turned to the Orphic tradition of a "detachable" soul, a tradition handed down by Pythagoras, Empedocles, and others.[14]

To utilize this tradition, says Dodds, Plato had to transform the Orphic self into the rational self. This was especially important because within the Orphic tradition there was a puritanical dimension that separated psyche and its desires, self from body. Although this influence certainly continued to be expressed in Plato's work, he made the issue more complicated—and more subtle and sophisticated—by locating desire within the psyche. This makes for real mental conflict, real psychology, and eventually real moral responsibility. Not psyche versus soma, but psyche versus psyche. In fact, it is this move that is the key to Plato's concept of the psyche. It is what makes it so rich, such a powerful challenge to the polis. Plato creates a complex psyche by locating desire within it, but he never figures out what to do with this desire. That the self might live in peace with its desires seems impossible, in large measure because these become the self's desires for itself, for its own perfection—desires whose intensity is exceeded only by the impossibility of their fulfillment, at least in the polis. Lacan has it just right, at least as far as Plato is concerned. In the end, the puritanical strain, which comes to mean separating the rational part of the psyche from the desiring part (as the Orphic tradition separated soul and body), seems to win out.

Dodds uses a bit of psychology to explain this. Under the extreme patriarchy of a feudal order, the son's obedience to his father was total and unquestioning. This pattern, however, began to break down somewhat in the post-Homeric era, as the father's claim became less total. Only then, Dodds argues, could one get the emergence of the Oedipus conflict, or rather, only then could one get any conscious awareness of the son's hostility toward father and his desire for mother. It was this psyche that Plato had available to draw upon to mix with the Orphic self so as to make the Orphic self somewhat more human and less detached.[15] Such a guilty psyche has the advantage of supporting a more complex view of the self. The disadvantage is that once one takes this guilt into the psyche, it becomes more difficult to get rid of it. It is in this context that splitting of the psyche becomes the functional equivalent of the old psyche-soma split. My argument does not depend upon Dodds's speculations, but the way in which they support each other is apparent. Both are concerned with the consequences of taking desire into the self.

David Claus's *Toward the Soul: An Inquiry into the Meaning of Psuche before Plato* is the most scholarly and systematic treatment of the subject in recent years. He does not show Dodds to be mistaken, but he does show that Plato's use of the term, particularly in the early dialogues, is more continuous with standard Greek usage than Dodds suggests. Otherwise expressed, there was more material to work with in the traditional Greek view of the psyche than Dodds recognizes. Thus it is less necessary to attribute what is new in Plato's view solely to his individual genius or to the Orphic tradition. One reason it is easy to miss this more sophisticated view of the psyche in the Greek tradition is that there are a multiplicity of soul words in Homer, such as *psyche, thumos, menos, kardia, noos, phren/phrenes*.[16] Of these, it is actually *psyche* that has one of the most restricted meanings, the physical life force, which when extinguished becomes a shade. It simply does not work to focus upon a particular word, such as *psyche*, in order to see how the Greeks understood the concept behind the term. Rather, one must look for a constellation of terms, how they are often substituted for one another, as well as the context of their use. Claus divides the way in which various soul words are used into three groups:

1. The physical life force itself, what keeps us going, what may be restored by nourishment and what may be extinguished by decay and violence.

2. The life force that is the seat of courage, desire, and extreme wrath.

3. The life force as the center of powerful emotions, especially joy and grief.

The same soul word, such as *kardia*, may sometimes be used in a very concrete, physical sense (group 1) and at other times refer to more subtle emotions (group 3), as when Tony Bennett sings "I left my heart in San Francisco." If one does not pay close attention to the context, as well as how words are substituted, one can easily overlook the complexity of their use.

Between Homer and Socrates, says Claus, the number of group 3 uses of the term *psyche*, as the seat of powerful emotions, is limited, owing in large measure to the close association of *psyche* and *shade* in Homer, an association so close that other meanings are pushed out. "There are," he says, "in the lyric poets and in Aeschylus about eight times as many instances of *thumos* in psychological contexts as there are of *psyche*."[17] Nevertheless, there are a number of sophisticated uses of the term (especially fragment 388 of Euripides), and even more of such related soul words as *noos*, *phrenes*, and *kardia*. It was not necessary, therefore, for Plato to go entirely outside the mainstream tradition to find support for his concept of the psyche. Conversely, this fact gives us license to interpret some of Plato's arguments about the psyche in a strategic fashion. Plato may sometimes be arguing for his new concept by linking it to more familiar ones, concepts not entirely alien from his. This seems to be particularly the case in the *Gorgias* (501b-c), where cookery is claimed to be an art aimed at the psyche (albeit in a way that does not promote virtue), a claim that makes no sense unless psyche and soma are seen as tightly bound, yet separate, a relationship the mainstream tradition would support.

Claus nevertheless concludes that we should not make too much of these pre-Socratic uses of the term *psyche* or of related words, either. And it is not only moderns who might make this mistake, reading back into classical uses more developed views. Aristotle, in *De Anima* (403a-411a), seems to assume that every mention of psyche by his pre-Socratic predecessors contains the full conceptual development of the term that is found in his own work.[18]

From what has been said it is evident that it is not because the psyche is compounded of the elements that knowledge belongs to it, nor is it correct or true to say that the psyche is moved. Knowledge, however, is an attribute of the psyche, and so are perception, opinion, desire, wish and appetition generally; animal locomotion also is produced by the psyche; and likewise growth, maturity, and decay. (*De Anima*, 411a26–31)

It is as though Aristotle assumes that because we can find references to each of these concepts in the work of the pre-Socratics, then each pre-Socratic view of the soul must contain all of these elements. This is not the case, either. In fact, the purpose of a healthy soul in the work of authors such as Democritus (B, 159, 170, 171, 187, 189[?], 212, passim) and Gorgias (*Encomium of Helen*) seems often to be as much to serve the healthy body as vice versa.[19]

This last view of the relationship between psyche and soma should not be unfamiliar. It is the dominant view in much of popular psychology today, including that represented in the magazine titled *Self*, in which it is important to have a good mental attitude and a good "self-image" because it will strengthen the immune system and make us generally healthier and happier. The self is valuable, from this perspective, because it is all the individual has ("I may not be much, but I'm all I've got") and perhaps all that the person can control. The notion that it might be ontologically higher than the body has long since been forgotten. This raises an interesting question that I will address in later chapters. Are modern teachings about the self best understood as a regression behind the Platonic self to a pre-Socratic separate but equal view of the relationship of psyche and soma?

The Dialogues

Even juggling the presumed order of composition of Plato's dialogues (for example, placing the *Timaeus* as a middle work, virtually contemporaneous with *The Republic*, a placement that seems quite convincing) does not produce an account of Plato's concept of the psyche that shows a coherent developmental line. Whereas presumably early works, such as the *Phaedo*, exhibit a less clear and sophisticated account of the psyche, the middle dialogues vary enormously in the sophistication with which they treat the topic. Although there exist theoretical grounds for claiming that one dialogue expresses a more mature, fully developed concept of the psyche than another, there exist no grounds for arguing that it came last—or first. It is assumed (with one partial exception) that the historical Socrates and Plato's Socrates are identical. Although this is unlikely to have been the case, there is insufficient evidence to proceed in any other fashion.

The Republic, Timaeus, and Phaedrus are dealt with in the next chapter, which does not ignore Philebus and The Laws, book 10. The Phaedo, of course, devotes a great deal of attention to the psyche, more sustained attention than any other dialogue, with the exception of the Timaeus. Nevertheless, I will not analyze it here, for it is essentially restricted to a single question: whether the psyche is immortal. Although it contains some interesting hypotheses on the relationship between psyche and soma, such as attunement, other dialogues treat this relationship in a more sophisticated fashion. The Apology contains Plato's most famous teaching about the psyche, that one's chief concern in life should be to care for it (30B). This, however, is the only reference to the psyche in the dialogue (some consider 40C a second reference); consequently the Apology will not play a major role in my discussion.

Three themes, not easily reconcilable, regarding the relationship between psyche and soma dominate the early ("Socratic") dialogues: (1) the psyche and the soma are separate (Protagoras, 313a), the psyche sometimes being regarded as the prisoner of the soma (Phaedo, 66b-68c, 80e, passim); (2) the psyche includes the soma as an integral part of itself (Charmides, 156e7–8); and (3) the soul, though separate from the body, leads it and is related to it in an intimate way (Gorgias, 464aff; Alcibiades 1, 129eff). Robinson suggests that these contradictory patterns reflect the shifting influence of the two views of the psyche that Plato drew on: the Homeric view, in which the soma and the psyche are tightly linked, and the Orphic view, in which the psyche is a virtual prisoner of the body.[20] Such an interpretation, though placing more emphasis than Claus on the Orphic tradition, is consonant with Claus's view that in these early dialogues Plato is using the traditional Greek view of the psyche as seat of the life force as a foundation from which to develop a more ambitious view. One sees this especially clearly in the Gorgias.

The Gorgias

The Gorgias begins to crystallize the issues with which we are concerned. Contrary to some interpretations, such as Kelsen's, the Gorgias does not support the thesis that the psyche is a prisoner of the soma. The psyche leads the body because it distinguishes between good and bad, whereas the body just seeks pleasure. Nevertheless, they are not opposite principles. They are similar enough that they can be frequently compared, not just contrasted, and the psyche is sufficiently embodied that cookery can be said to be aimed at the psyche (464b–465e). These considerations raise some questions. How much of Plato's argument is strictly rhetorical, designed to draw upon mainstream cultural views of an embodied psyche, but aimed at transcending these views? How much is simply confused, such as cookery for the psyche, the result of a conflation of archaic and early-fourth-century views? And how much is a genuine foreshadowing of Plato's position, elaborated in presumably later dialogues, that desire is of the psyche, not the body?

Although there is no fully satisfactory answer to these questions, themes are introduced in the *Gorgias* that will be developed further in later works. Plato's famous comparison of the psyche with a leaky jar—because it can never be filled or satisfied by the objects of desire (493a–494b)—establishes a strategy that dominates a number of dialogues. The pursuit of philosophy is desirable in this dialogue not because it is higher and better per se but because its goods (memory and belief) are the only ones that do not flow through the holes in the jar—that is, that can address the lack, the emptiness, at the core of the psyche. Plato's search, then, is the search for the sources of permanent and reliable satisfaction. Otherwise expressed, Plato quite often writes as if it were the purpose of self-knowledge to serve self-consciousness.

Socrates compares his love objects with those of Callicles (481c–482c). Callicles is in love with two objects, one individual, one abstract: Demos, son of Prilampes, and the Athenian *demos*. He can resist neither, always changing his opinion to mirror that of his beloved. Like Callicles, Socrates also has two love objects, one individual, one abstract: Alcibiades and philosophy. And though Socrates too has this tendency to mirror his beloved, he has found a way to turn this weakness to his advantage. He will love only the true and the good so that in mirroring them he will himself become just like them. This means, in effect, that Socrates will love only philosophy. For Plato, as for Kohut, almost all love relationships become selfobject relationships, usually one in which we assimilate ourselves to an ideal and so come to share in its perfection. There is little place here or in any of the other dialogues (as we shall see) for love objects: love of the unique particularity of the other qua other. The selfobject relations that Plato idealizes most are archaic, immature, strictly narcissistic. Indeed, it is worth asking (even if the answer is not entirely clear) whether Socrates' choice of love objects is, for this reason, even less mature than Callicles'.

It is frequently observed that in Plato's later work the language of the relationship of psyche to people and Ideas is heavily sexualized (*Republic*, 490ab; *Phaedrus*, 65b9, 66a6). As Robinson puts it, "mental contact is not enough; the sensation of *presence*, of total union . . . is an integral part of the experience."[21] Plato and Lacan share the same ideal—unmediated presence— even if they have reached very different conclusions about whether it may be realized. Consider, in this regard, how Plato uses the term *suneinai*, the ordinary term for sexual relations, to characterize not only sexual intercourse (*Symposium*, 211d6) but also intellectual intercourse with the beautiful and virtuous (212a2). But to call this language sexual is really to miss the point. This is not the language of sex. Or rather, the language of sex is itself an expression of the archaic idealizing selfobject transference. Indeed, the imagery of romantic love is virtually defined by this transference. Plato's is the language of an archaic merging with an idealized selfobject, in which the relation to the object is one of becoming like (*aphomoionsthai*), imitation (*mimeisthai*), and assimilation (*omoiosis*), terms that Plato also uses to characterize the relationship between psyche and Ideas (*Symposium*, 192c–193a; cf. *Republic*, 500c-d; *Theaetetus*, 176b).

Santas makes the same point somewhat differently, pointing out how Platonic love is entirely and completely determined by the beauty and desirability of its object—that is, strictly by its idealizability.

> Plato's theory, especially in the *Phaedrus*, allows and even directs the lover to benefit the beloved. But the beloved is still seen as an image of an abstract entity which remains the source of value for that love, the model that guides the lover. Love of the weak, the deformed, the sick, the untalented, even of the cruel and the arrogant, not only has no value, it seems, but is not even a theoretical possibility. Can the object so totally dominate the concept, define its nature and give it its only value?[22]

Our answer must be yes, but only when, as Plato does, we equate love with the idealizing selfobject transference, in which we love the other only insofar as he or she is what we would be. What kind of self loves only in this way?

Plato has already hinted at the answer: a self that seeks to fill the lack in itself by merging with its object, while being deeply afraid that its object is insufficiently reliable and worthy. Much of Plato's philosophy seeks to resolve this dilemma.

Philosophy as Defense of the Ego against the Desiring Subject?

Plato, it is apparent, does not create the psyche out of nothing. Instead, he renders the traditional Greek view far more sophisticated by taking desire into the psyche, thus transforming the conflict between the psyche and the soma into a conflict among different parts of the psyche. It is this view, whose most advanced expression is found in *The Republic*, that first allows genuine psyche-ology: the study of mental conflict. It is also, it might be noted, a view incompatible with the Socratic teaching that no one ever does wrong knowingly (*Protagoras*, 358c, Aristotle, N. *Ethics*, 1145b25–27, on Socrates' position). For Socrates, doing wrong is simply a matter of ignorance of the long-term effects of justice and injustice on the psyche. In Plato's account, on the other hand, one can know what is right and still be unable to do it, as the opposing parts of the mind are stronger. One suspects that the Platonic Socrates corresponds to the historical Socrates on this point, Plato himself holding the more psychologically sophisticated position, though this is impossible to know. Finally, Plato's view has the additional advantage of allowing desire to be conceptualized as a desire not merely for an external object but for the self. What leaks out of the jar is not merely the physical satisfaction that never lasts. It is the self. The self is porous to itself.

Plato is doing more than developing a more sophisticated view of the psyche. He is preparing the groundwork for splitting the psyche in the name of reason so that the reasoning self might soothe its dreadful lack in an archaic selfobject transference with abstract selfobjects—that is, selfobjects who will never disappoint, as they are not truly human. We see a key expression of this strategy (developed most fully in the *Phaedrus*) in Socrates' preference in the *Gorgias* for abstract love objects. Plato's greatness resides in his ability to transform the deepest needs of the self into the foundation of philosophy: "the *ressentiment* of metaphysicians is here creative." It is this that gives his philosophy its staying power, its perennial fascination. It speaks not merely to intellectual needs to understand the world but to the deepest needs of the self to plug the leaky jar that is the self. The danger is that this philosophy, no matter how brilliant and creative, may become an instance of narcissistic rage, coupled with retreat and denial, against the self who can never be fulfilled. Otherwise expressed, the danger is that philosophy itself becomes a defense of the ego against the subject. This too is a division of the psyche, with philosophy—reason at its most abstract—as the great divider. The Orphic tradition of the detachable soul becomes, in Plato's account, the divisible self.

O lastly over-strong against
thy self!—John Milton,
Paradise Lost [1]

CHAPTER FOUR

The Psyche
Divided against Itself

The Republic, Timaeus,
and *Phaedrus*

The three-part model of the psyche found in
The Republic is the most developed and sophisticated account in Plato's dialogues. It is not, however, unproblematic. *The Republic*'s account is sophisticated not because it divides the psyche into three parts but because Plato
takes a human entity, the polis, as psyche's selfobject. The three-part psyche
seems as much a result of this decision as its cause. How seriously Plato takes
the three-part psyche is difficult to determine and cannot be settled by
consulting issues of translation. Nevertheless, it should be noted, as George
Klosko points out, that the term *part* "is far too rigid for what Plato had in
mind." Although he uses several different terms, such as *eidos* (form) and
genos (kind), the Greek word for part, *meros*, is not used until 442b2, when
Plato is well into the discussion. [2] Plato, it is apparent, is not employing a
technical vocabulary and should not be analyzed as though he were, here or
elsewhere.

The first "part" of the psyche is reason (*logizetai*, 439d5; Plato uses many
other terms for this controlling principle, including *nous*). The second part is
desire (439d6–7, *alogiston* and *epithumetikon*, literally unreasoning and desiring). The third part is *thumos* (439e3), a term that at first seems to cover
too much territory, from pure anger, on the one hand, to feelings of noble
courage, self-respect, and righteous indignation, on the other. Yet the story
that Plato tells to explain this third element, often translated as "spirit" or
"ambition," captures it well. Recall that in Homeric Greek, *thumos* was
probably the most sophisticated self word. Leontion was on his way back to
Athens from the Piraeus when he saw some corpses lying on the ground with
the executioner standing near them. He wanted to look but held himself back
in disgust. Finally his desire got the better of him, and he ran over to the
corpses while saying to himself (that is, to his own eyes) "There you are,
curse you—a lovely sight! Have a real good look!" This is not an uncommon

phenomenon, continues Plato. We often see a man whose desires tell him to do one thing, and his reason, to do another that he knows is right. "It's like a struggle between political factions, with thumos fighting on the side of reason." Thumos is reason's natural auxiliary unless it is corrupted by bad upbringing (4393e–441a).

In the ideal polis of *The Republic*, the auxiliaries have a key role to play. They are enforcers, marked not so much by their reason or wisdom as by their unwavering commitment to the laws (*Republic*, 429b–430c). When the polis is the psyche's selfobject, as it is in *The Republic* (a more literal selfobject is hard to imagine; most of *The Republic* is organized around a parallel between the organization of classes in the polis and the organization of the parts of the psyche), then desire has a productive role to play in the psyche. Good desire can counterbalance bad desire if, that is, the individual is properly brought up, by which Plato means not merely good parenting but the influence of good customs and laws. That it is fair to characterize thumos as good desire finds support in the *Timaeus* (69c–70b), where thumos is characterized in precisely these terms. The big danger is that the elements of the mind will usurp each other. Although Plato's first concern is that bad desire will usurp reason, drawing upon good desire (thumos) for its energy (441b-c), the more common danger in the Greek world was actually that thumos would assume command. Thumos in command is hubris, the "Greek disease" as it has been called, the unrestrained struggle for individual (and to a lesser degree national) excellence that led to faction and such catastrophic decisions as Athens's invasion of Sicily during the Peloponnesian War.

The three-part mind is never again explained with such clarity (the chariot simile in the *Phaedrus* does not even come close). Robinson argues that this reveals that the three-part psyche is not central to Plato's program but serves primarily to justify by analogy a particular political arrangement. Although there may be some truth to this judgment when applied to the dialogue as a whole, it does not seem a fair characterization of the model of the psyche in *The Republic* (yet, even there, when the context is cosmological, Plato seems far from committed to the three-part psyche [612a4]). To the contrary, many have argued that it is really the argument about individual justice that is paramount in this work; the argument about justice in the polis serves primarily to support the former argument. One sees this most clearly in the conclusion to book nine, where Plato employs the well-governed polis as model for mature self-control. We do not allow children to run free, he says, until "we have established some kind of constitutional government in them, and have educated the best in them to be their guardian and ruler and take over from the best in us: then we give them their freedom" (591a). It is this use of the polis as a pattern for human subjectivity that makes it legitimate to regard it as a selfobject.

This interpretation, which makes the selfobject function of the city in speech central, is compatible with, though it does not depend upon, the interpretations of Bloom, Nichols, and others that the city in speech (or at least parts thereof) is counterfactual.[3] Plato is saying, in effect, that if there were to be a unitary and harmonious city, these are the deformations of human nature that would be required, which are obviously impossible, perhaps even undesirable. Whether or not Plato holds that the city in speech is possible and desirable, he clearly holds that the unity and harmony it represents can and should be internalized in the individual, or at least a few individuals (592b). In fact, the interpretations of Bloom and Nichols emphasize an important, albeit troubling point. If the city in speech was never intended as a political solution to the problem of justice, but strictly as a private, personal one, then the isolation of Plato's just man is even greater than is generally appreciated. *The Republic* is really about disconnecting a few men from the state so that they, like Socrates, might have a chance to be just individuals. The selfobject function of *The Republic* is not a supplement to its political teachings but an alternative to politics.

It has been frequently observed that the just man in Plato's *Republic* is remarkably unconcerned with the effects of his actions on others. His chief concern is to care for his psyche, to achieve the appropriate balance among the three parts and so live a life of happiness, even in a corrupt world (592a-b). Such individuals will, by the way, also make the best citizens, for they will be least likely to be led astray by their desires, or even by thumos. This, however, is almost a side effect: "And is not the reason for all this that each element within him is performing its proper function. . . . Justice, therefore, we may say, is a principle of this kind; its real concern is not with external actions, but with a man's inward self, his true concern and interest" (443a-d; cf. 589c-d for a similar argument).

We are now in a position to better understand an otherwise surprising aspect of the Platonic account of good citizenship. It depends not at all on the "socially constituted self" but, to the contrary, on citizens who care first for their own psyches. (To be sure, this is a model of good citizenship for the less than perfect polis, but this seems to be Plato's chief concern in *The Republic*, and it is certainly mine). *The Republic* is both selfobject and political program. As a political program it promotes a remarkably totalitarian and unfree regime. As selfobject, it posits an alternative: that individuals internalize this regime ("as a pattern in heaven, where he who wishes can see it and found it in his own heart") and so control themselves in lieu of control by others: "Then we give them their freedom" (591a). Kohut calls this phenomenon transmuting internalization. The question, of course, is whether Plato's version internalizes within the self the same type of harsh, totalitarian regime that the city in speech would impose externally on its citizens. If it does, must this encourage the rebellion of the lower orders of the mind, as Aristotle says it must in the polis (*Politics*, bk. 2, 1264a25–30)? Before we answer this question, however, it will be fruitful to consider first another dimension of Plato's political psychology.

Plato's Political Psychology

It would be inaccurate to characterize *The Republic* strictly as selfobject, though it is certainly that. It also contains a theory of the relationship between the psyche and the polis. It explains how the polis comes to serve as selfobject in the first place. Plato's theory is straightforward (548d–550c). Cultural, political, and economic changes in the polis are mediated through the family. For example, he says, suppose a young man lives in a state in which honor, achievement, and office are valued highly. He has a good father, but one not particularly ambitious, in part because the father recognizes that to succeed in such a state he would have to compromise himself. The son hears his mother complain that her husband has not achieved enough and that in general he "isn't a real man and is far too easygoing, and drones on with all the usual complaints women make in the circumstances" (549d-e). How will the son respond? He will seek some sort of psychological compromise, for he is "torn in two directions, his father's influence fostering the growth of his rational nature, and that of the others his desire and ambition." In such circumstances, says Plato, the son is likely to take a middle course, resigning "control of himself to the middle element and its competitive spirit, and so become an arrogant and ambitious man" (550a-c). Although this may be the middle course in terms of the triad of reason, spirit, and desire, it seems not so much a compromise between the paths of mother and father as a male version of mother's path. More on this point shortly.

Here is Plato's psyche-ology. Conflict among the three elements of the psyche is uncomfortable, creating a feeling of internal civil war. Conflict arises when parents represent different and conflicting values, and the child feels forced to choose between them. Boys will seek to resolve this conflict by some sort of compromise, a middle course that does not openly require the rejection of the values of either parent. In this case the middle course is achieved by allying thumos with desire rather than reason. This, of course, is the recipe for hubris. Although Plato associates this middle course with the Spartan regime, it seems applicable to the Athenian aristocracy, whose members (including the young men who sought instruction from Socrates and Plato) so often competed for individual honor, excellence, and political power at the expense of the polis. Alcibiades is the classic example. It is equally applicable because Plato, like most Athenian aristocrats, considered Sparta to be an aristocratic regime, and Athens a mass one. Plato goes on to characterize other typical families, each of which reflects different organizing principles of society, such as oligarchy or tyranny (550c–576b). In each case he is concerned with the way in which society, mediated by family, reproduces itself in the psyches of its citizens by influencing which of the three parts of the psyche is preeminent.

Plato, however, is not merely a diagnostician but also a therapist, seeking to mitigate the self-pathology fostered by the Athenian family. This is best seen by turning to Slater's study of what he calls the "oral narcissistic dilemma," the emotional conflict faced by the average Greek male (a conflict that may also lie behind the son's dilemma in Plato's "case study"). Slater calls attention to a fact that has puzzled many: the contrast between the utter exclusion of women from public life at Athens (there have been few societies more misogynic) and the forceful influence they exert in so many of the Greek plays. Drawing upon these plays as his primary source regarding the psychological dynamics of Athenian domestic life, Slater argues that Athens was a covert matriarchy as far as child rearing and the family were concerned. Men were afraid of women and rejected domestic life, spending most of their time in association with other men. Consequently, Athenian boys grew up in a female-dominated environment, in which the alienated, resentful women were both seductive and ridiculing toward their sons' achievements and ambitions, the result of displaced anger at their husbands.

The result was that the sons felt enveloped by mother and wished to be free; yet they were bound to her in desire and hate, a syndrome Slater analyzes, in roughly Freudian terms, as the "oral narcissistic dilemma." This dilemma, he continues, was greatly exacerbated by the agonal character of Greek culture. When the male child became an adolescent he was expected to reject all things female and to show his superiority by besting all others in almost every aspect of life—in effect, to become a super male.[4] Athenian culture, it appears, provided no space and no model (except perhaps in its idealization of male homosexual love)[5] of any relationship that stood between dependence and envelopment, on the one hand, and a wild and ambitious self-assertion, on the other.

A. W. H. Adkins's famous characterization of Plato's self-conscious task as that of civilizing the quest for individual excellence and so making the individual pursuit of *arete* more social and cooperative, less destructive of the values of the city, supports these considerations.[6] Plato does this by transforming *arete* from its traditional meaning of "competitive success over others" to its new meaning of *sophrosune*, "self-control," understood as the proper balance of the three parts of the psyche. One might argue that in so doing Plato is binding the pursuit of individual ambition to ideals and so creating a tension arc between ambitions and ideals where none existed before. But reflection upon Plato's core argument for sophrosune—that only it leads to *eudaimonia* and fulfillment—suggests that this interpretation is not quite right. Rather than bind ambition to mature ideals, Plato seeks to integrate archaic, narcissistic ambitions with mature ones. Otherwise expressed, he is seeking to heal a vertical split, as Kohut calls it, within the pole of ambitions, a split brought about by the interaction of faulty maternal empathy and the agonal culture.

Torn between his father's halfhearted ideals and his mother's frustrated ambition, Plato's typical Athenian aristocrat organizes himself around the immoderate pursuit of ambition: excellence, honor, and power. Plato's solution in *The Republic* (at least as far as the auxiliaries are concerned—that is, typical aristocrats like the son in the case study) is not to cultivate the pole of ideals, perhaps because this pole was even more impoverished in the typical male. Certainly the culture provided little support for a self organized around this pole. Plato's solution is instead to persuade the sons of Athenian aristocrats that sophrosune is the mark of a real man, because the real competition is within oneself between reason, spirit, and desire. Because this is the real field of competition, it is an appropriate arena in which to pursue one's ambitions. In short, one's chief competitor is always oneself, a point Plato stresses throughout *The Republic* from Socrates' encounter with Thrasymacus

(347e–350e) on. Plato's ideal is simple and attractive: naturally self-controlled men and women also make good citizens.

Civil War in Polis and Psyche

Aristotle argues that the city in speech reflects a unity more appropriate to the individual than to the polis (*Politics*, 1261a). The problem is that even in the individual the unity achieved by Plato is exaggerated, unnatural, and forced. The just individual is not merely not socially constituted; he has no real relationships at all. All relationships of power and passion are contained within the self. The communism of the ideal polis, when transposed to the individual, renders each individual his own little self-sufficient commune, all commerce being strictly intrapsychic. The model, as I argue in *Narcissism*, is really the inhuman autonomy of Socrates.[7] Not only is the individual isolated, but the internal balance that Plato writes of is actually the result of a perpetual agonal struggle of reason against desire. The desires, says Plato, long to reach out, to embrace something, to connect. It is the job of reason to prevent this, to constantly thrust away the objects of desire, as well as desire itself (437b-e). The goal may be psychic balance, but it is achieved only by relentless struggle against the self.

Why? Because what looks like a man from the outside remains a beast, or at least always potentially a beast, if it is not kept on a tight lead.

> Imagine a very complicated, many-headed sort of beast, with heads of wild and tame animals all around it, which it can produce and change at will. . . . Add two other sorts of creature, one a lion, the other a man. And let the many-headed creature be by far the largest, and the lion the next largest. . . . Then put the three together and combine them into a single creature. . . . Then give the whole the external appearance of one of the three, the man, so that to eyes unable to see anything beneath the outer shell it looks like a single creature, a man. (588c-e)

After all the talk of a well-balanced, harmonious self, modeled on the ideal polis, *this* is Plato's penultimate statement on the self in *The Republic*.[8] To be sure, it concludes with the hope men will internalize the ideal polis in their hearts (592b). But we now see more clearly that the city in speech is not so much integrated selfobject as defense object. The ideal polis, a model of harmony, unity, and order, when internalized serves not to promote genuine harmony at all. Rather, it serves as an ally of reason in its conflict against the self: harmony strictly on reason's terms, which is not real harmony at all.

It was noted in chapter 2 how idealization can serve as a vehicle of splitting, a defense against rage and desire. Shortly, Plato's idealization of various perfect Beings in the *Timaeus* and *Phaedrus* will be analyzed from this perspective. We see here that even the ideal polis, the city in speech, can perform this function. What is ironic, of course, is that though the ideal polis is characterized by unity and harmony, its psychological function is precisely the opposite: to split reason and desire in the attempt to secure the victory of the former over the latter with the aid of thumos, "reason's natural auxiliary." Why this does not work was grasped clearly by Aristotle, though, of course, he was writing of the city in speech as though Plato's Socrates meant exactly what he said (not the worst principle of interpretation!): "Must it not contain two states in one, each hostile to the other? He makes the guardians into a mere occupying garrison, while the husbandmen and artisans and the rest are the real citizens. But if so the suits and quarrels, and all the evils which Socrates affirms to exist in other states, will exist equally among them" (*Politics*, 1264a10–30).

The same principle holds true when the city in speech is regarded as selfobject. To split reason and desire only intensifies the archaic desires, rendering them even less susceptible to reason. As Kohut points out, it is precisely the isolation of archaic desires from the rest of the psyche (the vertical split within the pole of ambitions or ideals) that is the core pathology in most disorders of the self. It is this isolation that encourages these desires to live a life of their own, apparently subordinate to reason (that is, the individual is not psychotic) but actually using reason as their vehicle and ultimately rejecting its interpretation of reality. It is a double life in which reason and archaic desire hardly touch.

When introducing the three-part psyche, Plato rejects another possibility, sometimes but misleadingly called the holism of the psyche:

> What is difficult is to see whether we perform all these functions with the same part of us, or each with a different part. Do we learn with one part of us, feel angry with another, and desire the pleasures of eating and sex and the like with another? Or do we employ our mind [psyche] as a

whole when our energies are employed in any of these ways? These are questions it's difficult to answer satisfactorily. (436b)

It is Plato's great achievement to have rejected (albeit here in a somewhat tentative manner) the holism thesis, allowing desire to be taken into the psyche in such a way that it splits the psyche, setting one part against the other. This is his single most important teaching about the self, his great legacy, creating the possibility of psyche-ology: the study of mental conflict.

Nevertheless, Plato's account is misleading, as he assumes that mental conflict must always be between functional parts, such as reason versus desire. In reality, the conflict is more frequently between conflicting dyads of reason and desire, partial wholes, they might be called. Not reason versus desire, but reason as captured by archaic desire versus reason in the service of mature ambition, would be an example of how the conflict really works. It is this conflict that Kohut captures with the concept of a vertical split. Conversely, it is because Plato splits the psyche functionally that he assumes that reason can be separated out and split off without impoverishing reason or the psyche. In fact, doing so is tantamount to performing a lobotomy, carving up a whole where the joints are not. The result is a self who must constantly stand guard against its archaic desires, which isolated from reason grow ever more powerful.

If the leaky jar simile captures the way in which these desires can never be satisfied, then the simile of the occupying garrison invoked by Aristotle captures the relationship of reason and desire. Like political repression, psychic repression frequently only intensifies the desire to resist, even when this resistance is not well organized, perhaps even self-destructive. Like its political counterpart, talk of psychic harmony under these circumstances can be no more than an ideology.

The preceding aspects of *The Republic* all fall under the rubric self-consciousness, as Strauss calls it: concerned with human nature and its social relations. *The Republic* is also a work about self-knowledge: concerned with the nature of ultimate reality and one's place in it. What is so striking is the way in which the arguments associated with these two dimensions of experience barely touch, a point noticed by a number of commentators. Of the three arguments for the superiority of the just life, only the third even alludes to self-knowledge (576c–583b). The first two arguments, around which most of *The Republic* is built, assert that justice is good because it promotes mental harmony, understood as the balance of the three parts of the psyche, which is tantamount to eudaimonia. Nothing in these arguments requires self-knowledge, only self-consciousness. The third argument is that only balanced psyches, with reason in control, can experience the one truly lasting pleasure, the only one that does not flow out of the leaky jar almost as soon as it is poured in: knowledge. But, even here, as in the *Gorgias* (493a–494b), the purpose of self-knowledge is to serve self-consciousness. Taylor, in *Sources of the Self*, is thus mistaken when he argues that Plato's vision of the psyche is entirely outward looking, toward the psyche's place in the cosmos.[9] Though this is certainly a crucial dimension of Plato's thought, as the discussion of the *Timaeus* and *Phaedrus* reveals, it is a dimension in conflict and tension with the inward focus. This is important, as it suggests the possibility that the turn outward is a defense against the inner world (self-consciousness), a possibility that Taylor's formulation simply does not allow.

Timaeus

At the beginning of the *Timaeus*, Critias indicates that Timaeus' speech (which occupies virtually the entire dialogue) is to fall between two political discussions: Socrates on the education of the guardians (that is, *The Republic*) and Critias' own speech on citizenship (27a-c). It is evidently intended that Timaeus' cosmological speculations are to be an interlude in a discussion of man's political nature. This turns out not to be the case, and not only because the bulk of Critias' speech has apparently been lost. Rather, Timaeus characterizes the human psyche in such a way that politics becomes irrelevant. Self-knowledge rather than supplementing self-consciousness replaces it.

Timaeus begins by discussing the Creator, who makes the world in his own image. He does so because he is so perfect as to be free of jealousy; he is thus willing to create entities like himself (29e–30d). It seems fair to characterize the creator as a selfobject, in the same sense as the polis is in *The Republic*. The Creator creates the world body and the world psyche: the cosmos (32c–35c). Both are characterized by their narcissistic perfection. The body is smooth, round, with no needs at all, like those almost perfect beings sundered by Zeus in Aristophanes' tale in the *Symposium*, except that the world body is even more perfect, so perfect that it needs no legs or feet but always revolves around itself—it is its own axis, it own center. If the world body is an ideal of narcissistic perfection, then the world psyche is even more so. Like the world body, it is circular. It needs no friends, as it can converse with itself. Yet the world psyche is not quite perfect. Plato says that it has an in-between status, by which he means that it contains worldly stuff, as well as invisible, unchanging stuff (34c–36d). The details of this mixture are obscure, and much ink has been expended trying to figure it out. Suffice to say that the world psyche is a mixture of divine and earthly. Once again, Plato creates an ideal being, one that is especially easy to idealize, as it contains a dose of worldly stuff and so is just imperfect enough that a mortal might identify with it.

The most interesting selfobject is yet to come. It is the perfect mirroring selfobject, what Plato calls the receptacle and nurse of all generation (48b). At this point the reader may be wondering whether the author is not going too far, calling all these entities selfobjects. The way in which Plato describes the nurse of generation should change the skeptical reader's mind. First, he calls the receptacle a she (*aute*) and compares it to the mother, the father being the Creator (50c-e) whose relationship to the receptacle Plato characterizes by imagery of sexual intercourse (52d–53b). In addition, he refers to the product of the receptacle, generated by the Creator, as the child. This child is the outcome of the way the receptacle organizes the chaotic mix of divine and earthly substance (52d–53b). "We may liken the receiving principle to a mother, and the source or spring to a father, and the intermediate nature to a child," says Plato (50d). Later, he gives health advice to the individual psyche on the model of the receptacle, which he calls "foster mother and nurse of the universe." This mother keeps things in motion, so as to sort out like and like. The individual should do the same with his psyche: mental activity, along with the right kind of physical activity, keeps the parts of the psyche in motion, helping to purify it (88d–89e).

Plato, it is clear, intends the Creator, the world body-psyche, and the receptacle of generation to be selfobjects. Obviously, he does not intend them to be selfobjects in the sense that Kohut means. But if we mean by selfobjects not merely the entities of a particular theory but the more general idea that people, concepts, and ideas frequently serve as exemplars of ways to organize the self (as in the health tip noted above), and that individuals must identify (projective identification) with these people, concepts, or ideas in order to use them thusly, then Plato too is writing about selfobjects and the selfobject transference, and doing so quite consciously.

Plato introduces the receptacle of generation at 48e in order to fill in a gap in his account. His discussion of the Creator and world body-psyche has been too simple, he says. These objects explained the created world but failed to explain what gives this manifold and moving order its coherence. This is, of course, a problem that Plato has long been interested in. One might even call it a key problem of ancient metaphysics, the problem of the many and the one. How can something that changes retain its identity? It is a problem that also applies to the identity of the self as well as to every other thing. It is one of Locke's chief concerns in *An Essay concerning Human Understanding*. Plato assigns to the receptacle of generation the same function that Kohut assigns to the mother's mirroring of the infant: to respond to the young child's unintegrated, partial self with an integrated response, as though the child were a self, and so help the child sort out self from nonself, arranging both in a coherent pattern. Here, says Kohut, is how the self is formed, by a process of addition and subtraction, inclusion and exclusion.[10]

The receptacle of generation is such a mirror. She receives the impressions of things, giving them a form that they lacked; but she never becomes what she reflects (50b–51c). Like the ideal mother with whom Plato compares her (50d), the receptacle of generation is the perfect empathic mirror, giving structure and form to the ever-changing, disarticulated, chaotic world. But better than any mirror (including Lacan's, which only reflects the *illusion* of coherence), she reflects form when all she sees is chaos. And better than some mothers, she does not inappropriately merge with the object she is mirroring, which might make it more difficult for the object to sort out self and nonself. Lacan writes that in the mirror stage the child confuses not only himself with his image in the mirror but also himself with the image of his mother in the mirror, who is evidently holding him before it. The receptacle of generation is such a perfect mother that she forestalls both confusions: "Inasmuch as she always receives all things, she never departs at all from her own nature and never, in any way or at any time, assumes a form like that of any of the things which enter into her" (50b-c).

Plato posits a three-part psyche in this dialogue, even developing the concept slightly, locating reason in the head, desire in the belly, and thumos in the chest so that it might be closer to reason (69b–70b; cf. 89e). As Robinson points out, however, it is a three-part psyche in name only. Plato's characterization of the neck as "isthmus and boundary" between reason and the lower parts of the psyche means that this is actually a two-part model in which the second part, desire, is subdivided further into good and bad aspects. [11] This formulation is regrettable, though not because the three-part psyche is itself so important. Rather, the de facto transformation of the three-part psyche into two is evidence that Plato is seeking to isolate reason further, splitting it off from the rest of the psyche so that it might merge with its idealized counterpart, the idealized selfobject.

Seen from this perspective, reason becomes more than just one part of the divided psyche. It becomes the means of division, the abstract idea that splits the psyche, continuing to hold it apart and driving every aspect that is not identical with the idealized selfobject underground into the realm of desire. Thumos is no longer reason's natural auxiliary but just one more enemy. Tendencies in *The Republic* to isolate reason, restrained by the political context (that is, by the need to model a self able to live in society), become explicit when these constraints are removed. Expressed in the language of the psychology of the self, the archaic, idealizing selfobject transference seeks to assimilate the self to the idealized selfobject. To do so, the self must purify itself, splitting off all those aspects of the self, desire and thumos, that are alien from the ideal. Reason, as expressed in the idealizing selfobject transference, becomes not merely a search for the most abstract, pure, and universal expression of the good in order to assimilate itself to it. Reason also becomes the means by which the self splits off that aspect of itself that differs from its ideal: reason as the great divider. The virtual disappearance of the three-part psyche in this dialogue is not the cause of this phenomenon but its sign, in which all that is not reason is relegated to the lower regions, connected only by that skinny isthmus, the neck. [12]

Phaedrus

The problem posed by the *Phaedrus* is the problem that Strauss puts at the center of classical philosophy—that of self-knowledge. What is it, and how can it be achieved? Not only is self-knowledge the goal, but in this dialogue it seems opposed to self-consciousness. As Charles Griswold puts it in the finest book on the *Phaedrus* to come along in many years, "The myth [the soul as chariot] suggests that human nature cannot be understood historically as a process of social-political development." [13] It is significant, as commentators have pointed out, that the dialogue is one of the few to take place outside of the city. Self-knowledge, it seems, has nothing to do with the city or one's place in it.

Next to *The Republic*, the *Phaedrus* contains the most elaborate discussion of the three-part soul (246a–247e). Yet Robinson seems correct once again that this is not truly a three-part model, or rather, that it is three-part in name only, as the good steed is inseparable from the charioteer, having no function independent of the charioteer.[14] Thus, we would expect a model of the psyche in which reason and desire are split, reason fulfilling itself in an archaic merger with its ideal. This is precisely what we see, a claim made in full awareness of the fact that some readings of the *Phaedrus*, including Nussbaum's otherwise beautiful analysis in *The Fragility of Goodness*, hold that the dialogue unites reason and desire in the concrete love of another person. This is a nice story; it is what Plato should have said, but it is not what he said. My argument is best supported by a consideration of Plato's total idealization of the beloved. Extreme idealization, it will be recalled, is the medium of splitting and often a sign of suppressed rage.

> But when one . . . beholds a godlike face or bodily form that truly expresses beauty, first there comes upon him a shuddering and a measure of that awe which the vision inspired, and then reverence at the sign of a god, and but for fear of being deemed a very madman he would offer sacrifice to his beloved as to a holy image of the deity. . . . And so each selects a fair one for his love after his disposition and even as if the beloved himself were a god he fashions for himself as it were an image, and adorns it to be the object of his veneration and worship . . . thus creating in him the closest possible likeness to the god they worship. . . . Every lover is fain that his beloved should be of a nature like to his own god. (251a–253c)

One could argue, of course, that this is the Platonic equivalent of Victorian love poetry and as such is not to be taken too seriously (I would argue that the idealization in *both* should be taken seriously). The best way to settle this argument, however, is by looking not at the actual words of praise but at the selfobject transference involved: "So he loves, yet knows not what he loves; he does not understand, he cannot tell what has come upon him; like one that has caught a disease of the eye from another, he cannot account for it, *not realizing that his lover is as it were a mirror in which he beholds him-*

self" (255d-e; emphasis mine). This sounds like nothing so much as Narcissus gazing into the water, unsure whether he loves himself or another. As Ovid has Narcissus put it,

> Am I the lover
> Or beloved? Then why make love? Since I
> Am what I long for, then my riches are
> So great they make me poor.[15]

Here is evidence of an important and troubling point. In archaic selfobject transferences, idealization and grandiosity (love of another's ideal perfection coupled with the desire to share in it and so become, and perhaps even replace, the ideal) come very close together. It is as though the two poles of the bipolar self bend around and touch each other, but only in the archaic dimension. This would not be so important here except that it can be seen in other dialogues as well. The extreme idealization of abstract selfobjects, such as the Creator, seems mixed with an archaic grandiosity: to merge with it, to become part of it, and so also to become immortal, perfect. Such a part-object relationship contains more than a hint of violence, as if one could take desirable attributes from another, make them one's own, and throw the other away.

The selfobject transference upon which such a relationship is based is no longer simply a vehicle of archaic merger. When idealization is extreme and the other is regarded as a mortal god, the selfobject transference is evidently serving to support the defense of splitting, in which negative emotions, the opposite of those involved in idealization, are being confined to another part of the self. In a word, extreme idealization may be part of a schizoid defense against unintegrated desire, greed, envy, and rage, emotions driven further underground as the beloved is elevated further and further into the heavens. This is, of course, a theoretical assertion, based upon an analysis of the psychological functions served by the selfobject transference. It is supported by Lacan's insight that narcissistic rage may stem from envy of the perfection of the image in the mirror, as this alienated perfection and wholeness merely highlights the absence of these attributes in oneself.

Is there any evidence that the extreme idealization of the beloved in the *Phaedrus* is serving such a defensive function? Direct evidence is minimal, although Plato's characterization of how the ugly, wanton horse of desire is to be jerked to a halt so violently that his mouth and jaws drip with blood, forcing his body into a posture of submission, expresses more than a little aggression against the desiring self (253d–254e). In this account, by the way, the good horse is of no help to the charioteer, supporting further the thesis that the three-part soul has become only a formal assumption. In general, however, we must look elsewhere for unintegrated desire and rage: not in bloody words but in an attitude toward reality that devalues everything that is contingent, unstable, imperfect—that is, truly human. It is in this attitude that one sees what Theodor Adorno calls "idealism as rage" at a world too sparse to be dominated.

It might be asked, why call this attitude "rage"? Because the instability that Plato rejects is a source of pain (if our beloved is a person, he might fail to respond, die, fall in love with another, and so forth), a pain that stems not merely from unfulfilled desire but from a loss of permanent and reliable support to the self. The rage at issue is, of course, narcissistic rage, which stems from anger at a world that lacks constant and reliable selfobjects and so threatens the cohesion and stability of the self. Platonic idealism, understood as an approach that finds real value only in the ideal, abstract, universal, and unchanging, is not the only way in which narcissistic rage may be expressed. Nietzsche's "ressentiment of metaphysicians" and Creon's "temper that builds cities" (*astunomous orgas*) were mentioned earlier as examples.

It is surprising that Nussbaum would hold the *Phaedrus* to be the great exception: a work in which Plato values the worldly and contingent, and so too a psyche that can appreciate and model itself after such things. It is widely recognized by Nussbaum and others, such as Gregory Vlastos, that Plato's Socrates turns away from the love of real people in the *Symposium*, a dialogue that is only superficially about real love relations. As Vlastos puts it, "This seems to me the cardinal flaw in Plato's theory. It does not provide for love of whole persons, but only for love of that abstract version of persons which consists of the complex of their best qualities."[16] It is as though the best love is one that splits off attributes from those who have them, allowing the lover to merge with these attributes while ignoring the person who only accidentally possesses them. This requires some pretty complicated permutations of splitting and idealization in which reason once again becomes the great divider.

Why would Nussbaum see the *Phaedrus* as the exception? As she puts it, "Instead of loving one another as exemplars of beauty and goodness . . . these lovers [in the *Phaedrus*] love one another's character, memories, and aspirations—which are, as Aristotle too will say, what each person is 'in and of himself.' . . . They grasp the good and true not by transcending erotic madness, but inside a passionate life." [17] It cannot be because she is convinced from what Bernard Knox shows to be most unreliable evidence that Plato fell in love with Dion, a personal experience so overwhelming it led him to re-think his view of love. [18] Although this explanation appeals to Nussbaum, she recognizes it as pure speculation. In any case, Griswold comes closer to the mark when he claims on the basis of evidence previously cited that "when all is said and done, what the lover really wants is himself as he would like to be: himself fulfilled, whole, perfected, godlike." [19] The lover's apparent idealiza-tion of the beloved is actually ambition, grandiosity, and greed, masquerad-ing as the pursuit of an ideal. This is neither the first nor the last time in Plato's dialogues that the pursuit of an ideal is a cover for, or at least bound to, archaic ambition, narcissistic grandiosity. [20]

What has happened, I believe, is that Nussbaum, in the tradition repre-sented by Vlastos, focuses on how the lover in the *Phaedrus* does not abstract qualities from the person but rather appears to love the person who possesses these qualities, unlike the Socratic lover in the *Symposium*. In other words, she focuses on how the selfobject transference in the *Phaedrus* does not in-volve the part-object relationship seen in the *Symposium*, in which the be-loved and his qualities are split. This focus, however, leads her to overlook another, albeit closely related, way in which we can avoid truly loving an-other human being and so continue to avoid contingency, fragility, and the limits of real human relationships. By treating the other as a mirror of one's own grandiosity, "whole, perfected, and godlike," as Griswold puts it, we can also avoid dealing with a real person, dealing instead with the projection of our own desires. If the other is just a mirror, then I can find another any-where. The other need only be beautiful (and there are lots of those), for all the really good stuff is already in me. This conclusion fits the observations of Kohut and other analysts regarding archaic narcissistic object relations in which the other is not regarded as a real person at all but only a part object, valuable only to the degree he mirrors the narcissist's own grandiosity and hence readily replaceable. What I have added is greater emphasis on how such narcissistic themes are prevalent in primitive idealization as well.

Griswold captures the archaic, narcissistic, mirroring character of love in the *Phaedrus* so well that it is surprising that he would conclude that Plato has successfully blended self-knowledge with desire. Self-knowledge, he argues, is about what truly satisfies the whole psyche. To be rational is to know how to satisfy one's desires completely, which means to know how to be nourished by the divine. It is understanding oneself in this larger context that constitutes true self-knowledge and that is the basis for genuine satisfaction.[21] "Know thyself" means to know one's place in the cosmos. Self-knowledge and desire are not in conflict, as self-knowledge is about what truly satisfies: rational intercourse with Beings.

From such a vantage point one would not expect the three-part psyche to be very important. Or rather, other parts of the psyche are important only as they serve or impede reason's quest for intercourse with Beings. This is, in fact, precisely what Griswold suggests, although he is not troubled about it. Indeed, he argues that we might just as well talk about the four-part soul (the chariot being the fourth), as though it really does not matter how many parts the soul is said to have, for we all know that it is really one in the end: nous. As Griswold puts it, "Reason and desires are interdependent, as the myth makes abundantly clear. The mind cannot contemplate the truth until it is brought within sight of the truth by the soul, and the mind's contemplation of the truth nourishes the whole soul."[22] Note what "interdependent" means here: the rest of the psyche is valuable, but only insofar as it is merely a chariot, a vehicle for nous. As Plato puts it, true Being is "visible to nous alone, the pilot of the psyche" (247c7–8; cf. 253e5–6, 254c4–5). Or, as Griswold would seem to have it, reason's connection to psyche is itself only contingent.

Self-knowledge is not self-consciousness, as the political psychology of *The Republic* is not the whole of Plato's thought. But they are not opposites either. Self-conscious understanding of human nature, including its relationships with others, is indispensable in understanding how humanity fits into the cosmos. The problem with Plato's account is not merely that he divides them. It is that the self associated with self-consciousness, the three-part psyche, is itself split in the service of self-knowledge, so that the ambition that holds reason and desire, and hence the self, together is in effect equated with mere desire and split off in order to facilitate the unmediated experience of Being. Self-knowledge, understood as "the sensation of *presence*, of total union," as Robinson puts it, requires not just the transcendence of self-consciousness but its obliteration. From this opposition—not just a dualism, for self-knowledge seems to require the destruction of self-consciousness— Western thought has never recovered. As Tallis points out, this extremism of presence—"if I can't have it all, then I'll accept none"—is the oldest game in town. Plato and Lacan both play it; they just choose different sides.

This is, of course, not quite fair to Plato, for the self of *The Republic*, which takes the unity and balance of the ideal polis as its selfobject, is a self designed to live with the lack in itself. As Nichols says, "The just man who triumphs in the agon Socrates presents [in *The Republic*] both rules his 'many-headed beast' and is aware of his incompleteness."[23] But the cost is too high. Awareness of incompleteness leads not to its acceptance but to the attempt to transcend it via the abandonment of the self, an attempt given some of its impetus by the costs of its alternative: the life of the self as constant agon against itself. In Plato's account of the self-controlled self, we do not live with the lack. We perpetually struggle against that part of ourselves that would do anything to fill it, employing the ideal of psychic balance and harmony not so much as goal but as one more divisive weapon in the struggle. For Lacan the self is the symptom. For Plato it is the enemy, as it is so intensely needy. It is frequently argued that Plato, in the Orphic tradition, sees the body as prison. I have argued that it is not so simple, especially once desire is taken into the self. It is actually the self that becomes the prison—and prisoner to itself.

Against this conclusion, Socrates' advice to his guardians might be cited as evidence: "If any Guardian . . . tires of the restraint and security of the ideal life we have drawn for him, and is impelled by some senseless and extravagant idea of happiness . . . well, he will learn the wisdom of Hesiod's saying that the half is more than the whole" (*The Republic*, 466c). Surely Plato is concerned with teaching some to live with the lack in human existence, to accept that their jar can never be more than half full. In this world there can be no alternative; if one does not accept half, one will end up with nothing, like the tyrant. The problem is that even this apparently moderate solution is unstable, for all the reasons mentioned. In response it might be argued that it is actually Aristotle's polity that would make the better selfobject, as it does not depend upon the colonization of desire.[24] But only because it does not take desire—ultimately for the perfection of the self—as seriously as Plato does. Here is Plato's greatness. Although he has his ideal guardians split off desire, he never does so, at least not in such a way as to deny its power.

Conclusion

Other dialogues also have much to say about the psyche. The *Philebus* contains the clearest and most sophisticated argument that desire is based upon a lack or emptiness in psyche, not soma (34c–35d). *The Laws* X introduces the concept of the self-moving psyche, quite independent, it appears, of its creator (904a-e). It also contains an interesting discussion of the sun as an idealizable selfobject with its own psyche (898d–899b). The question of whether the psyche is immortal is a concern of a number of dialogues, most notably the *Phaedo*. Other dialogues, including *Meno* (86a–88c), *Laches* (185e–187e), *Crito* (47d–48a), *Charmides* (156dff), and *Protagoras* (313a-c), contain discussions of the psyche, generally questioning its relationship to the body. Clearly Plato's concept of the psyche could be elaborated further, filling at least one long book. But the dialogues examined here raise most of the important issues regarding the psyche that Plato sought to address, or at least those most relevant to my concerns.

Plato's concept of the psyche is richest when he is taking off from, and developing, traditional Greek thought on the psyche as life force. His view is less multidimensional the more he turns to the Orphic tradition. This is because in transforming the occult self into the rational self Plato splits reason and desire, as well as the self structure that is the culmination of the life force tradition: the three-part psyche in which thumos (an original life force term) is independent of desire. In response it might be argued that in several dialogues, especially the *Symposium* and *Phaedrus*, Plato makes desire—eros—itself a cosmological principle. Thus, the psyche can seek its cosmological tally without having to split off its desires; it need only purify them. This is not really a fair interpretation, however, as Santas points out.[25] In order to purify desire, Plato employs extreme idealization to split the psyche, resulting in the isolation of reason and the colonization of desire, hardly a genuine integration.

If desire is a psychic rather than somatic phenomenon, then knowledge, truth, and beauty—the things that belong to the psyche—are indeed the best soul food, an insight that seems fundamentally correct. What satisfies the psyche most is a relationship, understood as a selfobject transference, in which we participate in the truth, beauty, and knowledge we find in real individuals and real things. Otherwise expressed, what satisfies most is an opportunity to use individuals and things that are beautiful, knowledgeable, and truthful as sources of support for ourselves, so that we come to share these attributes—but without seeking to appropriate them greedily just for ourselves or obliterate ourselves in their pursuit. This is the closest that humans can come to filling the lack in themselves. And it is always temporary, or at least always contingent, dependent on the selfobject. It is this that Plato would avoid by separating attribute from person. For Plato, the goal remains *autarkeia*. "The Good" is self-sufficient, and he who participates in a good relationship should be, too (*Philebus*, 60c, 67a). In fact, of course, such a good relationship is really no relationship at all, a point that will not be overlooked in my study of Rousseau's account of Emile's love for Sophie.

Relationships with true and beautiful others satisfy because we may use the selfobject transference, in both its mirroring and idealizing aspects, to share in the selves of others. As Kohut puts it, "One cannot live many different kinds of lives, but one can be empathic with different types of personalities." [26] Empathy, the medium of the self-conscious selfobject transference, is the way we enrich ourselves by participating in the lives of others. The trick, to put it simply, is to know when to quit—that is, to know when one's attempt to assimilate oneself to the attributes of others begins to split the self or deny the otherness of the other. Once one steps out of the city, Plato does not seem to know where to quit. Inside the city, he does not know where to begin. The internalized polis becomes not the medium of these relationships but a defense against them, each self its own commune.

Are these the proper concerns of politics? Perhaps they should not be, but they are. Much politics at least tacitly claims as much. Nichols puts it well in *Socrates and the Political Community*: "The city pretends that man is simple enough that he can live merely as a citizen. It pretends that it is the whole that satisfies or completes man. By insisting that it fulfills man's eros, it destroys man's eros." [27] In a word, the city (and politics in general) lies, pretending it can meet needs that it can barely comprehend, meeting them only by perverting or trivializing them. It may be that the needs of the self and the needs of society are fundamentally incompatible, that the self must be sacrificed if a decent society is to exist. Although his language is somewhat different, referring not to the self but to its drives, this is Freud's thesis in *Civilization and Its Discontents*. And it is Hobbes's thesis, too. Plato, in *The Republic*, would deny it, arguing that good citizenship and eudaimonia converge in the balanced psyche. This, however, is the result of Plato's transformation of the conflict between self and society into an intrapsychic agon. Perhaps there is no solution. Perhaps this is the original *aporia*. There is no way out, but some ways of living with it are worse than others.

Nichols, like Bloom, interprets much of *The Republic* as a response to Aristophanes' *Clouds*. There the playwright comically criticizes Socrates' attempt to escape from all that is most human: contingency, uncertainty, and our attachment to the unique and particular. But, says Nichols, *The Republic* shows that not just philosophers but average citizens also wish to escape from these human things. Cephalus and Polemarchus want an "unchanging standard by which they can direct their lives," whereas Glaucon, while "not sharing Polemarchus' naive assurance that there is an unchanging standard by which he can guide his life . . . all the more intensely desires such a standard." The point of the city in speech, then, is to show "Aristophanes that the city itself leads to the abstractions from ordinary life that he attributed to philosophy." [28]

Whether or not the city in speech is counterfactual, Nichols makes an important point. Although the way in which Socrates and Plato propose to meet the needs of the self is strictly philosophical, these needs are universal. If they are not met by philosophy or religion, citizens will press these same demands upon the state, generally with even more deleterious consequences. Not only is the state not particularly efficient in meeting these needs, but it generally flattens and perverts them in order to address them at all (often in order to exploit them for its own ends): chauvinism in the place of national pride; the glorification of individual acquisitiveness in the place of mature ambition; the subordination of the individual to the group in the place of the common pursuit of the good. Otherwise expressed, the state seems much better at meeting the archaic needs of the self (for these are shared by all, are readily evoked by primitive symbolism, and so forth) than their mature counterpart. On this point Benjamin Constant's touching criticism of Rousseau is instructive. It hardly matters that *The Social Contract* brilliantly illuminates the paradoxes of democracy. In the hands of any one with an agenda, it can become only a pretext for suppression. [29]

Plato is not usually read as a theorist of the tension between self and society, but that is what he is. No theorist has penetrated more deeply into the sources of this tension in the needs of the self than Plato. Few theorists have told fewer lies (in Nichols's sense: that politics completes the self) than Plato. Perhaps it is the desire to save him from having told any lies at all that motivates Nichols and Bloom to treat the city in speech as purely counterfactual. On the contrary, I have suggested that Plato strays furthest from his own truth when he treats the victory of reason over desire as though it were a harmonious balance.

To be sure, others, such as Hobbes, capture the tension between self and society, never retreating from their own insights, never telling the lie. But Hobbes does so only by vastly simplifying the self and its longings. The question I will ask in the following chapters is whether one strand of the liberal tradition, that which runs from Hobbes through Locke to Rawls, makes any progress on the dilemma that confronted Plato: one overcomes the harsh totalitarianism of the city in speech only by internalizing it, founding it in one's own psyche. Calling it the dilemma that confronted Plato is important, for it becomes a dilemma only when one takes the self and its needs seriously, putting them at the center, as Plato does. Otherwise it is just a problem of trade-offs in institutional design. That it is a dilemma with which liberalism should be particularly concerned is apparent, as liberalism is that philosophy that claims to value the individual most. But does it value the self?

He is king over all the   CHAPTER FIVE

children of pride. —Job
Hobbes and the
Archaic Self

Laurence Berns has observed that "to the ex-
tent that modern liberalism teaches that all social and political obligations
are derived from and are in service of the individual rights of man, Hobbes
may be regarded as the founder of modern liberalism."[1]

From Berns's Straussian perspective, Thomas Hobbes is a liberal because
he transforms natural law from a "binding order prior to, and independent
of, human will" into a pure expression of will.[2] From the very different perspective of C. B. Macpherson, Hobbes is a liberal because he is the virtual
founder of possessive individualism, understood not in terms of material acquisitiveness but in terms of "conception of the individual as essentially the
proprietor of his own person or capacities, owing nothing to society for them.
The individual was seen neither as a moral whole, nor as part of a larger
social whole, but as an owner of himself."[3] Steven Lukes makes a similar
claim in his book, *Individualism*.[4]

A self-psychological perspective on Hobbes does not lead to strikingly new
conclusions. It does, however, allow us to begin to formulate the relationships between Hobbesian liberalism and the liberalism of Locke and Rawls in
a more subtle and complex manner. This, though, is the task of three chapters, not just one. Hobbes *is* a liberal. But to write in these terms is similar to
writing about the self in the abstract "metaphysical" language of contemporary debates. It is not false, but it is so abstract that it is not especially revealing and sometimes is misleading. How one conceptualizes the individual self
that is the ground of rights and the locus of will is not a mere detail; rather, it
makes all the difference in the world, Otherwise expressed, the distinction
between self-consciousness and self-knowledge is insufficient. What kind of
self-consciousness has rights, and should have rights, is crucial.

Mechanical Man

It is common to approach Hobbes via the question of the unity of his thought,
particularly in *Leviathan*. Do the theology (over half of *Leviathan* is con-

cerned with religion, 371 of the 714 pages in the Molesworth edition)[5] and materialist metaphysics support the political theory? The standard view still seems to be that of George Robertson, who argued over a century ago that they do not. Most interpreters since then, says David Johnston, "have agreed that the systematic pretensions of his philosophy are little more than a veil designed to disguise the cracks in an essentially syncretic amalgamation of ideas."[6] In *The Rhetoric of Leviathan*, Johnston challenges this conclusion, arguing that it is a unified work in which theology and materialist metaphysics serve the political theory. This becomes apparent, however, only after it is recognized that this service is rhetorical and polemical, not deductive and scientific.

The theology and materialist metaphysics, Johnston continues, promote a view of human beings as rational machines. Only when they come to view themselves in this fashion are the arguments and threats of the sovereign compelling. Only then do they fear violent death above all else and not, for example, eternal damnation. The theology and materialist metaphysics are designed to persuade people to view themselves as Hobbes views them: soulless machines, for whom neither dishonor nor damnation have any meaning. My argument is in accord with that of Johnston, with one important caveat, or rather elaboration. The disparate elements of Hobbes's account serve not merely to render humans soulless. They also render them selfless, without a self. Only then, Hobbes seems to say—that is, only when the self has disappeared from the scene as one more superstition, one more myth— can there be social peace.

As Berns points out, Hobbes is the first to define the state as a person, "an Artificiall Man."[7] In this sense his approach is the opposite of Plato's, who defines the person in terms of the state. Knowing this about Hobbes, but knowing nothing else, one might conclude that he was a theorist of organic solidarity, of the state as a community of souls. In fact, of course, Hobbes's state is nothing of the kind. It is rather "a loose collection of individuals," as Sheldon Wolin puts it, united only by the sovereign, whom Hobbes calls the "Artificiall *Soul*" of the state.[8] Why does Hobbes's view of the state as an artificial person not lead him to see the state as an organic unity? In large measure because Hobbes views the *person* as a fragile machine of loosely connected parts. Because the person is an artificial machine to begin with, one should not be surprised that the state reflects this. In Hobbes's case we can read the selfobject transference right to left (state to person) or left to right (person to state), and it reads the same.

Hobbes's mechanical view is seen most dramatically in his account of the seemingly least mechanical of human experiences, those intimate, inward, subjective experiences that we know as dreams and fantasies. Thus, he explains imagination in terms of (actually a deduction from) the law of inertia: "When a body is once in motion, it moveth, unless something else hinder it, eternally . . . so also it happeneth on that motion, which is made in the internal parts of a man, when he sees, dreams, etc. For after the object is removed, or the eye shut, we still retain an image of the thing seen."[9] Imagination is, therefore, "nothing but decaying sense," the sense organs slowly returning to rest after stimulation. In a similar fashion Hobbes explains memory.

The standard reading of this aspect of Hobbes's work does not, of course, interpret Hobbes's mechanical account of human beings as an expression of extreme alienation from the self. Rather, his mechanical view is seen as a methodological achievement, albeit a naive one, the result of his accidental discovery of a book on geometry (in which valid conclusions could be derived from a few assumptions apparent to all) and his encounter with Galileo, in which he learned not merely the resoluto-compositive method but the principle that motion, not rest, is the natural state of things, and so forth. It was experiences such as these that provided Hobbes with the levers necessary to overthrow the schools. Indeed, even those who sharply disagree with Hobbes's conclusions frequently see his method as an achievement. R. S. Peters, for example, wrote, "To suggest that man is a machine was a great step forward in thought. Even though the hypothesis is probably untenable, it marked the beginning of the effort to use scientific methods and objective concepts in the sphere of human behavior. In the seventeenth century this was a novel undertaking, as well as a dangerous one."[10] Were Hobbes a pure and unalloyed scientist of humankind, such an interpretation might have more validity. In fact, what is so interesting is that Hobbes came to these conclusions *not* after a scientific study of people but from introspection and the study of history (today, for example, one might reach conclusions similar to Hobbes's after studying firing patterns of neurons as revealed by the encephalogram). With Hobbes, the most humane mode of self-study leads to the most mechanical of results: it is this discrepancy that is the key.

Wisdom, says Hobbes, comes not from reading books, but from reading men. And how does one learn to read men? By reading oneself.

But there is another saying not of late understood, by which they might learn truly to read one another, if they would take the pains: and that is

Nosce teipsum: Read thy self. . . . whosoever looketh into himself, and considereth what he doth, when he does *think, opine, reason, hope, feare,* &c, and upon what grounds, he shall thereby read and know, what are the thoughts, and Passions of all other men, upon the like occasions.[11]

It is introspection, coupled with his study of history (Hobbes was the first to translate Thucydides into English from the Greek), that led Hobbes to conclude that above all else, man seeks power over other men. And it is the importance of this and similar insights that leads him to conclude that while it is "harder than to learn any Language, or Science," nothing is more important than to see in oneself the nature of all mankind. This is especially important for political leaders. He "that is to govern a whole Nation, must read in himself, not this, or that particular man; but Man-kind." And nothing is more important for the social theorist, "for this kind of Doctrine, admitteth no other Demonstration" than reflection.[12]

Today some social scientists are measuring blood serotonin levels as a way of better understanding aggression and the will for power generally. Preliminary findings suggest that politicians have higher levels than others. These scientists are using physiological and behavioral methods to generate physiological and behavioral conclusions.[13] Whatever one may think of such methods, they do not necessarily reflect an alienation from the self: the self is an important part of human nature, but it is not the whole story; the physiological basis is also real. This is not Hobbes's approach. He uses not mechanical models to reach mechanical conclusions but, rather, introspective methods to reach mechanical conclusions. More accurately put, Hobbes uses introspection and reflection to arrive at the *simile* of man as a machine, for, of course, he never observed the mechanisms per se. One might better compare Hobbes's approach to a psychological version of the phenomenological reduction, in which Hobbes "brackets" our extraneous fears, hopes, dreams, and desires to get down to our most basic emotions. And what does he find: a fearful, brittle machine, one whose most intimate, subjective processes are akin to a machine, one that must always keep going, lest it perish.

In Hobbes's defense one might refer to his praise of Thucydides, who never enters "into men's hearts further than the acts themselves evidently guide him . . . [for] the inward motive . . . is but conjectural."[14] That is, Hobbes is not writing of the self per se. He is simply constructing a model that explains what he sees as parsimoniously as possible. This, however, is not the case. Hobbes claims to probe deeply, using mechanical processes not as mere explanatory models but as entities, essences, the stuff man is made of. Since these models are actually no more than similes, however, it seems fair to characterize Hobbes's account as a description of a self-state, how he experiences the self, not just his own but the nature of the self in general. This conclusion is supported by analyzing the selfobject transference: the state (as clear a selfobject in Hobbes's account as the polis is in Plato's) is as inorganic, so to speak, as man. These considerations gain indirect support from Kohut's study of patients whom, it seems, must always keep going: they must always be active, never stopping for a moment, whether the activity is sex, work, politics, or whatever. Generally, there is a frenetic tone to such activity. Often, says Kohut, the activity is an attempt to revivify the self, to combat a feeling of deadness, a lifeless mechanical quality, at the core of the self.[15] If this is so, then perhaps the threat to the Hobbesian self stems not merely from without but from within: from a sense that the self is threatened by deadness from within, by its own lifeless, mechanical quality. Changes in Hobbes's world that might have led him to see the self in this fashion are considered below.

The Fatherless Society

Johnston's argument that Hobbes's mechanical materialism is not so much science as rhetoric supports my argument. *The Elements of Law* (consisting of two treatises, *Human Nature* and *De Corpore Politico*), first circulated about 1640 but not published until a decade later, as well as *De Cive* (1642), reveal that Hobbes's mechanical materialism was not merely a rhetorical strategy but a serious program. Nevertheless, by the time he wrote *Leviathan* (1651) the primary function of his materialism was polemical: to persuade the literate public that only if man understands himself as a rational machine may he have social peace, for only then will his fear of death be sufficiently strong to control his behavior. It is this that helps explain the frequently noted and otherwise puzzling fact that while Hobbes inveighs against metaphor and "Poesy" throughout *Leviathan*, the book is filled with it. Indeed, even the title is metaphor, drawn from the Book of Job (41:1). *Leviathan* is not so much the foundation of Hobbes's science as its practical application. In order for it to be applied, however, men must first be convinced that they are the mere machines that Hobbes apparently believes they are. This is the task of *Leviathan*. That men require so much convincing of this would seem to speak against its status as natural fact. But perhaps it is inappropriate to push Hobbes's argument quite so hard. It is more fruitful to see this apparent confusion not as a sign of a failed argument but as a symptom of Hobbes's era, and perhaps of ours as well.

Only when men understand themselves as machines, Hobbes argues, do all those transcendent values that men have shown themselves willing to die for disappear. Physical existence, survival, is the only value left, a value simple and straightforward enough that it can be manipulated and controlled in the name of social peace. The question arises, however, as to what made Hobbes think he might persuade the literate public of this fact. The answer, Johnston suggests, has to do with the changes taking place in the era in which Hobbes wrote, changes to which Hobbes was remarkably attuned. "England was, in Hobbes's view . . . undergoing a cultural revolution—a period of dissolution in social ties and ethical norms as well as in political authority more absolute than anything ever previously experienced by his fellows." [16] In such an era, as old self-understandings are overthrown, it is more likely that a new one can take their place. It is to this new self-understanding that *Leviathan* is dedicated.

What was the old self-understanding, and why did its loss create so much anxiety? The answer is as familiar as it is important. The old self-understanding was based upon the security of the medieval order, in which individuals understood themselves in terms of tradition, status, and the "Great Chain of Being." Lovejoy, in his lectures on this topic, points out that this concept was not merely an ideology, though, of course, it was that, too. The idea of the Great Chain of Being went hand in glove with the belief, held since Plato, that the universe is whole, rational, and intelligible. Lovejoy quotes Soame Jenyns on this point: "The universe resembles a large and well-regulated family, in which all the officers and servants, and even the domestic animals, are subservient to each other in a proper subordination; each enjoys the privileges and perquisites peculiar to his place, and at the same time contributes, by that just subordination, to the magnificence and happiness of the whole." [17] It was this belief that was coming apart in Hobbes's era, though it would persist as an intellectual legacy for another 150 years. In such a world, not merely intellectual certainties but social ones as well seemed to be dissolving. No longer did the ideal of reciprocal obligation and constraint mark the relationships among the classes. Lovejoy quotes a verse of "an appropriate quality" to exemplify the ideal that was being undermined:

> The meanest slaves or they who hedge and ditch,
> Are useful, by their sweat, to feed the rich;
> The rich, in due return, impart their store,
> Which comfortably feeds the lab'ring poor.
> Nor let the rich the lowest slave disdain,
> He's equally a link of nature's chain;
> Labours to the same end, joins in one view,
> And both alike the will divine pursue.[18]

Opposed to this order was the emerging market society, which at least at first did little to help the "lab'ring poor" and much to destroy the idea of mutual obligation. Less important in this context than whether these duties were actually performed was the function of the Great Chain of Being as symbolic selfobject: a center of gravity, a way for the self to know its place in the world. It was this that was being lost to the fragmenting forces of the market, in which everything was up for grabs, everything subject to renegotiation, even the self. Obeying its own inhuman rules, the emerging market society was experienced by many as lifeless and mechanical, especially in contrast to the medieval order, which, Lovejoy points out, was frequently experienced in an organic fashion, itself a living organism.[19]

Hobbes's view of the weakness of the family supports these considerations. Although his atomistic individualism is usually stressed, he actually paid considerable attention to the family.[20] In fact, Schochet argues that the patriarchal element in Hobbes's thought is so strong that it is a mistake to see the state of nature as a state of free individuals. Rather, it is "composed of familial social units," which remove the individual from the state of nature, an insight employed by Filmer to argue against Hobbes's own conclusions drawn from assumptions regarding natural freedom, equality, and consent.[21] Yet in the end this seems a tendentious interpretation. Even if one interprets the state of nature as a state of war of every family against every family rather than, as Hobbes says, "every man against every man," the conclusion is the same. The family is "radically defective and always on the brink of dissolution," for it cannot protect its family members; it cannot save them from human predators. It is for this reason that Hobbes concludes that the Fifth

Commandment is optional in the state of nature, dependent, evidently, upon the degree of actual protection offered.[22] That is, honor and respect are reduced to a question of power, the pattern that one observes time and again in Hobbes's work.

In a series of works on contemporary culture, Christopher Lasch has argued that it is the decline of the family, particularly the loss of its ability to protect and insulate the child from the outside world, that leads to *The Culture of Narcissism*. Recall that narcissism is not egoism but the most common expression of self-pathology, what Lasch calls *The Minimal Self*. Such a self expends all its energies trying to protect its fragile coherence and autonomy, usually by shrinking the realm over which autonomy and control are exercised. An obsessive focus on diet and exercise, for example, may reflect a belief that there is no other aspect of life subject to one's control and that whatever control one is able to exert must be total. It is this demand for total control, whatever the sphere, that is narcissistic.

Lasch goes on to argue that though this decline of the family, understood as its inability to protect the individual from extrafamilial forces, is most advanced in the ghetto, the difference between ghetto and middle-class families should not be exaggerated.

> Most of the evidence supports Rainwater's conclusion that poor black people find it almost impossible to develop a sense of family solidarity. "They did not regard themselves," Rainwater writes of one St. Louis family, "as a solitary unit separate from the outside world. Instead their home territory was readily invaded by anyone who established a relationship with one of them, and the children were ready to derogate and demean other family members." . . . These observations describe . . . the conditions of middle-class life as well. . . . It originates in the invasion of the family by the marketplace and the street, the crumbling of the walls that once provided a protected space in which to raise children, and the perversion of the most intimate relationships by the calculating, manipulative spirit that has long been ascendent in business life.[23]

Lasch is, of course, not the only theorist who has addressed this topic. Indeed, Lasch's account owes much to the Frankfurt school of critical theory's study of the "fatherless society" (*vaterlose Gesellschaft*) in which the concrete authority of the father has been replaced by the abstract authority of the state and its administrative and bureaucratic agencies, such as schools and welfare agencies. The result, say Max Horkheimer, Theodor Adorno, and Herbert Marcuse, is that the young child no longer develops his ego in a protracted, highly personalized conflict with father. Father becomes less relevant, less able to protect the family, as the child is presocialized by the state and mass media, whose authority is both less identifiable and less resistible.[24] No longer associated with a particular human being, authority becomes part of the taken-for-granted background, just the way things are.

In his classic *Hobbes*, Richard Peters argues that Hobbes was writing during a similar period in which "the momentous social changes which were then in full swing could be graphically described as the *rise of the fatherless society*. Patriarchalism, as a system of authority spreading beyond the family to all institutions, was on the wane."[25] To be sure, there is a difference between the decline of patriarchalism as a universal principle of social organization and the decline of patriarchalism *within* the family. It is the difference of three hundred years between Hobbes's era and our own. Despite this difference, however, there seems to be a continuity in the types of issues that it raises for the self. Tradition, status, the Great Chain of Being, my station and its duties, patriarchy as a model for every relationship of authority (attractive, in part, because patriarchy reminds us that those in authority have corresponding duties)—these may not seem like ideals to us, but only because our ideals have changed. In Hobbes's world these ideals provided the "narrative unity" that MacIntyre writes of in *After Virtue*. What would take their place?

Although the ideals are different, our situation today seems not dissimilar. In the absence of reliable ideals around which to build a self, power and control become the only standards. Only power, it seems, can stem the sense of loss of control over self and world, as any ideals that might constrain this quest for power have long since lost their force, except perhaps as one of a number of "alternative life-styles." The full development of the self, it seems, requires that those it idealizes combine power and ideals, so that the latter are not impotent and the former not meaningless. Ideals that have power; power that is governed by ideals personified by Plato as philosopher kings): this seems to be the magic combination as far as self-development is concerned. Without it, the self never truly distinguishes ambitions and ideals, always seeking power for its own sake, or—as is more usually the case—pursuing power in the name of ideals. Traditionally, the role of combining ambitions and ideals has been associated with the father, but there is no reason this need be the case. The risk is not that the role will be shared by mother but that it will be filled by no one.

The Perversion of the Aristotelian Virtues

It is by no means pathological to pursue power, and on occasion Hobbes's treatment of power is benign. For example, at the beginning of chapter 10 of *Leviathan*, Hobbes defines power thusly: "The Power *of a Man* (to take it Universally,) is his present means, to obtain some future apparent Good." [26] That is, power is efficacy, the ability to realize one's ambitions. Without a feeling of power, the self would be thrown back into narcissistic fantasies of omnipotence or its counterpart, the idealization of another's power for its own sake. To be without any power is to not be a self at all. This, however, is not the leading concept of power in *Leviathan*. It quickly slides over into power pursued for its own sake, as a scarce resource in a zero-sum game, in which it becomes simply the degree to which one man's "Faculties of Body, or Mind" exceed those of another. The more power I have, the less you must have. Why do men seek ever more power? Some, it appears, because power is a means to ever more intensive delight. For many, however, it appears that power is not sought either for its own sake or as the means to endless delights. Rather, they seek power, and ever more power, as a defense against others: [27] "And the cause of this, is not alwayes that a man hopes for a more intensive delight, than he has already attained to; or that he cannot be content with a moderate power: but because he cannot assure the power and means to live well, which he hath present, without the acquisition of more." [28]

Although most may seek power in order to live well, in the end this Aristotelian motivation cannot hold, as the competitive character of society reduces all men to the pursuit of power for its own sake. Thus, in a cruel parody of Aristotle's *Ethics*, chapter 10 of *Leviathan* reduces most of the virtues with which Aristotle was concerned—reputation, patriotism, liberality, affability, prudence, nobility, eloquence, attractiveness, dignity—to the common denominator of power. Affability is power because it gains the affection of those who may be helpful, and prudence is power because others will submit themselves to the prudent man more readily. Thus, power as a means to more intensive delight becomes an end in itself. To protect what one has, and ultimately one's life, one can never have too much power.

One sees the corruption of the classical ideal nowhere more clearly than in Hobbes's treatment of honor in *Leviathan*. In his early works, such as the introduction to his translation of Thucydides' *History* ("the crown and end of his humanist period," as Strauss says),[29] Hobbes interpreted honor as tantamount to the heroic virtues of valor and noble descent. A link to the Aristotelian conception was thus maintained, at least as mediated by what Strauss calls "Renaissance Aristotelianism," which tended to equate the virtues of the courtly aristocrat with virtue per se.[30] By the time he wrote *Leviathan*, however, honor had been reduced to power, or rather, the appearance of power.

> *Honourable* is whatsoever possession, action, or quality, is an argument and signe of Power. . . . Dominion, and Victory is Honourable; because acquired by Power. . . . Riches, are Honourable; for they are Power; and Servitude, for need or fear, is Dishonourable. . . . Nor does it alter the case of Honour, whether an action (so it be great and difficult, and consequently a signe of much power) be just or unjust: for Honour consisteth onely in the opinion of Power.[31]

One might be tempted to confuse Hobbes and Nietzsche here until one remembers that power for Nietzsche is a means by which to perform noble ends: to become a great-souled man. For Hobbes, on the other hand, power serves not to enlarge the soul or self but only to protect it. Hobbes's view of power, coupled with his egalitarianism (men are distinguished not by the quality or intensity of their desires but by their power: "From this equality of ability, ariseth equality of hope in the attaining of our Ends"), guarantees that power is the only standard.

In several recent works, most notably Jessica Benjamin's *The Bonds of Love*, the Hegelian dialectic of mutual recognition serves as a model by which the self is formed.[32] Benjamin compares this dialectic to psychoanalyst Margaret Mahler's account of self-development, but it might just as well be compared with Kohut's—or better yet Lacan's. In *The Political Philosophy of Hobbes*, Strauss also turns to Hegel's account in the *Phenomenology of Mind*, quoting from it as follows:

> Self-consciousness exists in itself and for itself, in that, and by the fact that it exists for another self-consciousness; that is to say, it *is* only by being acknowledged or "recognized" . . . each is indeed certain of its own self but not of the other, and hence its own certainty is still without

truth. . . . The relationship of both self-consciousnesses is in this way so constituted that they prove themselves and each other through a life-and-death struggle. They must enter into this struggle, for they must bring their certainty of themselves, and certainty of being for themselves, to the level of objective truth, and make this a fact both in the case of the other and in their own case as well.[33]

Strauss claims that Hobbes's account of the self is the foundation of Hegel's dialectic of mutual recognition (whether Strauss's claim is historically accurate is not important here). Unlike Descartes, Hobbes gets down to basics, in which the self's "life-and-death struggle" with others for its recognition is first and foremost a struggle for physical survival. This *is* life, and consciousness of life is consciousness of this struggle. Or as Strauss puts it, Hobbes sees "fear of violent death as the only adequate self-consciousness."[34]

To see the issue as one of mutual recognition suggests that the issue is a little more subtle than life and death, even in Hobbes. One does not (at least as an adult) require another's recognition to secure one's physical life. One does need recognition to secure the self. In short, the issue is not just physical survival; it is the way in which lack of recognition inflicts narcissistic injury. These considerations find support in an interesting place: again in Hobbes's introduction to his translation of Thucydides' *History*.[35] There he suggests that envy is as powerful a motive as fear; envy, fear, and honor—all seem to have virtually the same primacy in this account. Conversely, in *Leviathan* Hobbes argues that to evoke another's envy is as dangerous as to threaten his life: both invite preemptive attack.[36] Envy, it will be recalled, is a reaction to the narcissistic injury that occurs when our excellence compares unfavorably to that of others. That is, it is a reaction to an assault on one's honor.

Is my argument that Hobbes is really writing about fear of narcissistic injury, not fear of death? A passage in *The Elements of Law*, a work in which Hobbes's view of the self differs very little from that in *Leviathan*, would seem to support this claim. There he argues that the desire to escape humiliation may be stronger than the fear of death.

REVENGEFULNESS is that passion which ariseth from an expectation or imagination of making him that hath hurt us, to find his own action hurtful to himself. . . . For though it be not hard, by returning evil for evil, to make one's adversary displeased with his own fact; yet to make him acknowledge the same, is so difficult, *that many a man had rather die than do it.*[37]

From this perspective, honor becomes at least as important as life, with violent death (which Hobbes defines in terms of the possession and invasion of one's body by another)[38] being the ultimate narcissistic injury. Is this my argument? The answer is yes and no, to put it as unambiguously as possible. At the archaic level of self-development about which Hobbes is writing, there is no distinction between power and honor, and there is really none between power, honor, and the self. All are wrapped up together in that omniwhole that Kohut writes of, in which ideals, ambitions, omnipotence, and the worth of the self are one. One sees this even in the title of chapter 10, "Of Power, Worth, Dignity, Honour, *and* Worthinesse"—the great equation, it might be called. It is not that Hobbes is *really* concerned with narcissistic injury or fear of violent death or honor rather than power. It is that they tend to become one in his account. Violent death is not so much the most extreme manifestation of narcissistic injury as the paradigm of all narcissistic injury. When one suffers narcissistic injury, one's weakness is exposed to self and others, making one vulnerable to them. It is this vulnerability to invasion and appropriation that seems to be the fundamental fear, honor and power being equated by virtue of their status as bulwarks against them.

The self implicit in Hobbes's account is hardly subtle and indeed quite catastrophic. The pole of ideals is missing, and the pole of ambitions is reduced to its most archaic dimension: the pursuit of power for its own sake, or rather, for the sake of depriving others of the power to inflict narcissistic injury on us. Yet, as is so often the case with the self, archaic aspects are not isolated. Whether cause or effect (or perhaps neither, but instead part of a mutually elaborative developmental pattern), an archaic orientation in one dimension is often associated with other archaic perceptions. This is what makes diagnosis easier, albeit sometimes too easy, ignoring the idiosyncratic way in which archaic and mature aspects of the psyche may be combined. Hobbes's concept of the self, however, has few mature elements with which the archaic might combine. Quite the contrary, the self's obsession with power is associated with a rather narcissistic, unclear distinction between self and world: as though the whole world were but a mirror of one's own passions. In his "Discourse on Human Nature," Hobbes characterizes the passions in terms of their objects. Yet, as Peters suggests, the object of the passions in Hobbes's account is ultimately the self. Or rather, the self is inseparable from what we desire, being fused with all the objects of our desire. Hobbes, says Peters,

> injected into his account a bizarre kind of egocentricity. For Hobbes, in all cases of passions the notion of "self" was part of the content of cognition. He seemed to think that all such "phantasms" of objects, by reference to which the passions are to be distinguished, involve the thought of ourselves doing something or of our power to do something. Pity is thus seen as grief arising from our imagining ourselves in the same predicament as that of the one pitied. . . . Furthermore, how the highly sophisticated and *narcissistic* type of appraisal involved in the passions is to be reconciled with any attempt to represent them all as movements of the body and of some internal substance in the head is very difficult to determine.[39]

Hobbes is not entirely wrong, of course. Pity does seem to depend, in good measure, on our ability to identify with the suffering of others, as Rousseau grasped so clearly. In Hobbes's account, however, pity and other passions do not *depend* on the ability to identify with others. Rather, we relate passionately to the world only to the degree that everything in it happens to us. It is not merely that there are only selfobjects in Hobbes's world. It is that the entire world is perceived only in terms of how it makes us feel. In response it might be argued that this is always the case. This is what subjectivity means, why objectivity is so difficult, if not impossible. Perhaps, but once again it seems a matter of degree. To passionately relate to the world strictly in terms of how every event induces in me the experience of myself having certain passions seems both narcissistic and schizoid, dissociated—as though unless I experience myself having these emotions, then I don't know I have them and don't know that I am alive. But perhaps this has become the norm. *People* magazine, *USA Today,* most television news, is about asking others how they *feel* (after winning the lottery, losing a baby) so that viewers or readers might finally feel something, too (*Time* magazine advertises itself with the slogan "*Time* cries and lets you care"); then they can convince themselves that they are alive, human, not just a machine. Hobbes seems to see the passions in a similar fashion. Only his account implies that we split ourselves off from our passions in order to know that we are having them. But perhaps this split was always there in Hobbes's account of the self.

Strauss and Allan Bloom, among others, have captured well the way in which Hobbes makes *feeling* central. As Bloom writes in his chapter on "The Self" in *The Closing of the American Mind*,

> Freud was unknowingly following in the lines of Hobbes, who said that each man should look to what *he feels*—*feels*, not thinks; *he*, not another. Self is more feeling than reason, and is in the first place defined as the contrary of other. "Be yourself." Astonishingly, Hobbes is the first propagandist for bohemia and preacher of sincerity or authenticity. . . . "Feel!" Hobbes said. In particular you should imagine how you feel when another man holds a gun to your temple and threatens to shoot you. That concentrates all of the self in a single point, tells us what counts. . . . This experience helps much more to "set priorities" than does any knowledge of the soul or any of its alleged emanations such as conscience.[40]

Bloom, however, does not tell us why Hobbes argues thusly—that by feeling we know we are alive, not just one more machine. Only the Hobbesian self cannot really feel, or does not have enough confidence in itself to merely feel. It must observe itself feeling, an act of alienation in the midst of an experience valued because it overcomes alienation.

Civil Society Changes the Structure of the Self Not at All

One might agree with much of this analysis, but respond by arguing that it has confused the state of nature with civil society under the sovereign. It is the point of Hobbes's theory, after all, to create a society with sufficient security so that individuals need not devote all their time to the pursuit of power. For it is not merely danger from other men but the perpetual pursuit of power to the exclusion of all else that makes the life of man in the state of nature "solitary, poore, nasty, brutish, and short."[41] Hobbes argues, probably correctly, that under the sovereign, trade, commerce, art, and literature may flourish. Berns points out that Hobbes evidently "looked forward to a much milder regime than his total arming of the sovereign power would suggest."[42] Yet, though Hobbes may expect that the sovereign's regime will be mild, this evidently does not lead to fundamental changes in the self-structure of its citizens. Security and the relief from fear do not lead to self-development, a troubling point taken up again in the chapter on Rawls.

To be sure, behavior changes under the sovereign: from constant vigilance and preemptive attack to a concern with money-making and the like. This, though, reflects only the fact that except in the most severe disorders of the self, reality testing and ego adaptation (understood as a function, not a structure) remain intact. What does not change in civil society is the fundamentally archaic, narcissistic character structure of the citizens in which every issue continues to be reduced to one of power. Only now it is not the self's power but the sovereign's that is idealized.

Kohut shows why this shift involves no basic change. To seek all that is powerful for oneself or to idealize mere power in others, sharing in it via an archaic idealizing selfobject transference, are really different versions of the same psychological constellation. The most common self-disorder, says Kohut (and, I would add, social pathology), is archaic ambition masquerading as the mature pursuit of ideals. Furthermore, it makes little difference whether we pursue this ambition in our own lives or idealize it in others whom we follow and obey. The archaic psychological dynamics are the same. It is not difficult to discover this equation of power and goodness; it is all around us. The Frankfurt school claimed to find it in the "ideal" of the bourgeois father (an important point: patriarchy should not be idealized, even when what follows may be worse, the *vaterlose Gesellschaft*). Horkheimer writes that "when the child respects in his father's strength a moral relationship and thus learns to love what his reason recognizes to be a fact, he is experiencing his first training for the bourgeois authority relationship."[43] This equation is found throughout Hobbes's account of life under the sovereign. In the real world of sovereignty, citizens may have contempt for their leaders. In Hobbes's ideal world they glory in the reflected radiance of his power.

In chapter 18 of *Leviathan*, Hobbes stresses that the sovereign is pure will, unconstrained by law. This is, of course, the most primitive experience of power, how we first experience the power of parents and others, as well as how we would first exert our power. Against this interpretation Hobbes's emphasis on consent might be noted. It is through consent that we make the sovereign's power our own: "But by this Institution of a Common-wealth, every particular man is Author of all the Soveraigne doth; and consequently he that complaineth of injury from his Soveraigne, complaineth of that whereof he himselfe is Author."[44] This, it might be argued, is evidence of the citizens' mature identification with the sovereign. But it is too sudden, too unrealistic, too idealistic in the psychological sense. Pretending to appeal to mature reflection, Hobbes actually invokes archaic identification as grounds of submission, as though to say, "It is not enough that you accept the power of the sovereign. You must identify with it even when it is turned against you." Here is the real ground of the social contract: not just consent but submission.[45]

In the same chapter, Hobbes compares the sovereign to the sun, outshining all others: "As in the presence of the Master, the Servants are equall, and without any honour at all; So are the Subjects in the presence of the Soveraign. And though they shine some more, some lesse, when they are out of his sight; yet in his presence, they shine no more than the Starres in presence of the Sun."[46] Not only is this notion of power as illumination or brilliance a familiar narcissistic image (analysts have commented that the fantasy of being the source of all illumination, a virtual sun-king, or the only character with a spotlight on him is common among those with narcissistic personality disorder), but the appeal here is surely to the petit-bourgeois authoritarian personality who loves to see the mighty humbled by the still more exalted, but who is slavish in his obedience to the truly powerful. As Wolin observes, there is in Hobbes's account something of the mentality of Fallada's *kleiner Mann:* "the little man who rejoiced when the proud and mighty were humbled . . . who watched without complaint the growing distance between subject and sovereign, resentful only when the sovereign failed to maintain equality between citizens."[47] The citizens rejoice because they have identified themselves with the still more powerful sovereign, as though they shared in his ability to humble the mighty and so reduce their own envy.

Hobbes goes on to argue in chapter 21 that there is liberty only where the sovereign is silent.[48] Again, the conceptualization of power is narcissistic, in which the powerful have no limits (they can go wherever they want, do whatever they want), and the people have no boundaries, being subject to the intrusion of the sovereign in any way, at any place, at any time. This combination of no limits and no boundaries is perhaps the typical narcissistic fantasy, in which the otherness of the other is denied. This is seen in Hobbes's account of the passions. It is also, as *The Story of O* reminds us, a sadomasochistic fantasy. The most telling aspects of Hobbes's account of the sovereign, though, is perhaps the least subtle. It is Hobbes's claim in chapter 21 that "the Obligation of Subjects to the Soveraign, is understood to last as long, and no longer, than the power lasteth, by which he is able to protect them."[49] We recall that this is the same standard by which the validity of the

Fifth Commandment is evaluated. Power—to overawe others and to protect us from others—is the only standard, the only morality, the only basis of obligation. The notion that we might have a duty, when the sovereign is weakened, to come to his aid, to support him with our power, is totally absent.

Wolin argues that these considerations show the Hobbesian concept of power to be in the end hollow: "If sovereign power were effective because it induced withdrawal, how could the sovereign ever hope to join his subjects' wills to his in the pursuit of a common endeavor." [50]

But if it is a hollow concept of power, it is also a hollow concept of the self of the citizens, frightened, passive, vicariously participating in the subjugation and humiliation of the powerful by the still more powerful sovereign. The notion that right is separable from might, that citizens might have obligations, not just the duty to stand aside—all this and more is missing in Hobbes's account. Citizens have no sense of their own power; they overcome their narcissistic injury not by developing realistic (that is, limited) mature powers, but by identifying with the mighty. Hobbes's account of life under the sovereign is usually seen as an account of an authoritarian regime, not a totalitarian one. The liberties of citizens depend on the silence of the laws, and Hobbes apparently believes that over most private things the laws will be quiet. Nevertheless, though the sovereign's regime is not totalitarian, it fosters and depends upon selves who would find themselves at home under totalitarianism.

Religion

The standard reading of the relation between Hobbes's treatment of religion and his political theory is that of Peters, who argues that Hobbes is concerned that these irrational forces not challenge the rational power of the sovereign. Jesus gave authority to his followers to teach and preach. The danger arises when spiritual authority seeks to challenge the state or operate independently of it. "Most of his Scriptural exegeses were directed towards establishing these points," Peters says. [51] This is not incorrect, but Johnston puts it a little more precisely. Hobbes is not merely concerned with preventing religious leaders from challenging the sovereign; he seeks to overcome religious superstition in general, particularly the belief that man possesses an immortal soul, a spiritual or divine element. Hobbes's argument is aimed at the literate public, seeking to convince them that man is as much a material, corporal substance as the universe, no more and no less.[52]

> The World, (I mean not the Earth onely, that denominates the Lovers of it *Worldly men*, but the *Universe*, that is, the whole masse of all things that are) is Corporeall, that is to say, Body; . . . And because the Universe is All, that which is no part of it, is *Nothing*; and consequently *no where*. Nor does it follow from hence, that Spirits are *nothing:* for they have dimensions, and therefore really Bodies.[53]

Spirit is as real as one's body; there is hardly any difference between them. Hence (the implication is unavoidable) the soul cannot be eternal, since all substances are subject to change. The soul, like any spirit, is an ordinary, corporal substance—a body.[54] Cebes had it right all along, one might say (*Phaedo*, 70a).

If this is so, then men need no longer be afraid of the imaginary sanctions associated with Christian mythology and exploited by religious leaders. True or not, if people believe in these sanctions, they will not hesitate to disobey their sovereign. The sovereign may threaten death, but how can this compare to the threat of eternal damnation? If, however, men can be brought to believe that there is no greater punishment than death, they will respond to the sovereign's threats. As Johnston says, "Hobbes's refounding of Christianity was an attempt to transform men and women into the rational and predictable beings they would have to be before his vision of political society could ever be realized."[55] This required that Hobbes challenge those aspects of Christianity hostile to absolute sovereignty and that he demonstrate that man is strictly a machine, without soul or spirit. Only such beings fear violent death most of all because physical life—their body—is all they have left. There are no values worth dying for, no ambitions worth risking one's life for. Scientific, materialistic reduction becomes a psychological reduction as well, as the self is reduced to its body. It is this that makes rational politics possible, as all fear the same thing in the same way: the sovereign, who controls the fate of the body.

Although the overlap between self and soul in Hobbes is less complete than in Plato, it seems clear that in eliminating the soul Hobbes also eliminates the self. In eliminating any vestige of inwardness, of psyche that is not identical with body, Hobbes eliminates both self and soul. In a sense, he is a seventeenth-century Lacan, demystifying the self so that only a machine is left. Alan Ryan has argued that the premodernist Hobbes was actually the first postmodernist.[56] Ryan was referring to Hobbes's nominalism, but he could have been speaking of his view of the self as well. When the self has disappeared, Hobbes seems to say, then we can have social peace and only then. It is all the things valued by the self, such as honor or avoiding eternal damnation, that become more important than life itself, and it is this that makes society ungovernable, even by the sovereign.

Hobbes seems to believe this account of the self. It is not just a magnificent myth or a noble lie. His earlier works, such as *The Elements*, present essentially the same view in a nonpolemical context, in which the goal is to persuade not the literate public but the intellectual elite (though it should not be forgotten that Plato's magnificent myth was also aimed at the elite). Although Hobbes evidently believes his materialistic account of the self, he apparently does not believe that it is enough or that it will really convince. If he did, there would be no need to idealize the sovereign's power, as discussed above. If man were just a rational machine, Hobbes's rational arguments would be enough. But the idealization of the power of the sovereign appeals to a nonrational dimension. It is the political equivalent of superstition, so to speak, appealing to the most archaic, primitive aspects of the self. In the end Hobbes does not seem to believe that most selves can do without superstitions.

Reason

From an epistemological perspective, Hobbes's view of reason and rationality is unclear, Strauss arguing that Hobbes never denied that reason is incapable of establishing or justifying norms.[57] Certainly Hobbes believed that his system was based on rational, scientific analysis and deduction. By the "impotence of reason" Hobbes was referring not so much to its epistemological status as to its practical weakness in the face of the passions: its inability to withstand will, interest, desire, and thus, as we have just seen, its inability to calculate accurately the true interests of the body: "For I doubt not, but if it had been a thing contrary to any man's right of dominion, or to the interest of men to have dominion, *That the three Angles of a Triangle should be equall to two Angles of a Square*; that doctrine should have been, if not disputed, yet by the burning of all books of Geometry, suppressed, as farre as he whom it concerned was able."[58]

Although the apparent political irrelevance of geometry protects it, the same cannot be said of philosophy, ethics, religion, and the social studies, activities in which people define good and bad, right and wrong, as it pleases them. Or, as Hobbes puts it, "names have their constitution, not from the species of things, but from the will and consent of man." Otherwise expressed, "Good and evil are names given to things to signify the inclination or aversion of them by whom they were given."[59] The result is not merely political anarchy but conceptual and intellectual anarchy as well. Furthermore, it is a problem that has gotten worse in the modern world, as everyman comes to believe that he is capable of what once only priests, philosophers, and kings were: to define good and bad. There is only one solution: the Great Definer, a sovereign dispenser of common meanings, a "publique reason." It is the task of the sovereign to keep not merely political order but also the conceptual and linguistic order upon which the political order depends.

It has been frequently suggested that Thucydides' account of the civil war in Corcyra served as inspiration for Hobbes's concept of the state of nature. About this war (actually, violent anarchy) Thucydides says that "to fit in with the change of events, words, too, had to change their usual meanings."[60] Control the definitions of words, and one has a leg up on political control. By defining once and for all the meaning of "*meum* and *tuum*, right and wrong, good and bad," the sovereign creates order out of chaos. He does so, however, only by an act of will and power. What is right and wrong, good and bad, becomes arbitrary, the will of the most powerful. Reason is the will of the sovereign. Period. This is why Wolin concludes that "at bottom, then, a deep irrationalism pervaded Hobbesian society, for the sovereign could assign any content he wished to public meanings."[61] Reason has disappeared, absorbed by power and will in the name of stability. And though the idealization of reason is certainly problematic, as countless critics have shown, its separation from ideals, its equation with the will, is hardly an improvement.

In this light it may be useful to reconsider Macpherson's argument that Hobbes does not commit the naturalistic fallacy. The fallacy that Hobbes is charged with by so many critics concerns, of course, his claim that once the individual transfers his rights to the sovereign, "then is he said to be OBLIGED, or BOUND, not to hinder those, to whom such RIGHT is granted . . . from the benefit of it: and that he *Ought*, and it is his DUTY, not to make voyd that voluntary act of his own."[62] In short, "Hobbes believes that he has deduced moral obligation from fact, ought from is," for none of Hobbes's characterizations of human nature contains or implies "ought" statements.[63] In response, Macpherson argues that Hobbes is writing of a world in which "is" is the only standard, the "is" of natural equality. In such a world it is perfectly logical to conclude that one ought to obey the sovereign if one has consented to do so. "Ought" means here only "you ought to do so if you want to survive." This is all it can mean. There is no fallacy, as the distinction between "ought" and "is" upon which it is based does not exist in Hobbes's world.[64] Nor, I have argued, are Hobbesian selves capable of making this distinction, except in the prudential fashion to which MacIntyre refers—"I ought to do it if I want to survive."

MacIntyre makes a related point. As noted in chapter 1, what appeals to MacIntyre about traditions is that

> they give their members something more basic than arguments and justifications to ground their moral convictions in; they actually create persons whose nature is such that certain things count without question as reasons, justifications and criticisms of conduct—they generate the dispositions of thought and character on which reasoning of that kind depends, and thus provide a confidence in the results which reason alone is powerless to bestow.[65]

Nagel criticizes MacIntyre for the potential irrationalism of such a position. And perhaps it is irrational if we regard reason as possibly and properly living a life of its own. How much better it is (how much more in accord with the reality of the fact that only selves reason) to approach the epistemological status of reason through the developmental status of the self. If we approach reason through the self, then we ask not what is the fullest and most perfect expression of reason but what is the fullest and most perfect expression of the self who reasons. What is wanted is deep, subtle, manifold, and sophisticated selves, for such selves are most likely to be persuaded strictly by good reasons. Conversely, one-dimensional archaic selves are best convinced by one-dimensional reasons, such as those that make no distinction between "is" and "ought." Plato and Aristotle fully appreciated this point. Their conception of the good man was inseparable from their understanding of right reason. Only good men can reason well.

To be sure, the classics understood reason as an objective principle, not a subjective faculty, a view (at least in the case of Plato) based upon the separation of self-consciousness and self-knowledge, which is an assumption not without cost to the self who reasons. Bloom, along with many others, holds that only by returning to the classic concept of objective reason can the self be rescued from liberals such as Hobbes (or Locke) who transform it into a

bundle of feelings. Subjective reason and subjective selves, whose primitive
passions set their priorities, are inseparable. Against this position I have pro-
posed a normative model of the self, one that posits the inseparability of reason and the self who reasons. This need not trivialize reason, but only the
trivial reasons of trivial selves. My project resembles MacIntyre's, but rather
than blending rationality and tradition, it blends reason and the self, a mixture that to many will be even more troublesome than MacIntyre's. This is
why I devoted so much attention in chapter 1 to demonstrating that this
blend is not an endorsement of wild self-assertion. Rather, it stands closer to
the classical conception of mature self-consciousness. This, in turn, required
the demonstration that mature self-consciousness can be distinguished from
self-knowledge, a major theme of chapter 4.

The Frontispiece

The famous frontispiece of the 1651 edition of the *Leviathan* shows the
sovereign as a huge figure towering above his surroundings like some
regal Gulliver, brandishing in one hand the military sword, in the other
the sceptre of justice. Nestled in the valley below lies a tiny, thriving
city, its geometrical tidiness clearly symbolizing the peace and order
made possible by the giant looming in the background. . . . Yet there is
another feature of the frontispiece worth noting. The sovereign's powerful body is, so to speak, not his own; its outline is completely filled in by
the miniature figures of his subjects.[66]

Wolin interprets the significance of this along lines already suggested. The
sovereign's power is a myth, more rhetoric than reality. Real power depends
not merely on citizens' willingness to stand aside but on their active cooperation. My perspective views the significance of the frontispiece (actually, the
engraved title page) somewhat differently. From the perspective of the psychology of the self, the frontispiece is ironic because it at once suggests and
denies the truth: that the real threat comes not from others but from within
ourselves. It is the intensity of our fear that retards the development of the
mature self, the only force (other than the sovereign) powerful enough to
quell the narcissistic rage and aggression that stems from fear: fear at our vulnerability and rage that we lack the power to master either others or ourselves.
    Wolin emphasizes the symbolic importance of the fact that the sovereign's

body is not his own; it is entirely composed of the bodies of his citizens. Furthermore,

> each subject is clearly discernible in the body of the sovereign. The citizens are not swallowed up in an anonymous mass, nor sacramentally merged into a mystical body. Each remains a discrete individual and each retains his identity in an absolute way. What is suggested here is that the substance of power assigned the sovereign was less impressive than the rhetoric surrounding it.[67]

Does this contradict my interpretation that citizens fuse with the sovereign in order to overcome their narcissistic injury? Not really. The distinctness of each citizen within the sovereign's body suggests the thesis of this chapter: under the sovereign nothing changes. The selves of the citizens are not transformed. The amelioration of their fear does not promote the self-development that leads them to better distinguish "is" and "ought," right and might. They remain self-psychologically the same, even as they idealize the sovereign's power rather than their own.

That the sovereign's power is actually far less than they imagine, that much of his power stems from their own, is, of course, what Hobbes would have his citizens forget—or rather, be self-psychologically incapable of apprehending. For the archaic self, power is an all-or-nothing matter: if I do not have all the power, then someone else must (this is why the narcissist prefers absolute control over himself to mere influence over the world). The relation between this way of thinking and the inability to distinguish right and might is apparent. So too is the way this deficit in Hobbes's citizens makes them less capable of challenging the sovereign as well as less capable of aiding him.

Conclusion

The first sentences of Hobbes's introduction to *Leviathan* read as follows:

> Nature (the Art whereby God hath made and governes the World) is by the *Art* of man, as in many other things, so in this also imitated, that it can make an Artificial Animal. For seeing life is but a motion of Limbs, the beginning whereof is in some principall part within; why may we not say, that all *Automata* (Engines that move themselves by springs

and wheeles as doth a watch) have an artificiall life? For what is the *Heart*, but a *Spring*; and the *Nerves* so many *Strings*; and the *Joynts*, but so many *Wheeles*. . . . *Art* goes yet further, imitating that Rationall and most excellent worke of Nature, *Man*. For by Art is created that great LEVIATHAN called a COMMON-WEALTH, or STATE, (in latine CIVITAS) which is but an Artificiall Man . . . and in which, the *Sovereignty* is an Artificiall *Soul*, as giving life and motion to the whole body.[68]

One sees in this passage most of the themes discussed in this chapter: the sense that at its core the body is not only a machine but a lifeless machine, inorganic, without a soul. Although lifeless, it is nonetheless dangerous to itself and others. For this reason it must be constrained by, and psychologically contained in, a more powerful machine that can control it. This more powerful machine is, however, made in the image of its maker: lifeless, mechanical, its soul, the sovereign, being in the end nothing but power, the power to keep going.

My approach in this chapter, and throughout the book, has been to read the selfobject transference from right to left, as it were, to see in the selfobject chosen by the author the nature of the self. Occasionally this has required some fairly aggressive interpretation, but not in Hobbes's case. The artificial mechanical *Leviathan*, whose soul is concerned only with the power to keep going ("life and motion"), mirrors the self that Hobbes writes of almost perfectly, as he tells us it will on the first page.

In fact, *Leviathan* mirrors the self in another important respect as well. Civil society, Hobbes tells us, is not natural but artificial, an entity whose coherence and order is maintained against the centrifugal forces of fear and desire only by power. It seems that Hobbes's concept of the self is similar. It too seems almost unnatural: fragile, mechanical, brittle ("For if we look on men full-grown, and consider how brittle the frame of our human body is . . ."),[69] vulnerable, threatened by others and by the intensity of its own fear, rage, and desire, an intensity made all the worse by the absence of any mature self to contain these emotions. Thus, they must be contained by another, who is vastly more powerful, but in the end just as mechanical, lifeless, artificial. This is why the self never grows in Hobbes's account. In the end the state remains the containing, controlling other, a defense object, not an internalizable selfobject.

Is the Hobbesian self human nature? Macpherson argues that though

Hobbes thought he was writing about human nature per se, he was actually writing about human nature under early capitalism, the emergence of the "possessive market society." Within these historical constraints Hobbes assessed human nature accurately; he simply mistook human nature under capitalism for human nature per se. Hobbes's model, says Macpherson, "requires a model of society which not only permits continued invasion of each by each but also compels the moderate men to invade; that the only model which satisfies these requirements is the possessive market society, which corresponds in essentials to modern competitive market societies."[70]

This puts it too narrowly, for Macpherson never shows that human nature is not roughly as Hobbes describes. He shows only that the nature that Hobbes describes is given especially free reign in market societies. What Macpherson wants to do is reverse the arrow of influence. It is competitive market societies that cause people to behave in the way that Hobbes described. Get rid of these societies, and one can transform the human nature that Hobbes thought was a given. Perhaps Macpherson is correct, but nothing in his argument supports his claim, and some commonsensical observations work against it.

Who has not seen the type of behavior that Hobbes describes in bureaucracies and even families? Indeed, bureaucracies, including (of course) those in socialist societies, seem to be the natural home of Hobbesian man. Joseph Heller's *Something Happened* is Hobbes as farce instead of tragedy. One could argue, of course, much as Lasch does, that every aspect of contemporary society has been invaded by the market, contaminated with its value. Although this is not entirely untrue, it risks rendering Macpherson's argument a tautology, such that nothing could show it false. One might take a wider perspective, looking at various nonmarket societies throughout history. Thucydides' *History*, for example, describes the type of invasive, power-hungry behavior Hobbes wrote of on almost every page. Greece was a competitive society, an agonal culture, but it was hardly a competitive *market* society. Although Macpherson seems mistaken in his attempt to equate the Hobbesian self with the capitalist self, the preceding considerations do not support the opposite conclusion either: that Hobbes was writing about human nature per se. The self is how human nature appears to us in history, at least insofar as we can know it in the human studies. The self that Hobbes writes of is always present, always a force to be reckoned with. Which is another way of saying that fear, rage, desire, and the pursuit of power will always be with us and that Hobbes's account of these passions is brilliant. What is not a constant is the structure of the self—that is, how it deals with its passions.

Everything that Hobbes says is true. The question is how we come to terms with this truth. Everything he says is true because he is writing about the archaic self, a self that never disappears, never loses its force, but is ideally integrated with its more mature counterpart, the genuine bipolar self. Hobbes never seeks this integration. Locke and Rawls do. In this sense their liberalism is fundamentally different. The question is whether they come to terms with Hobbes's truths about the archaic self in a way that respects Hobbes's insights. Locke develops a genuine bipolar self. He does so, however, by splitting off aspects of Hobbes's archaic self via what Kohut calls a vertical split within the pole of ambitions. Locke is also willing to render the self terribly dependent on the opinions of others in order to control it. Rawls, with his maximin solution to the problem of the original position, actually better comes to terms with Hobbes's truths, the truths of fear, rage, and desire. The question is whether Rawls, unlike Hobbes, does so in such a way that allows further self-development.

Here, then, is the problem faced by this strand of liberalism, "liberal traditionalism" it has been called: how to come to terms with Hobbes's truths about the self without making them the whole truth or splitting them off and denying them. Is it possible to do this while respecting the integrity of the self? Or is the only alternative to the rule of the sovereign the internalization of the sovereign within—that is, Plato's solution in *The Republic*: superego in place of superstate. Perhaps there is a third solution, what Nichols calls the lie: that the state can meet the needs of the self if the self dedicates itself to the state. But is there yet another solution, one that does not depend on the lie? Perhaps there is, but it is not Rousseau's, who avoids Hobbes's conclusions only by denying the differences among people that evoke narcissistic injury in the first place.

This you may learn from his
writings; which will also tell
you whatever else there is to be
said of him. —From the epitaph
of John Locke

CHAPTER SIX

Locke and the
Self Held Hostage

Allan Bloom observes that John Locke was perhaps the earliest thinker to use the term *self* in the modern sense. The self is among the most important discoveries made in the state of nature, but we have been unable to capture it. "We go back and back, ever farther, hunting the self as it retreats into the forest, just a step ahead of us."[1] The reason, suggests Bloom, is that the self is ultimately a pale substitute for the soul (psyche). We chase the shadow because we have forgotten the substance. In one respect Bloom is correct. For the self-contained psyche of Plato's *Republic*, Locke substitutes a psyche dependent for its self-esteem upon the opinion of others and in this sense utterly conventional: a concern with a reputation for virtue is virtue. It is as though Glaucon and Adeimantus wrote *The Republic* or Locke's *Some Thoughts concerning Education*.

Yet this discontinuity between Plato and Locke does not support the conclusion that Hobbes and Locke are continuous. Bloom, following Strauss, argues that they are, as both substitute feeling for thinking, a distinction roughly comparable to that between the modern self and the classical psyche:

> Once the old virtues were refuted . . . Hobbes and Locke assumed that most men would immediately agree that their self-preservative desires are real, that they come from within and take primacy over any other desire. The true self is not only good for individuals but provides a basis for consensus not provided by religions or philosophies. Locke's substitute for the virtuous man, the rational and industrious one, is the perfect expression of this solution.[2]

In fact, Locke's view of the self differs decisively from Hobbes's. In place of Hobbes's archaic self Locke posits a genuine bipolar self, in which ideals are more than ambition in disguise and ambition seeks more than power. And as important, Locke's self possesses self-consciousness, knowing not merely that it feels but that it has a history, what MacIntyre calls a "narrative unity." This is seen most clearly in *An Essay concerning Human Understanding*, the last topic of this chapter.

Yet the Lockean self is far from ideal; it is characterized by a profound vertical split within the pole of ambitions, serving to deny the continuity between the desire to master and dominate others (the theme of *Thoughts concerning Education*) and the desire to acquire ever more property (a theme of the *Second Treatise*). The result is the idealization of acquisition for its own sake, as though it were an ideal and innocent form of domination, a sure sign of self-mastery rather than the mastery of others. Ultimately Locke's strategy for self-control fails, in part for the reasons usually cited. It depended, for example, upon a medieval religious constraint on acquisition that had lost its grip even as Locke wrote. From the perspective of the psychology of the self, however, Locke's strategy fails for another reason, one internal to the structure of the Lockean self. Lockean man is flawed from the beginning. In this sense he is tragic (which means that his character possesses noble elements), not merely the victim of modernity or capitalism. The Lockean self is based upon the unrealistic idealization of acquisition as a particularly innocent and pure form of domination. It is inauthentic, denying what it relentlessly pursues: mastery of others. To be sure, this inauthenticity finds a great deal of support in the ideology of the possessive market society, as Macpherson calls it. But this is really the point. The Lockean concept of the self, like all concepts of the self, exists not in a vacuum but in a particular historical context. Analyzing the self is one way of getting a slightly different perspective on this context, particularly how disparate and contradictory elements in a society's ideology combine with, exploit, and reinforce the fears, rages, and desires of the self.

One of the most striking things about the secondary literature on Locke is not merely the diversity but the polarity of opinions. For Vaughan, Locke is an anarchic individualist, for whom the individual is the only value. For Kendall, on the other hand, Locke is a more thoroughgoing (and hence more dangerous) theorist of the general will than Rousseau. Macpherson sees Locke as a defender of possessive individualism, whereas Dunn sees the key to Locke's theory in the religious doctrine of the calling. Strauss looks at Locke and sees Hobbes. [3] My account of the Lockean self does not reconcile these conflicting interpretations. My interpretation does not show that they do not really conflict at all, but are actually different aspects of a seamless whole. To show this wholeness is the power of Macpherson's interpretation and its limit—the latter because to render smooth and whole an account filled with conflict and contradiction is to misrepresent this account, especially if the account derives much of its significance from its contradictions.

All this is not to say that contradiction is good. It is to say that if we fail to appreciate the contradictions in Locke's account, we fail to fully appreciate its significance. Not merely Bloom but all who argue that Locke is *really* this or that type of theorist (individualist, collectivist, Hobbes manque) make this mistake. Macpherson states that "it seems more reasonable to conclude that Locke was able to take both positions about human nature because he had in mind simultaneously two conceptions of society."[4] "More reasonable" is only good, of course, when the object of study is best illuminated by rendering it rational. It is this that I question. One advantage of approaching Locke via the psychology of the self is that it embraces contradiction. This is what the self is about: holding ambivalent and contradictory passions together in some sort of pattern. Some patterns are better than others because they require less splitting and denial. But all are based on ambivalence and contradiction: between, for example, archaic desires and mature ideals. In fact, it is the archaic self, the Hobbesian self, that is least contradictory, as it lacks mature ideals in the first place. This obviously does not make it more desirable.

The Bipolar Self: *Second Treatise of Government*

There is no clearer, more transparent use of a symbolic selfobject in all of political theory than Locke's concept of property—that is, "Lives, Liberties, and Estates, which I call by the general name, *Property*."[5] Slightly less obvious, but almost as important, is Locke's understanding of God and his relationship to man in terms of the selfobject transference. Just as property is man's selfobject, says Locke, so are we God's property, or in effect, God's selfobject. This ability to understand oneself as God's selfobject turns out to be central to Locke's concept of reason, which is best understood as the ability to take a God's-eye view: to see things as one might see them were part of one's self, the valuing and judging part, shared with God.

The basic structure of Locke's concept of the self is unfolded in his *Second Treatise of Government*, and it is with this essay that I begin, even though many details of this structure are developed only in other works, particularly his *Thoughts concerning Education* and *An Essay concerning Human Understanding*. (The next section on Locke's concept of the self in the *Second Treatise* may, therefore, seem sketchy, but many of the details are filled in in subsequent sections on *Thoughts* and *An Essay*.) As far as the psychology of the self is concerned, the key point to remember is that the bipolar self is characterized both by the poles of ideals and ambitions and by a sectorial distinction *within* each pole between archaic and mature aspects of ideals and ambitions. All mature selves are characterized by such a vertical division or split. The question is always one of degree: how isolated is the archaic sector from its mature counterpart? If the split is severe, the mature elements cannot temper or bind the archaic ones, serving instead to rationalize their pursuit.[6]

The Idealizing Pole

In the more archaic sector of the idealizing pole, the self understands itself as God's property, God's selfobject. As Locke puts it, "Men being all the Workmanship of one Omnipotent, and infinitely wise Maker: All the Servants of one Sovereign Master, sent into the World by his order and about his business, *they are his Property*, whose Workmanship they are, made to last during his, not one another's Pleasure."[7] The self is valuable because it is the workmanship of an ideal, all-powerful, all-knowing object, who makes us in his image. Being his property we are subject to his laws. The element of fusion with an ideal apparent in this formulation becomes more apparent when one considers how Locke conceptualizes legitimate property in the first place: as the outcome of mixing oneself with an inanimate object.[8] Only in this case the "oneself" is God, and the result is animate humans mixed with God and belonging to him.

In the more mature sector of the idealizing pole, man becomes a person, capable of formulating and following his own rules, albeit under the guidance of God. Otherwise expressed, God becomes man's selfobject, not vice versa, a shift marked by a movement from passivity to activity, from following orders to internalizing them. Locke addresses this shift in terms of the difference between a man and a person. A person, says Locke, is "a Forensick term appropriating Actions and their Merit."[9] A person is a man who is responsible for his own actions, who claims and exerts ownership over them: "In this *personal Identity* is founded . . ."[10] Such persons, argues John Yolton, are no longer merely God's property; they become their own property.

While he had asserted earlier in this same treatise [*Second Treatise of Government*] that men are the property of God since they are his workmanship, he apparently did not feel that fact was incompatible with my person being *my* property as well. *Men* are God's property, *persons* are not. Person is, as we have seen, the most perfect form of moral man, the standard of humanity. When we appropriate our actions as our own through consciousness, we are exerting effort, laboring as it were, and accepting responsibility for what we are as moral agents. [11]

The moral freedom of the person to which Locke refers is the outcome of an act of psychological labor, of appropriation in which we make an external standard our own by mixing ourselves with it. In so doing we come to conceive of ourselves differently: not as the objects of this standard but as its subjects. The transformation is from passivity to activity, from being acted upon to acting, but it is not a movement from reliance upon an idealized selfobject to autonomy. Rather, the shift is from seeing oneself as the selfobject of another to having a selfobject. As we would appropriate a piece of property by mixing ourselves with it, so we may appropriate a selfobject, making it more truly part of ourselves, what Kohut calls transmuting internalization—and that is labor.

The Pole of Ambitions

Behind the love of liberty, says Locke, lies the love of power and domination. Not only, he continues in *Thoughts concerning Education*, does the child have desires; he has the desire to bend others to his will. It is not enough simply to have all that one wants; one must have constant evidence of the power of one's will over another to feel truly free.

> I told you before that Children love *Liberty*. . . . I now tell you, they love something more; and that is Dominion: And this is the first Original of most vicious Habits, that are ordinary and natural. This Love of *Power* and Dominion shews itself very early, and that in these Two Things. . . . They would have their Desires submitted to by others. Another thing wherein they shew their love of Dominion, is their desire to have things to be theirs; they would have Propriety and Possession, pleasing themselves with the Power that seems to give, and the Right they thereby have, to dispose of them, as they please. [12]

Here is the basis of the pole of ambitions in both its archaic and mature sectors. In the archaic sector, the self wants omnipotence: the power to bend another's will to its own. The self also wishes to own and dispose of everything that catches its fancy and perhaps everything that catches the fancy of others, so that the self might have further evidence of its power. Will and desire are like Hobbes's concept of power: relational goods in a zero-sum game, valuable primarily in terms of how they transform others into means for my ends. What does the self desire? Most of all to transform others into instruments of its desire, a desire marked not so much by a lust for things as by a wish to evince its will.

Locke recognizes that "these two Roots of almost all the Injustice and Contention, that so disturb Humane Life, are not early to be weeded out." [13] In *Thoughts concerning Education*, Locke seeks to extirpate greed itself, or at least its most egregious manifestations. One sees this, for example, in his placement of a variety of restrictions on how the child is to treat his first property: his toys. They should not be in his custody; he should play with only one toy at a time and that to be chosen by his parent; and he should make most of his toys. Locke hopes that this will teach the child that while he may enjoy his playthings, he does not have dominion over them. He is to see that property is a "gift" from those who have power, and that this gift is not free but requires labor. Finally, he is to be discouraged from a desire for variety for its own sake, playing with only one toy at a time, for example. [14] The goal of these rather heavy-handed pedagogical techniques is to quell, via the formation of good habits, the apparently natural desire for unlimited possession: "Covetousness, and the Desire of having in our Possession, and under our Dominion, more than we have need of, being the Root of all Evil, should be early and carefully weeded out, and the contrary Quality of a Readiness to impart to others, implanted." [15]

The tone and strategy in the *Second Treatise* is puzzlingly different, however. As both Macpherson and Tarcov point out, in this work covetousness is defined as the desire to possess what *others* have labored for (that is, trespass), and unlimited acquisition is rationalized by means of the introduction of money, which allows infinite accumulation without spoilage. [16] If, however, we focus upon the self-psychological function of acquisition, this difference becomes more understandable, if no less contradictory. The program of the *Second Treatise* is not to quell the desire for unlimited mastery, domination, and acquisition but to rechannel it (sublimation) into the acquisition of property, as innocent and benign an expression of mastery as can be found, for it creates more for all without limiting anyone's freedom. [17] The acquisition of property is innocent dominion, for it carries with it no authority to dominate others. In fact, Locke spends a great deal of energy in the *Two Treatises* trying to separate power and property, arguing, for example, that even if Filmer were correct that God gave Adam and his descendants "*Private Dominion* over the earth," this would not justify political power: power over the lives of persons. [18]

In the face of the objection of Macpherson and numerous others that this is a disingenuous distinction in a world of scarce resources, in which control of property must lead to power over others, Yolton argues that Locke is making a conceptual distinction. Like the underlaborer in philosophy, Locke is distinguishing two concepts that Filmer ran together, power and property. [19] This is not an adequate explanation. Yet it may pay to examine further Locke's idealization of the innocence and purity of acquisition, for there is a conceptual issue at stake: the distinction between the material reality of acquisition and its symbolic significance. A primary reason for Locke's regarding the acquisition of property as an innocent form of mastery is that it requires self-mastery, delayed gratification, all those things that have come to be known under the rubric "puritan work ethic." Acquisition is hard work, requiring that the individual control himself and subjecting his willfulness and his desire for pleasure to the demands of the market and nature. From this perspective there seems to be some basis to Dunn's claim that Locke understood the labor of acquisition as a calling, in which man makes recompense for his sinfulness by performing his assigned task in life as well as possible. [20] Or rather, Locke's is a heavily secularized and psychologized version of this doctrine, in which the amount one is able to acquire is evidence of the value of one's self, of one's worth as a person. It serves as evidence not so much of one's election by God as of the degree to which one has mastered oneself—the degree to which one has sublimated the desire for the mastery of others into self-mastery. *This* is virtue for Locke.

There is a contradiction here! The more I acquire, the more I prove that I have mastered my greedy and acquisitive nature. It would be less contradictory, certainly, in a world in which "there was still enough, and as good left" over for others, but even in this world Locke's account would not lose its contradiction, as it is not merely economic but psychological. The psychoanalyst Janine Chasseguet-Smirgel writes of how the pervert comes to terms with his perversion by idealizing it. [21] Her point is that ideals are so powerful that often the only way we can violate them is by an act of psychological reversal, in which we convince ourselves that bad is good. Property is hardly a perversion, but Locke's reasoning appears to be similar. The desire to master and dominate others, to make them instruments of our will, cannot be overcome; it can, however, be rechanneled into acquisition. But rather than leaving it at this, Locke takes great pains to idealize this rechanneling, as though to cleanse it of its origins entirely. The result is a vertical split in the self, in which the continuity of motives in mastery, domination, and acquisition is denied. This vertical split is reflected in the discontinuity between *Thoughts* and the *Second Treatise* on the morality of acquisitiveness, as though children could be taught what adults could not be expected to remember.

Property and Denial

Locke argues that by mixing our labor with property we mix ourselves with it and so make it ours, an extension of ourselves. The property every man has in his own person becomes mixed with the property he has worked on: "Man (by being Master of himself, and *Proprietor* of his own Person, and the actions of *Labour* of it) had still in himself the great *Foundation of Property*."[22] Just as Locke regards the property that each man has in his own person as a God-given right, so he extends this protection to the property acquired through labor, so that "Man being born, as has been proved, with a Title to perfect freedom, and an uncontrouled enjoyment of all the Rights and Privileges of the Law of Nature, equally with any other Man, or Number of Men in the World, hath by Nature a Power, not only to preserve his property, that is, his Life, Liberty and Estate."[23]

   In short, property is a symbolic selfobject, representing man's most fundamental natural rights, rights so profound they may never be justly abridged by others. Yet this is not the whole story. In an astute remark, Laslett observes that far from being an inalienable right, property is in fact the *most* alienable aspect of the person.[24] We can sell it, trade it, or give it away, and it may justly be taken from us. To be sure, there is considerable debate over how much social regulation of property is permissible under Locke's account (redistributive taxation seems questionable, proportional taxation acceptable,[25] but it is in any case quite extensive. As Laslett puts it, "even the minutest control of property by political authority can be reconciled with the doctrine of *Two Treatises*. . . . If it is permissible to look on his use of the concept 'property' as symbolic, as has been suggested, then the symbolic system seems to express all human rights as market commodities."[26]

What Locke seems to be doing is using property as the symbolic expression of a psychological fact: not merely that all rights are up for sale but that the self is at once intimate and public, private and shared, social and individual, one and many. This is the interpretation of that famous liberal political theorist Norman O. Brown, who in *Love's Body* argues that Locke sees our mixing of ourselves with property as symbol and metaphor for mixing ourselves with others.[27] Here then is another reason Locke regards the acquisition of property as an expression of innocent dominion: it is a sign of successful socialization, a measure of the degree to which one is willing to share oneself with others. The man who has the most property has, in a sense, shared himself most with others, which means not merely that he has produced more value for others to share in but also that he has made himself more vulnerable to others. For no matter how much property he has, the majority may still regulate it; and the more he has, the more there is to regulate. Acquisition of property is innocent, then, in a way that mastery over others is not because in acquiring property we make ourselves not less but more vulnerable to others, perpetually susceptible to the control of the majority. This way of thinking is very different from that of Hobbes, for whom all activities of the self are oriented toward the reduction of vulnerability. For Locke, acquisition is morally redeemed by the way it testifies to a willingness to render the self vulnerable to society—that is, a willingness to be social.

Macpherson argues that the individualist (e.g., Vaughan) and collectivist (e.g., Kendall) interpretations of Locke are both correct. Because Locke intended that only property owners vote, he had few qualms about subjecting the individual to the collective. As Macpherson says, individuals who have "the means to realize their personalities (that is, the propertied)" do not need to reserve any rights against civil society, as this society is set up to protect only them in the first place. Once one recognizes that civil society for Locke is a means by which some (property owners) will realize their individuality at the expense of others (non–property owners), most of the inconsistencies and mysteries in Locke's account disappear. Locke's individualism, according to Macpherson, "asserts an individuality that can be realized fully only in accumulating property, and therefore, realized only by some at the expense of the individuality of others."[28] The full development of the selves of some is achieved at the expense of the development of the selves of others.

Such an interpretation, though not incorrect, fails adequately to address the consequences to the selves of the privileged. And though the privileged were in Locke's day, as our own, a minority, today most individuals in the liberal democracies are accumulators, possessive individualists. Thus, it is wise to worry about the effects of Locke's unrealistic and idealized picture of acquisition on their psyches, too. The primary psychological effect of Locke's idealized portrait of acquisition is splitting. And the best evidence of splitting is excessive idealization and the Manichaeism frequently associated with it: the good has no connection to the bad, a sign that the archaic and mature sectors of at least one pole of the self are not well integrated, the archaic desires being walled off out of fear that they will run amok and contaminate the ideal. This seems to be precisely what is going on in Locke's account of property, in which the greedy, acquisitive, domineering aspects of the self are somehow rendered pure and blameless when channeled into industrious, self-denying acquisition.

One might argue that this split is an effect, not a cause, of an economic system that allows the free development of some selves only at the expense of others. Locke is forced into idealizing the innocence of the acquisition in order to avoid confronting the hypocrisy of a system that proclaims universal rights but practices differential ones. True enough, but this becomes an explanation only when we appreciate why hypocrisy is such an important defense in the first place in Locke's account. Individuals might, after all, simply admit the unfairness of it all and be done with it. Individuals are hypocritical not merely in order to deny the discrepancy between ideal and reality but in order to deny their own greed and avarice, their own lack of self-mastery. Ideologies defend the system. Hypocrisy defends the self that lives in it. Or rather, ideologies reinforce the splitting of the self by giving hypocrisy its rationalizations. Finally, it should not be overlooked that the splitting in question takes place *within* the pole of ambitions (it is a vertical split), not just between ideals, and ambitions. We deny the continuity between our desire for domination and our mature acquisitive activities by splitting off and idealizing the latter. Splitting, then, is about denying our own greed and lack of self-control, not just the injustice of a system from which we happen to benefit.

Tarcov concludes his essay on Locke's *Thoughts concerning Education* this way:

Even if we recognize Lockean decency and realism, we may be apt to regard the moral virtues toward which he directed education as merely bourgeois or middle-class morality, hard and narrow, low and colorless. He may offend our moral taste by seeming to slight imagination, passion, and sexuality in favor of reason, self-expression in favor of self-denial, beauty in favor of utility. . . . Locke saw that we have to be willing to deny our desires, face our fears, endure our pains, and take pains in labor to preserve our equal liberty and avoid being either tyrants or slaves. Lack of that self-mastery makes us prone to prey on the rights of others and willing to surrender our own. For Locke, passion and imagination make us subject to the authority of others, exploited by their ambition and covetousness. [29]

Tarcov does not regard the valorization of self-mastery and self-denial that he finds in Locke especially problematic. The preceding considerations show why it is, quite independently of whether one admires the genuine expression of these virtues. Self-mastery and self-denial in Locke seem frequently inauthentic, based upon the idealized pursuit of a purified version of what is being denied.

Reason, Natural Law, and the Isolation of the Idealizing Pole

Neither reason nor natural law, key topics in many studies of Locke, has been emphasized. Nevertheless, it may be useful to consider briefly the implications of Locke's concept of the self for these topics. It is frequently held that Locke became more and more skeptical about the reach of reason. In his early (1664) *Essays on the Law of Nature,* he asserts that the tenets of natural law are capable of demonstration and that anyone who used his sense perception and reason could know them. Conversely, he states that "the law of nature cannot be known by tradition." [30] Locke never demonstrated a single natural law, however, unless one wants to count the very general claim (actually, an assertion, serving as a premise) in the *Second Treatise,* referred to earlier, in which the law of nature tells us that we are not to harm one another. Furthermore, Locke never again made the attempt to establish particular laws. He apparently intended that his *Essay concerning Human Understanding* (1690) would conclude with a rational demonstration of the law of nature, but abandoned the attempt, suppressing the chapter in which the attempt was announced. [31] Dunn suggests that Locke never pursued this program because he came to realize that it was impossible. In any case, one may read Locke's late (1697) *Reasonableness of Christianity* as the alternative: faith, not reason, is the path to natural truths. As Locke puts it there, "It is plain, in fact, that human reason unassisted failed men in its great and proper business of morality. It never from unquestionable principles, by clear deductions, made out an entire body of the law of nature."[32] My interpretation is compatible with this sequence, but puts it in a somewhat different light, suggesting that Locke ended up not so far from where he began.

Locke seems to have always understood reason and revelation as two sides of the same coin. As he writes in *An Essay*, hardly a fideist tract, "*Reason* is natural *Revelation*, whereby the eternal Father of Light, and Foundation of all Knowledge communicated to Mankind that portion of Truth, which he has laid within the reach of their natural Faculties." Conversely, he goes on to characterize revelation as "natural *Reason*, enlarged by a new set of Discoveries communicated by God immediately, which *Reason* vouches the Truth of, by the Testimony and Proofs it gives, that they come from GOD."[33] How could reason stand so close to revelation? How could Locke hang so much of his argument on the power of reason to know natural law, be unable to conclude this argument, and yet apparently find this no great embarrassment, or at least no cause to revise his thinking?

Laslett suggests the answer in the introduction to his collation of the *Two Treatises*, arguing that reason for Locke is not so much about being able to *prove* the existence of God and his laws as about being able to take a God's-eye view of things, including one's own interests.[34] Expressed in terms of the selfobject transference, reason is the ability to take the perspective of the idealized self object, to make the God's-eye perspective one's own. This ability may be expressed in two dimensions, that of the archaic and the mature idealizing selfobject transferences, which seem roughly to correspond to the distinction between faith and reason in Locke's account, particularly insofar as they are not opposites or alternatives but flow into each other, as reason and revelation do.

What precisely does taking a God's-eye view mean for Locke? Primarily it means to be able to distinguish between one's private interests and the public interest, pursuing the latter when acting in a public capacity. Hancey states that "the participating citizen is to guide his actions in the 'forum' by the greater good of mankind which is the law of nature."[35] The issue is one of perspective, not justification. Taking a God's-eye view means conceptualizing ideals as the capacity to look down on oneself and others from above, seeing oneself as one among many, all with valid interests. Expressed in psychoanalytic terms, it is about the ability to bind the narcissistic pursuit of ambition with ideals, ideals that remind each individual that he lives among others who also have value, for they too are made in God's image. This perspective also helps explain why Locke's early disparagement of tradition as a mode of access to natural law is absent in his later works. Tradition, too, is a way of standing back from the immediate interests of the self, seeing the self as part of a larger whole, such as the Great Chain of Being.

If the idealizing pole of the self is so mature and coherent in Locke's account, then why is the Lockean self so hypocritical? Part of the answer has to do with the abstract character of natural law itself. Right, respect, and moral equality are compatible with great actual inequality and always have been. But the more fundamental reason has to do with the fact that ideals can't bind what they can't find. Split-off and archaic ambitions are immune not only to mature ambition but also to the mature ideals that would bind them. A profound vertical split in one pole of the self will affect its ability to maintain its connection to the other, a point insufficiently emphasized in Kohut's account of *How Analysis Cures*, which is frequently by restoring only one pole to health. From this perspective, Plato is right to see the fundamental problem of moral life as the problem of desire. All the ideals in the world cannot bind archaic desire if they cannot find it.

Thoughts concerning Education

Nathan Tarcov opens his essay on Locke's *Thoughts* by asking what the relation might be between Locke's *Thoughts* and his political interests. Originally written by the bachelor Locke as a series of letters to Edward Clarke on how best to raise his eight-year-old son, *Thoughts* nowhere connects the two issues. Tarcov suggests that the link is best seen in one of Locke's minor educational writings, "Some Thoughts concerning Reading and Study for a Gentleman," where Locke distinguishes between two dimensions of politics: the founding of civil society and its successful governance. The *Two Treatises* are presumably about the first dimension, *Thoughts concerning Education* about the second. Locke's brief comment, in "The Epistle Dedicatory" to the *Thoughts*, that "the Welfare and Prosperity of the Nation . . . much depends on" how children are bred, supports this view. [36] My perspective puts it even more simply. *Thoughts* is about an upbringing that will support, via trans-muting internalization, a self-structure compatible with the civil society that Locke writes of in the *Second Treatise*.

Although one might be tempted, along these lines, to see the child that Locke writes of in *Thoughts* as analogous to man in the state of nature in the *Second Treatise*, this would be misleading. As with Hobbes, the state of nature and civil society are continuous. The state of nature is a way of saying some things about human nature that one does not always wish to say out loud, so to speak. Or, as Macpherson has written,

> Natural . . . is not the opposite of social or civil. . . . The natural con-dition of mankind is within man now, not set apart in some distant time or place.

> Locke read back into the state of nature, in a generalized form, the as-sumptions he made about differential rights and rationality in existing society. [37]

Locke's *Thoughts* is actually a far better guide to his views on human nature than the state of nature in the *Second Treatise*. (Originally begun in 1684 and published in 1693, *Thoughts* would have been begun only a couple of years after the *Second Treatise*, according to Laslett's dating.)

Although Tarcov takes pains to downplay its harshness, much of Locke's *Thoughts* seems stringent indeed, even by the standards of the day. One reader wrote Locke saying that he found his recommendation that the child *never* be given the object of its desire quite cruel. [38] In fact, this is really the theme of *Thoughts*: to deny children their desires so that they would be able, upon reaching adulthood, to deny themselves: "As the Strength of the Body lies chiefly in being able to endure Hardships, so also does that of the Mind. And the great Principle and foundation of all Vertue and Worth, is placed in this, that a Man is able *to deny himself* his own Desires, cross his own In-clinations, and purely follow what Reason directs as best, tho' the Appetite lean the other way." [39] Rebutting Yolton, who interprets this passage as mean-ing that reason and desire almost never meet, Tarcov suggests that Locke re-mains a hedonist in the Aristotelian sense, in which reason and happiness coincide but only in the long run. In any case, Clarke, who apparently fol-lowed Locke's advice, does not seem to have thought that his son turned out very well (among other things, Edward, Jr., suffered from melancholy) and sent the young man to Locke for remedial work some years later. Locke sent the boy back home. [40]

Locke's educational psychology is straightforward. Submission to another can develop the habit of rational self-control. This psychology is implemented by denying children whatever they ask for. "Whatever they were importunate for, they should be sure, for that very Reason, to be denied." By this Locke seems to mean anything they fancy, such as this or that particular food, rather than food per se. This, though, is only half the strategy; the other half is equally important. One should supply them with "whatsoever might innocently delight them," provided that they have not requested it and that the delights are not "rewards of this or that particular Performance." [41] Such innocent delights are to serve as evidence of the parents' esteem. In this way children are to be conditioned to associate esteem with pleasure and delight. The goal, says Locke, is to

> make the Sense of *Esteem* or *Disgrace* sink the deeper, and be of the more Weight, other *agreeable* or *disagreeable things should accompany these different States*; not as particular Rewards and Punishments of this or that particular, but as necessarily belonging to, and constantly attending one, who by his Carriage has brought himself into a State of Disgrace or Commendation. [42]

In his commentary on the *Thoughts*, Axtell points to a passage on this point in Locke's diary, where Locke asserts that "credit and reputation . . . shame and disgrace," are "the principal spring from which the acting of men take their rise, the rule they conduct them by, and the end to which they direct them." It is this, he continues, that makes Hurons endure unexpressible torments, that makes merchants in one country and soldiers in another, that makes men and women wear uncomfortable clothes and study difficult subjects. [43] In short, it is concern with reputation that makes the world go around, that sets the standard of value on all things, especially the excellences of the self. This is not bad psychology, capturing both the sheer power of narcissistic ambition and the way its expression is culturally variable.

Locke sets the selfobject transference to work ordering society and teaching children and later adults to esteem in themselves what others esteem in them. One might call this Cooley's looking-glass self, but Kohut's perspective really runs deeper: the self's narcissistic ambitions are made dependent upon the approval of others. In this way people are socialized, which means (as with property) rendered vulnerable to others, almost part of them. Such a strategy is, of course, the opposite of Plato's, which makes self-esteem and self-mastery a personal affair. It is also the opposite of Rousseau's in *Emile*, a work directed against Locke's *Thoughts*. Does this make Rousseau's strategy similar to Plato's? Yes, especially insofar as both see autarky as the solution to amour propre (pride, vanity), which Bloom equates with thumos.

Why does Locke found society upon the outer-directed man, more concerned with a reputation for virtue than virtue itself? Or rather, upon a man who can see no difference between them? One could argue that Locke is a modern, and this is what moderns do. Having less confidence in reason, moderns are more concerned with stability than virtue. So they aim lower: not the good society but the stable one. This, however, seems not so much an explanation as a definition. In any case, Locke seems profoundly impressed with the intensity of the desire for mastery and domination, as well as how socially disruptive it can be. Tarcov downplays this point a bit, pointing out that Locke writes that men are "desirous to be Masters of *themselves* and others."[44] But what Locke seems to mean is only that individuals do not wish *others* to master them: self-mastery is here tantamount to freedom, not self-control. Or rather, we control ourselves only so that we won't suffer the still greater narcissistic injury of being controlled by others. On this point, at least, Locke and Rousseau are in agreement.

In Hobbes's world, mutual freedom brings ruin to all, as everyone seeks mastery over others in order to avoid being mastered himself, resulting in the war of all against all. Locke sees that the situation is more subtle because he has a considerably more subtle appreciation of the self: it desires not only to live, to remain in motion, but to think well of itself, to realize its nuclear ambitions. And as important, he appreciates more fully the operation of the selfobject transference (though, of course, he does not call it that). Self-esteem is at almost every moment dependent on the evaluations of others. Or at least children can be raised to make it so. "Habits woven into the very Principles of Nature," Locke characterizes it, which literally makes no sense, but is probably best interpreted as the development of latent potentials, in this case the rearing of children to be more dependent than need be upon others for their self-esteem.[45] In this way individuals are made dependent on each other for the coherence of their very selves, at least insofar as coherence depends on self-esteem, which Kohut tells us is so. Furthermore, though we can use force to physically master others, we usually cannot induce them to esteem us through force (though sometimes others are so psychologically subjugated that we can). Individuals are, in a sense, held hostage to one another's admiration. The result is civil peace, albeit at considerable cost to the ideal of the self as an autonomous, free-thinking being, what Taylor calls a second-order evaluator.

Of course, Locke is not the only liberal to see the opinions of others as the alternative to Hobbes's Leviathan. Adam Smith's "impartial spectator" serves the same purpose, reminding us that "it is only by consulting this judge within, that we can ever see what relates to ourselves in its proper shape and dimensions; or that we can ever make any proper comparison between our own interests and those of other people."[46] This is, of course, precisely what Locke's ideal parents aim to teach. Nor is it always bad. It may support the ability to take a God's-eye view or, as Smith has it, to grasp that "we are but one of the multitude, in no respect better than any other in it. . . . It is from him [the impartial spectator] that we learn the real littleness of ourselves, and of whatever relates to ourselves, and the natural misrepresentations of self-love can be corrected only by the eye of this impartial spectator."[47] The problem is that in Locke's hands, at least, this perspective is as much designed to weaken the self as it is to strengthen its ability to live *sub specie aeternitatis*. To see oneself in this fashion, the self must, Locke seems to believe, be weakened, split vertically within the pole of ambitions. Identification with ideals is not enough; the desires are too strong.

The process Locke relies on may also be explained in terms of projective identification, the psychological mechanism behind the selfobject transference. In projective identification we put a part of ourselves into another, who becomes a caretaker of that part, in this case, our esteem. When this process is mutual the result is interdependence—my esteem depends upon your response, and vice versa. It is this sharing that binds society, making social cooperation possible, as my sense of self-esteem depends upon your voluntary corroboration of it. Projective identification also serves to stabilize the other, making him more predictable, more like myself, by putting a part of myself in him and finding it there. We value the same things in each other, expect the same things from each other, and finding it there value each other in the same way (if not to the same degree) as we value ourselves. Projective identification is not pathological. To the contrary, it is the glue that holds groups together. It may also enrich the self, allowing us to more fully share ourselves with others, and them to share with us. Pathology is once again a matter of the degree to which projective identification fragments or impoverishes the self, locating too much of it in too many others. Locke, it appears, intends to fragment the self in order to render it less cohesive, a point that will become clearer in the next section.

Continuity with Hobbes

The continuity, or discontinuity, between Hobbes and Locke is, of course, a subject of considerable dispute. Occasionally the issue is treated as one of pure definition, in which it is argued that because Hobbes is the first liberal and Locke is also a liberal their analyses must be continuous: both transform natural law from an objective principle into a subjective act of will, such a profound transformation that the differences between them hardly matter. [48] Another well-known argument for their continuity is that of Macpherson, who claims that Hobbes and Locke are both theorists of nascent capitalism. Believing they are exploring human nature, each is actually formulating a model of human beings compatible with competitive, individualistic market society. [49] From the perspective of the psychology of the self, the continuity between them is more contradictory. Locke's model of the self is fundamentally different: a genuine bipolar self, with a well-developed idealizing pole and a severe vertical split in the pole of ambitions, which tends to render its ideals abstract, disconnected.

Were Hobbesian and Lockean selves to find themselves in the analyst's consulting room, the former would likely be diagnosed as a severe pathological narcissist (a borderline personality disorder), the latter as a case of moderate self-pathology, a significantly less severe disorder, more akin to what Freud called a neurosis. What is ironic is that it is all the things that the Lockean self shares with its Hobbesian counterpart that produce his neurosis. The Lockean self never comes to terms with the Hobbesian self within him. Nor does political theory.

Thoughts concerning Education is based on the insight that children (as well as adults who are not properly educated) want not merely to be free and have their way. They wish to dominate and master others both to get the things they want and to demonstrate the superiority of their wills. [50] As with Hobbes, the reasoning is relational, relative, and zero-sum: I demonstrate the strength of my will only by bending another to it. Indeed, aspects of Locke's thought are more Hobbesian than Hobbes. (There is something wonderfully complex about Locke: recall that Kendall regards Locke as a greater theorist of the general will than Rousseau.) As Macpherson points out, Hobbes seems to hold that most people seek power not to dominate others but to protect themselves from those who would dominate them. Since power is a scarce resource in a zero-sum game, one must forever increase one's power or lose it to those in search of more intensive delight. For Locke, on the other hand, we seek mastery and control not primarily out of fear but out of a desire to express and realize our freedom by bending the will of others to our own. Freedom is more than simply the absence of constraint, unless the mere existence of others living lives independent of our own is to count as a constraint.

Freedom, in the *Thoughts*, is the freedom to use others as means to our own ends, to experience the entire world as an instrument of our will. The researches of Kohut and others into the primitive, narcissistic layers of the personality suggest that Locke is far from mistaken. Behind the fear that others would use us as instruments of their own purposes lies the usually unconscious knowledge that a part of us wishes to use others in a similar fashion (Rawls will be interpreted along these lines in the next chapter). Hobbes stops at the fear. Locke grasps that behind this fear of others often stands a fear of our own archaic desires.

Macpherson takes pains to demonstrate that Locke views the desires as being as powerful and socially disruptive as Hobbes does. "For Locke, like Hobbes, held that men are moved primarily by appetite and aversion; the appetites are so strong that if they were left to their full swing, they would carry men to the overturning of all morality." Further evidence, says Macpherson, is found in the fact that the state of war lies just behind Locke's state of nature. "The difference between the state of nature and the Hobbesian state of war·has virtually disappeared."[51] My considerations strengthen this claim. Hobbes's self is so inchoate that fear, desire, and the will to power are one. Locke's self is more mature, but still wants power: for its own sake, for the narcissistic satisfaction, not just as defense. In this regard, the Lockean self is actually more frightening. Its fears are apparently less, and it *still* wants to master others.

Locke's solution is to thwart transmuting internalization, so that children never truly internalize their parents' mirroring admiration as self-esteem. Recall that the child is never to be given what he wants, but is only to be capriciously indulged. Or so the child thinks. Actually, the child is to be associatively conditioned to equate virtue with external reward.[52] The result is a child, and adult, whose self-esteem depends on something that neither domination nor mastery can acquire from others: a *reputation* for virtue, what others think of him. Of course, such an understanding of virtue has nothing to do with the classical ideal. About this Strauss and Bloom are absolutely correct.

In general, Tarcov emphasizes the difference between Hobbes and Locke, pointing out, for example, that in focusing on the family in *Thoughts*, Locke is concerned with expressions of self-love more subtle and sophisticated than the concern for self-preservation. Yet Tarcov too appreciates the continuity between them, arguing that the Lockean virtues "are founded on two fundamental insights: that almost everything that is of value comes from human labor and that there are more and stronger men in the world than oneself."[53]

In fact, any serious political theory must maintain continuity with Hobbes—that is, with the archaic self. The question is how. Locke fears that even mature ambition will be unable to restrain its archaic counterpart and thus seeks to cripple the pole of ambitions by splitting it in half. But such a strategy devalues the self it claims to protect, and moreover it does not work. In the real world the split within the pole of ambitions encourages the self to purify and idealize its quest for mastery rather than abandon it, a major theme of the *Second Treatise*. Thus, Locke's strategy encourages hypocrisy. It also trivializes virtue, equating a reputation for it with the real thing—Plato's problem, not his solution. But the question remains: is there any way to do it better?

Plato does better, neither trivializing virtue nor sacrificing the autonomy and freedom of the psyche whose value he teaches. Yet Plato's solution is unstable, not just for all the reasons usually given (for example, it depends on a unique coupling of polis and cosmology) but for self-psychological reasons as well. It is overly harsh against the self and is also based on a split in the self (in this respect Plato does sacrifice the psyche), which makes the inherent lack in being more painful, encouraging further the regressive retreat to an archaic selfobject transference with beings. Does this make the socially constituted self the solution? Or is it just a more thoroughgoing version of Locke's solution: split the archaic Hobbesian elements off, rendering the self so dependent on others' esteem that it dare not express these elements, all the while lying to the self that political participation can meet all its real needs? We cannot know the answer until someone takes pains to develop the socially constituted self in sufficient detail that it can be analyzed via the selfobject transference.

This is what Rousseau did, and his answer is addressed in chapter 8. His answer is in one respect honest, never indulging in cheap versions of the lie that Nichols writes of: that the self can fulfill itself through the state. In Rousseau's account the self comes first; society is legitimate only to the degree it respects the natural integrity of the self. Are modern communitarians, especially the "new communitarians" that Gutmann writes of, as honest? Or do they seek the coincidence of self and society on the cheap, so to speak, flattening and trivializing the needs of the self in a way that Rousseau never does? It is hard to tell. But perhaps this is the point. If one writes only of abstract, metaphysical selves, one need not face the hard choices and the harsh realities. They can be abstracted away, and abstraction serves as splitting and idealization, as we saw in chapter 2. Nor must one confront the archaic Hobbesian self within.

One sees an instance of this last point in Locke's *Essay concerning Human Understanding*. It is a beautiful account of the self, for the same reason that Plato's account is especially beautiful when he steps outside the city: it transcends via abstraction all the base and ugly things that tie the self to the world. Actually, Locke's account in *An Essay* is considerably more abstract than Plato's, transcending the passions as well. Finally, like Plato's account, Locke's *Essay* contains brilliant insights into the self, albeit in an abstract philosophical framework that serves only to dull them.

Locke's *Essay* and Identity

As Dunn suggests, Hobbes is far more the ghostly adversary in *An Essay concerning Human Understanding* than he is in the *Two Treatises*. [54] In *Two Treatises*, Locke shares much with Filmer. Each strenuously denies, for example, that we are born into a moral vacuum; but neither seriously argues against the possibility that we are. For this reason, says Dunn, both Locke and Filmer remain at the level of ideology in their political works. What Dunn says about the ideological character of *Two Treatises* vis-à-vis *An Essay* fits my concerns as well. In *Two Treatises*, self-identity is conceptualized in terms that are conditioned by life in a competitive market society still not quite free of the medieval order. In *An Essay*, self-identity is understood in more abstract terms: our ability to appropriate and reappropriate our own consciousness. Although abstract, these terms are not, of course, necessarily universal. Appropriation and reappropriation are more universal than capitalist production (Marx had a few words to say about them), but they reflect a view of self as active agent in the world, which may not be universal.

Of the twenty-eight sections in Locke's famous chapter on "Identity and Diversity," added to the second, 1794, edition, twenty-two are devoted to the question of personal identity: what makes a person the same person over time?[55] Among the questions addressed are the following: Were a prince's consciousness transferred to a cobbler's body, who would be the person, the prince or the cobbler? (Answer: the prince.) If someone were to think Socrates' thoughts, would he be Socrates? (Yes, if he thought the exact same thoughts.) How much of his body can a person lose and still be the same person? (Apparently all.) If the person's consciousness were in his little finger and the little finger were chopped off, would the little finger be the person? (Yes.) If Socrates asleep and Socrates awake have entirely different consciousnesses, are they really two different persons? (Yes.) Of the many examples and hypotheses in this chapter, most concern the transmigration of souls. If, as Plato suggests in the *Phaedo*, the soul never dies but is constantly occupying new bodies, are we dealing with one self or many? (If the soul cannot remember any of its past lives, then just one.)

It is clear that Locke is concerned with the issue at hand, the identity of the self. He addresses this issue in a sophisticated fashion, raising many more issues and possibilities in a far more subtle way than would be necessary were he merely trying to discover or create an entity that might *have* empirical experience. Nothing could be further from the truth than Bloom's claim that Locke, even before Hume, invented the self in order to postulate an entity that might contain its experiences: "Locke appears to have invented the self to provide unity in continuity for the ceaseless temporal succession of sense impressions that would disappear into nothingness if there were no place to hold them."[56] Locke's concept of personal identity is actually concerned with explaining how a man may be a responsive moral agent—"a Forensick" person.[57]

This is not the place to enter into the debate over the degree to which *An Essay* is actually a defense of empiricism. Although Lovejoy's claim that Locke in his epistemology was "essentially a Platonist" seems exaggerated, it is important to note that Locke was by no means a thoroughgoing empiricist, at least not as the term has come down to us in the English tradition. This point is easily missed, as Dunn points out, when we read Locke's *Essay* backwards, from the perspective of the history of philosophy, as the first (or perhaps second, if we count Hobbes) "splendid contribution to the great line of English empiricism." [58] Part of the reason Locke's empiricism is so heavily stressed certainly has to do with the doctrine he is attacking: an especially extreme form of innatism that would have various substantive propositions already wired in. It is this that leads Locke to stress sense experience, even though it turns out that much of this experience is actually internal, more akin to what we would today call reflection or introspection. As Jenkins has written:

> Ideas of reflection, on the other hand, are those produced by what we would now call introspection. . . . He is referring in particular to the ideas the mind can receive by observing its own mechanisms. It is the "perception of the operations of our own minds with us" [II.1.4]. Such ideas include thinking, doubting, perception itself, believing, reasoning, knowing, and willing. Although, strictly speaking, such ideas are not derived by sensory means, Locke is not averse to calling this source of ideas an internal sense. [59]

It is this perspective that allows us to see the continuity between Locke's epistemological concerns and those regarding personal identity. Personal identity is not merely the container of experience; it is the *subject* of experience. Earlier in *An Essay* Locke calls this subject "Spiritual *Substance*," arguing that though the concept may be difficult to apprehend "we can no more conclude its non-Existence than we can, for the same reason, deny the Existence of Body: It being as rational to affirm, there is no body, because we have no clear and distinct *Idea* of the *Substance* of Matter; as to say, there is no Spirit, because we have no clear and distinct *Idea* of the *Substance* of a Spirit." [60]

Personal identity is discovered by the same method we employ to make epistemological discoveries, including the discovery of spiritual substance: reflection on the internal sources of those operations that organize and evaluate knowledge. Personal identity is discovered by the same method because it is virtually the thing: not the container that contains "Thinking, Reasoning, Fearing, etc." but the subject who experiences these things. Personal identity is neither just one more epistemological assumption nor a supraordinate holding concept. It is the subject of human understanding and the agent of moral responsibility. The difference between Hobbes's reflections and Locke's on the origins of experience could not be more striking. Hobbes finds a machine, Locke a subject. But is there an element of idealization and de-nial by abstraction in Locke's account?

In *Locke and the Scriblerians: Identity and Consciousness in Early Eighteenth-Century Britain*, Christopher Foxe points out what a challenge the Lockean concept of self-consciousness posed to the Christian tradition, in which it is God who grants identity (a position to which Locke holds in the *Second Treatise*). How could God punish or reward such an insubstantial self? "By 'shifting the locus of the personality from the indivisible soul to the floating ideas of an ever-changing consciousness,' Locke seemed to have imagined a self no longer accountable to God."[61] Does this mean that Bloom's assessment is correct, that Locke's concept of the self remains an empty container to which nothing sticks? No, the Lockean self is character-ized by activity, by its ability to reappropriate its experiences. Nothing sticks, but everything can be recalled. Through recollection the self continually makes itself anew—not out of nothing but out of itself. Here is the weakness of Bloom's approach and perhaps that of Straussians in general to this issue. Their categories are so dichotomous that if the self is not characterized as the correlate of objective reason, then it is no self at all.

Locke's answer to the question of what makes a person the same person over changes in time and space is straightforward: consciousness. The mere fact that we believe that we are talking about the same body is insufficient. "Nothing but consciousness can unite remote Existences into the same Per-son, the Identity of Substance [i.e., the same body] will not do it. For what-ever Substance there is, however framed, without consciousness, there is no Person."[62] A standard objection to this formulation has been to equate con-sciousness with memory, leading to the obvious objection (because the conclusion is so counterintuitive) that if one should forget what one has done, or misremember, believing that one has done something one has not, then it is not really the same person who did it. The eighteenth-century phi-losopher Joseph Butler added an important point to this argument, noting that a memory claim contains within it an assertion of identity (that is, "I remember"), and therefore it cannot be treated as an independent premise from which identity can be derived.

It is, however, by no means obvious that Locke intends to equate con-sciousness and memory, as Jenkins suggests.[63] In fact, Locke seems to make a clear distinction between them, arguing that "for whatsoever any Substance has thought or done, which I cannot recollect, and by my consciousness make my own Thought and Action, it will no more belong to me, whether a part of me thought or did it, than if it had been thought or done by any other immaterial Being any where existing."[64] Recollection and conscious appropriation ("by my consciousness make my own Thought and Action") appear to be separate events, sequential stages in the establishment of identity, but clearly distinct. Not recollection or memory but its conscious appropriation makes identity, which seems to have been Butler's point in the first place. But what is this conscious appropriation that Locke is referring to? It seems to be nothing more and nothing less than the sense of self as a being with continuity over time, able to act in the world and to be responsible for its actions. This is, we recall, roughly how Kohut defined a self.

It might be argued that this answer comes close to being a tautology. What makes it more is Locke's appreciation of the fact that the sense of self is an achievement, an act of appropriation that is never final but must be constantly renewed, reappropriated: not product but process. Otherwise expressed, if the self is not memory but conscious appropriation of memory, then the self is involved in constant labor, constantly reappropriating its memories (for they are never all in consciousness all at once), reorganizing them, rearranging them to fit new understandings of the self based on new experience. Some memories become more important, some fade into the background, some are reinterpreted (misremembered or perhaps remembered more accurately), recreated, all to fit one's current understanding of one's self. The self is the outcome of appropriative labor. Unlike Locke's account of labor and the self in the *Second Treatise*, the object of appropriation is not first alienated in property. In *An Essay* the target of appropriation is the right target.

One of Locke's stronger claims regarding consciousness and identity is that

if the same *Socrates* waking and sleeping do not partake of the same *consciousness*, *Socrates* waking and sleeping is not the same Person. And to punish *Socrates* waking, for what sleeping *Socrates* thought, and waking *Socrates* was never conscious of, would be no more of Right, than to punish one Twin for what his brother-Twin did, whereof he knew nothing, because their outsides were so like, that they could not be distinguished; for such Twins have been seen. [65]

Consciousness here obviously cannot be equivalent to a normal waking state, or every person would indeed be two persons, which is clearly not Locke's point. Rather, consciousness seems to be a much more subtle sense of continuity: that all the different experiences of oneself, including dreams, somehow fit together. Or as Locke puts it, "nothing but consciousness can unite remote Existences into the same Person." [66] One is reminded here of Kohut's wonder that at sixty-eight years he is the same self as when he was a child, even though so much has changed.

> I'm an old man. My hair is grey. My muscles are feeble. Yet I know I am the same person I was when I was 18, and 22, and six, when I was running and jumping. It's still in me and a part of me. There is no discontinuity. I have totally changed and yet my conviction that I have remained the same is absolute. I never feel myself chopped up in that way. . . . You know, when you think about it, that little six-year-old boy in Vienna and the six-year-old boys in Vienna now have much more in common than the six-year-old boy that I was and the 68-year-old man that I am now. We have very little in common, it seems to me. And yet, I feel we have everything in common, not only that, but that we are the same. It isn't somebody else. I'm not estranged from that. I may not remember much about the boy anymore, but he is still within me. [67]

What holds these two Kohuts together, so that they are one? What holds the waking and sleeping Socrates together? Consciousness, understood in terms characterized above.

One cannot avoid the impression that Kohut protests too much (though it should be noted that this is a transcription of an interview given shortly before his death, when he was very ill). One can imagine Lacan seeing Kohut's assertion as an act of bad faith, an instance of wild self-assertion in the face of death, the symbolic epitome of disintegration and disunity. Similarly, Locke's standard of consciousness is too high, too demanding. We never put all the "remote Existences" together. In a sense Socrates dreaming is not the same person as Socrates awake, though there is considerable overlap. It is the degree of overlap that we should be concerned with. Locke wants too much and so plays into the hands of those, such as Lacan, who would see standards such as Locke's as acts of denial. What is valuable about Locke's account is not his demanding standard of identity and personhood. Or rather, this standard is valuable primarily in contrast to the mechanical self in Hobbes's account, and the "bundle" self in Hume's, the next "splendid contribution to the great line of English empiricism." What is valuable about Locke's account is its emphasis on process, the way in which we must constantly appropriate and reappropriate our experiences in order to ensure what Jenkins refers to as the survival of identity. [68] The self is not necessarily fragile, by no means necessarily a lie. It is, however, not so much an achievement as a process in which we reinterpret the meaning of the past in terms of the events and crises of the present (particularly as these impact upon our ambitions and ideals) in order to project ourselves into the future—that is, to see the meaning of going on, the purpose of our lives, and ultimately the meaning of our deaths.

Conclusion: Identity and Responsibility

Locke's thesis in *An Essay* is that consciousness makes a self because in joining disparate experiences it allows one to take responsibility for one's actions, allowing the self to be a "Forensick" person. Why does Bloom not appreciate this aspect of Locke's account? Perhaps because doing so would undermine Bloom's position that a substantial view of the self is inseparable from its participation in objective reason; the only alternative is pure feeling. Confronting the sophistication of Locke's account readily reveals this interpretation to be wrong. In fact, the problem with Locke's account is that there is not enough feeling, or rather, not enough appreciation of how feeling may interfere with conscious appropriation of the self, leading to only partial appropriation: the appropriation of pieces, fragments.

At an abstract, philosophical, "metaphysical" level, the problem of the self is indeed the problem of who is a self and how much unity such selves possess. But to analyze this question independently of an analysis of how this unity is actually achieved is to avoid all the most interesting and important questions. For example, is it achieved by splitting off the desire, fear, and rage that would threaten this unity? Are the self's ideals genuine, or do they serve to reinforce splitting or disguise the pursuit of ambition? These are questions that cannot even be properly formulated about such abstract, philosophical selves as those that appear in *An Essay*. One facet of Plato's greatness is his ability to combine great abstraction about the self with great detail. Locke does, too, only this combination is divided among different accounts, political and philosophical, that never fit together as Plato's do. This makes Locke's view of the self less brilliant, but not therefore necessarily less true.

Why, it might be asked, is the split self found in Locke's political writings, including *Thoughts*, so bad? Is it because such selves are anxious and unhappy? This is part of the reason. The more important reason is that such selves are less likely to be the morally responsible individual that Locke creates in *An Essay*, a "Forensick" person. Why this is so can be explained by looking at Freud's account of the relation between repression and morality (recall the fundamental similarity between repression and splitting; splitting is a more extreme form of repression, as it isolates desire even more thoroughly). Freud argued that "anyone who has succeeded in educating himself to truth about himself is permanently defended against the danger of immorality, even though his standard of morality may differ in some respect from that which is customary in society."[69] Freud's statement contains more than a hint of the Socratic "no one ever does wrong knowingly," a position that simply does not accord with most of what Freud says about the way in which the mind is divided against itself. Nevertheless, he makes an important point. Immorality is often encouraged by hypocrisy, and hypocrisy is rendered so much easier—almost automatic—when we deny to ourselves what we are doing.

Behind Freud's assertion, as Jeffrey Abramson points out, is the insight that repression isolates our desires from the possibility of rational reflection. Or, as it was expressed earlier, ideals can't bind what they can't find. Abramson quotes Paul Ricoeur on the salutary consequences of psychoanalytic insight: "There is . . . opened up a clearing of truthfulness, in which the lies of the ideals and idols are brought to light. . . . This truthfulness is undoubtedly not the whole of ethics but at least it is the threshold."[70] The fundamental problem with the abstract, philosophical, metaphysical approach to the self in *An Essay*, as well as in Sandel's *Liberalism and the Limits of Justice*, is that it does not allow us to find the lies. Conversely, political theory in the tradition of Plato, Hobbes, and Locke (in his political writings, including *Thoughts*), concerned with the details of real selves that love, hate, envy, split, idealize, and so forth, brings forth the lies—or at least allows the critic to find them. Like a good scientific hypothesis, we learn more from a precise statement about the self, no matter how flawed (and is it always clear that the flaw is in the theory, not in ourselves?), than from vague abstractions.

Who's not sat tense before
his own heart's curtain?
—Rainer Maria Rilke,
Duino Elegies

CHAPTER SEVEN

Rawls

Justice as Fearfulness

Charles Taylor argues, as pointed out in chapter 1, that academic accounts of the self are frequently alienated from experience because the academic is not really concerned with understanding or explaining the self at all. Not what concept best captures the manifold experiences of the self but what concept best allows us to predict or derive an esteemed value, such as the inviolability of the individual, determines the theorist's assumptions.[1] Although Sandel criticizes John Rawls for doing just this, I argued in chapter 1 that Sandel's concept of the self is also alienated from experience, only rather than deriving inviolable individuality, Sandel derives community. In this chapter I shall argue the converse. Rawls's concept of the self is actually remarkably substantial. His "original position" makes a number of concrete and challenging claims about the self. In fact, it comes close to the state of nature that so many political theorists have written of: a literary device by which to make claims about human nature. The abstract, "metaphysical" aspects of Rawls's account of the self in the original position are best seen as literary disguise: a way of saying some rather frightening things about the self without appearing to do so. Unfortunately, this literary disguise functions too well, allowing Rawls to avoid confronting his own insights.

To be sure, such an interpretation goes against Rawls's own interpretation of his work, particularly in recent years. Rather than arguing that his apparently "metaphysical" account is actually substantive, Rawls argues in "Justice as Fairness: Political, Not Metaphysical" that the original position is not intended as an account of the self at all. The original position behind the veil of ignorance is a "device of representation," by which rights, not selves, are at stake. A *Theory of Justice* does make assumptions about the self, he says, but these are the standard assumptions made about the self by liberal democratic polities. For example, subjects can take responsibility for their values and actions and possess the capacity for a sense of justice and the capacity to form a conception of the good. This is, says Rawls, a "political conception of the person." Such a conception "of citizens as free and equal persons need not involve, so I believe, questions of philosophical psychology or a meta-physical doctrine of the nature of the self. . . . Thus, justice as fairness delib-erately stays on the surface, philosophically speaking."[2]

I argue below that this reinterpretation does not do Rawls's conception of the self justice. Although the "conception of the person" in A *Theory of Justice* may stay on the philosophical or metaphysical surface, it does not stay on the psychological surface. Quite the contrary, it expresses deep psychological insight into the way in which fear stands as a barrier to justice. Thus, my argument defends Rawls in a manner different from, and in some ways the opposite of, the way he defends himself. No claim is being made that Rawls is intentionally disguising his account of the self or that he "unconsciously" understood the self in a way he no longer recognizes. The argument is simply that Rawls's original position may fruitfully be read—whatever his intention and state of mind then and now—as making some substantive, challenging, and frightening claims about the self, claims so Hobbesian that Rawls employs a literary fiction, the original position, to render them less threatening.

There is much discussion today about the "regime character of liberalism," the way in which liberal institutions influence almost every aspect of the society of which they are a part, including the selves of its members. Sometimes this is called "partisan liberalism" in order to suggest the way in which liberal principles have consequences for everything else: all the way up, as it were, to the realm of metaphysics and philosophy and all the way down to the nature of the selves who compose such regimes. Against "partisan liberalism" is sometimes set "political liberalism," presumably Rawls's position (if he is indeed a liberal), it being argued that the demands that liberalism makes on regimes and selves are real but minimal. Charles Larmore's critique of the "cult of wholeness" in *Patterns of Moral Complexity* exemplifies this position.[3] Once again my approach is in some ways the opposite, or at least it starts from the opposite direction, asking not about the "regime character of liberalism," but about the "regime character of the self." Given that the self is a certain way, and not just any way, what sort of regime can best support it, making it as whole, free, and civil as possible? This is the tradition of the state of nature theorists, such as Hobbes, Locke, and Rousseau. They start with the real self and build a regime on this basis.

Rawls too is a state of nature theorist. The state of nature is the original position, and the nature in question is human nature: the self, human nature insofar as we can know it as a subject of humane study. Rawls states that "the original position of equality corresponds to the state of nature in the traditional theory of the social contract."[4] It is, above all, the equality of our fear that Rawls is concerned with. In this respect too he is like Hobbes.

Before proceeding further, I need to clarify the term that appeared in quotation marks in the preceding section, "metaphysical." Strictly speaking, the term does not make sense when applied to the self, at least in the current context (it does in the case of Plato). As Rawls points out, metaphysics generally proceeds at such a high level of abstraction (e.g., realism versus idealism) that particular metaphysical doctrines rarely imply particular views of the self.[5] Because it has become part of the jargon of the debate among Sandel, Rawls, and others, I shall continue to use the term. I shall, however, use it here only in a casual sense, to connote views of the self that are abstract, vague, and insubstantial, unconnected to the ways in which the self is experienced, discussed, or written about in everyday life. Generally, such metaphysical views of the self stem from the circumstances identified by Taylor, in which the self is conceptualized strictly in terms that fit the larger theoretical agenda of the theorist. Such an approach need not lead to an abstract and insubstantial view of the self, but it may. Although I argue that the metaphysical character of Rawls's account of the self serves largely as a guise behind which to say some rather shocking things about the self, it is not merely a guise. In the end it prevents Rawls from fully appreciating the import of his account. His metaphysical view of the self performs the splitting and idealizing function that is performed by reason in Plato's account. It is a defense.

Self-Esteem and Self-Defense

> Therefore the parties in the original position would wish to avoid at almost any cost the social conditions that undermine self-respect.[6]

In *Politics and Vision*, Sheldon Wolin argues that it is incorrect to see liberalism as an account of the individual's pursuit of pleasure. Although Locke grants pleasure and pain equal status as sources of motivation, later liberals return to Hobbes, insofar as they make fear and anxiety central. James Mill, Jeremy Bentham, and Benjamin Franklin extend this anxiety so that it is equally concerned with the preservation of possessions and status. Says Wolin, "Liberal man moved in a world where pain and deprivation threatened him from all sides. His fears were compressed into a single demand: social and political arrangements must ease his anxieties by securing property and status against all threats excepting those posed by the competitive chase itself."[7] From this perspective, possessive individualism stems ultimately not from greed and desire but from fear. We accumulate so much in order to protect ourselves from its loss, a loss that sometimes seems tantamount to the loss of life itself, a point suggested by Locke's virtual equation of life and property, as well as by Hobbes's virtual equation of narcissistic injury and death. Psychoanalytic studies of primordial greed, as Kohut calls it, that see greed as the self's most primitive defense against narcissistic injury (as though the self could preserve its esteem and sense of well-being only by incorporating all that is good in the world) support this observation.[8]

Rawls may be seen as addressing this problem, founding a society in which the threat of narcissistic injury (loss of self-esteem and all that supports it, such as status and possessions) is mitigated and so reducing the greed and fear that stand in the way of justice. The aspect of Rawls's system being referred to is, of course, the maximin solution to the bargaining game behind the veil of ignorance. Before proceeding further, however, I must address a possible objection to this argument. Rawls's system is so complex, his mode of argumentation so sophisticated, it could be argued that to focus almost exclusively on this one aspect of A *Theory of Justice* must be misleading. After all, Rawls takes great care to defend the two principles of justice from several perspectives, including the rational reconstruction of everyday moral consciousness. Indeed, reflective equilibrium, as Rawls calls it, claims that the maximin solution is not merely the rational solution of a bargaining game but one that corresponds to our deepest moral intuitions about fairness. Nevertheless, it is not misleading to focus on the maximin solution. Robert Paul Wolff points out that an early paper reveals that this was not Rawls's first solution, but it is clearly at the argumentative center of A *Theory of Justice*. It is the solution that all the other arguments are designed to support.[9]

The maximin solution addresses the anxiety that Wolin puts squarely at the center of liberalism. The maximin principle, says Rawls, is based on a situation of "grave risks," in which we must worry about the "worst that can happen." And what is this? That a malevolent "enemy is to assign [the individual] his place" in society and so deprive him of the resources necessary for life and self-respect. In such circumstances, individuals are "forced to protect themselves" by assuming that the others with whom they are dealing are this enemy.[10] Rawls's is the language of paranoid anxiety. Paranoid, because one is assuming the other is hostile and malevolent strictly on the basis of one's own fearful imagination regarding how one might behave in similar circumstances (greedy and punitive), since this is almost the only information one has. Rawls's general laws of psychology, which concern how we love those who love us and treat us well, remain operative behind the veil of ignorance but provide no grounds for such anxiety.[11] We must conclude that the self must find its reasons for anxiety elsewhere, and the only "elsewhere" left behind the veil is the self itself. Since this anxiety seems to be an attribute of human nature and not the risk-averse concerns of a few neurotics, it is precisely the type of thing that one could know in the original position.[12] The original position captures the way in which we attribute and project all that threatens our self-esteem to the malevolence of others. It captures, in other words, the self's most primitive fears of, and defenses against, narcissistic injury.

It might be argued that this interpretation takes a few words from Rawls out of context. It is important to note, however, that at issue here is not just a few words but the whole way of thinking behind the maximin solution. Recall what maximin means: to maximize the minimum one can expect to receive from a rational opponent. And who is a rational opponent? One who would take all for himself, if he could, leaving me with nothing. Maximin is thus a conservative strategy, aimed at avoiding the worst outcome. For Rawls, as for the liberals that Wolin writes of, the "nothing" that I fear I may be left with is not simply material but spiritual or psychological: that I will be deprived of the resources for self-respect.

The maximin solution, it has been frequently argued, is remarkably conservative. Average expected utility, perhaps with a floor constraint, seems a much more reasonable solution. Certainly this is the solution that several experimental tests of Rawls's scheme seem to converge on.[13] So, why maximin? Since average expected utility also generates a solution, the reason cannot be strictly theoretical—that is, it cannot be that only maximin allows a determinate solution. If we regard the original position as telling us something important about the self, then the answer has to do with the intensity of the fear that it represents. Individuals are so risk-averse because they see the world through the prism of their fears rather than their opportunities. The threat of narcissistic injury (i.e., loss of self-respect) is so threatening, so catastrophic, that it forecloses every other issue, defines every other possibility. One might as well ask why Hobbes saw fear of violent death, and not the opportunity to balance the various pleasures of life (of which security is but one), as the paramount motive. The answer is because both Hobbes and Rawls possess profound insight into the way in which the threatened self comes to define every issue, every ideal, every possibility, and every institution in terms of how it can mitigate this threat that seems to flood the self, rendering everything else secondary, derivative.

Rawls's arguments against average expected utility as a solution support these considerations. No matter how much more individuals would receive under average expected utility with a floor, vis-à-vis the difference principle, average expected utility has the overwhelming disadvantage of conceptually regarding some people as means to others' ends.[14] To be the unwilling means to another's ends, no matter how well compensated, is to suffer narcissistic injury. Indeed, this is a virtual definition of narcissistic injury: to be treated as a means, not an end. Kant was not without psychological insight. Otherwise expressed, what individuals fear most is not a loss of resources; this is just a sign. They fear most being on the receiving end of what Locke tells us all individuals want to do: master others, bend them to one's will, and so feel confirmed in the power of one's will. Since all fear this, they sign a contract eliminating this possibility for all: the difference principle. Furthermore, it is a contract all can live up to, unlike average expected utility. Echoing Hobbes's comments on the weakness of words to bind men to their covenants, Rawls argues that contracts that treat some as means to others' ends "exceed the capacity of human nature. How can the parties possibly know, or be sufficiently sure, that they can keep such an agreement?"[15] They cannot be sure because the narcissistic injury associated with being treated as a means is likely to be such a source of fear and rage that it will override all else.

To be sure, Rawls himself does not argue that the original position is best seen as a way of coping with the hostile effects of others' willfulness. Quite the contrary, he states that "persons in the original position do not, of course, assume that their initial place in society is decided by a malevolent opponent. As I note below, they should not reason from false premises."[16] But in defending the maximin solution in this way, Rawls is making my point. Of course, the individual does not know that his enemy is malevolent. All he knows are his own hopes and fears, which include how he might act were he to have the tantalizing absolute power to determine the fate of others. In other words, the original position is a screen, virtually empty of content, like a Rorschach test, and so a perfectly neutral vehicle by which to capture the desires and anxieties of those behind it. My argument is that Rawls's original position is an artistic literary achievement, whether intended as such or not. Like all great art, it abstracts from distracting particulars to leave us face to face with reality, in this case our own fear, including our fear that we would use any absolute power given to us to exploit others ruthlessly. Thus, we assume others would do the same. Furthermore, like so many great works of art, A *Theory of Justice* makes its point in a way that does not force this insight onto us, an effort that can only intensify denial. Rather, Rawls expresses a challenging and threatening hypothesis—that society is at base an instrument by which we obtain some relief from our fearful selves—in the dry and formal language of game theory, even offering an "of course, people don't really assume the world is so malevolent" to reassure us. He denies what he has just asserted and so makes the assertion more persuasive. Here is the difference between ideology and art.

Viewing the maximin solution as an attempt to address the anxieties of the liberal self does not deny the importance of Rawls's other argumentative strategies, rational reconstruction and reflective equilibrium. They, too, are part of the work of art. The preceding considerations, however, should cause us to reinterpret the role played by these arguments. Reflective equilibrium suggests that our confidence in the two principles as a solution to the problem of justice is enhanced to the degree that it corresponds to more intuitive as well as more philosophically familiar thinking about the problem, such as Kant's categorical imperative. But instead of calling it reflective equilibrium we might better call it causal necessity. It is not that the maximin solution merely *corresponds* to more abstract thinking about the problem. Rather, the maximin solution *allows* more abstract thinking about the problem, by addressing the fear and greed that stands in the way of such solutions. By mitigating the intense paranoid fear characteristic of the liberal self, the fear that it will lose all to its enemies, Rawls allows this self to begin to think about justice in terms that regard the other's interests as being as worthy as one's own. "If he does not treat me as an instrument of his ends, then I need not treat him as an instrument of mine," the thinking might run. The maximin solution is at the core of Rawls's scheme not merely for the formal analytic reasons that so many find attractive (it is clever, brainy, elegant, and so forth) but for sound psychological reasons as well. Only by mitigating the anxieties of the liberal self can we begin to talk about justice in terms more abstract and universal than the self-interest of the fearful.

Envy

Rawls rightly makes envy important. It is the only one of the "special psychologies" that he systematically explores (the psychological assumptions that, though empirically observable, contradict the rationality assumption in the original position; thus, an argument must be made as to why it is not unrealistic to exclude these assumptions from both the original position and the well-ordered society). Rawls makes envy important because he makes self-respect important: "On several occasions I have mentioned that perhaps the most important primary good is that of self-respect. . . . Without it nothing may seem worth doing, or if some things have value for us, we lack the will to strive for them. All desire and activity become empty and vain, and we sink into apathy and cynicism."[17] Envy is what we feel when we lack self-respect. Acting from envy, we would deprive others of their self-respect and all that supports it, such as autonomy and primary goods, even if doing so does not enhance our own esteem, except by contrast. Misery loves company.

Carefully distinguishing among envy, jealousy, and greed, Rawls argues that envy (more precisely, the subtype Rawls calls "rancorous envy") stems not merely from an absence of resources compared to others but from a deep loss of self-esteem, coupled with a feeling of impotence: that one can do nothing to alter one's fate and restore one's esteem.[18] The result is a desire to take goodness from others, even if one cannot obtain it for oneself, even if doing so will spoil things for everyone. Rawls goes on to argue convincingly that such rancorous envy will not occur in the well-ordered society, as the less fortunate are not regarded as inferior beings (Sandel would argue that all are regarded as equally worthless), the difference principle would not support vast discrepancies in wealth and opportunity, and so forth. Rawls also argues that envy can rationally and reasonably be assumed to be absent from the original position. Were it not, then the solution would be not the difference principle but absolute equality, the outcome most expressive of envy, as Freud suggests.[19] As Rawls reminds us, Freud argued that social justice is founded on envy.[20] We obey the law, deny ourselves, so that, as Freud puts it, "others may have to do without . . . as well." Rawls concludes that envy is not an inherent barrier to justice and the well-ordered society but only a rational consequence (Rawls calls it "excusable envy") of the coupling of great inequality with contempt for the less equal.

Something is quite right in Rawls's account, and something wrong, too. He is right to see envy as a genuine problem, recognizing that it may be fostered by society, not just bad parents—that is, emotional life is not reducible to the events of childhood. Where Rawls goes wrong—and this is really a symptom of something else—is in making too many distinctions. He distinguishes among at least six kinds of envy (benign envy, emulative envy, envy proper or rancorous envy, excusable envy, resentful envy, as well as just plain envy), as well as a number of related emotions, such as spite, jealousy, resentment (not the same as resentful envy), and grudgingness. It is as though Rawls would tame envy by categorizing it to death, rending it into dozens of harmless pieces. Thus, he rejects Freud's claim that envy is the ground of social justice by making a series of distinctions among envy, jealousy, and resentment, arguing that Freud is really talking about resentment. This is, of course, a familiar philosophical tactic, parsing a threatening idea until nothing remains, as though the problem were all in the confusions of our minds. Of course, the problem *is* in our minds, but not in this sense.

In fact, Rawls tames envy in a much more powerful way, much as he tames the feared loss of self-esteem that is its source. Envy, Rawls tells us, stems from grave wounds to one's self-esteem, coupled with feelings of impotence. Psychoanalysts call these wounds narcissistic injuries. And what is the original position designed to secure? Sufficient self-respect and resources (esteem and potency) to be able to begin to think about justice in terms more universal and caring than the self-interest of the fearful. Rawls argues that the two principles of justice chosen in the original position show that envy will not be a barrier to justice in the well-ordered society. But, in fact, the original position *shows* no such thing. Rather, what it *does* is provide sufficient protection from narcissistic injury to mitigate the envy that stands in the way of justice. Once again, the original position is the cause, not the effect or expression, of justice. The original position is best understood not as an abstract theoretical construct but as deep psychological insight into the barriers to justice posed by fear and aggression, of which envy is an extreme case, the most virulent of the "special psychologies."

At the core of Rawls's inviolable self is a self terrified of violation of its life, possessions, status, and self-respect. The result, as Hobbes recognized, is the constant pursuit of power, as only power and more power over others can quell this fear. Goodness thus comes to be equated with power, an equation that becomes even more compelling as competing sources of goodness, such as religion, decline in influence. In such a world, Hobbes's world, values other than power and its instruments become not so much bad as worthless. Not Manichaean ideology but a one-dimensional culture is the result, in which the world is divided into that which presumably enhances power (such as money, fame, or primary goods) and that which does not. The deleterious effects of such a worldview on community are apparent.

It is against the fear of powerlessness in the face of power that Rawls's original position is designed to protect us. And now we see that this fear not only stands in the way of justice. It also helps undermine a cultural tradition that can give order and meaning to our lives and selves. For though the equation of power and goodness may reinforce the self's defenses, it can hardly support a culture and society adequate to give meaning and continuity to human experience—that is, provide the values that help constitute the self. The only continuity such a view can express is one measured by power in which whatever increases power is good, and whatever decreases it is bad. In the end such a view can only support a half-self, a unipolar self, in which every ideal is measured by standards of primitive ambition: the growth of the self's power.

Kohut's observations on how emotional growth can be measured by the degree to which ideals are defined in terms other than those that enhance the power and perfection of the subject are relevant here. Whether the individual can make these distinctions, says Kohut, depends in good measure on the degree to which he can overcome his fear of narcissistic injury.[21] In everyday language, this is the degree to which he is secure in his self-esteem, so that he need not devote his entire self to its protection. Rawls's original position recognizes this truth, seeking to mitigate, via the provision of objective security measures (maximin), the fear that stands in the way of justice—or at least in the way of a concept of justice more ideal than the mutual self-protection of the fearful. Once again these security measures are best seen not as attributes of the well-ordered society but as necessary conditions for its existence.

Rawls as State of Nature Theorist

If the state of nature is an account of the self (that is, human nature insofar as we may know it by humane study), then Rawls may be read as arguing that man is at heart a fearful narcissist, desperately in need of confirmation of his self-esteem, profoundly vulnerable to narcissistic injury, and eagerly awaiting confirmation of his worth from others and so terribly dependent on them. In *Some Thoughts concerning Education,* Locke argues that men and women must be trained to depend upon the evaluations of others. Rawls, on the contrary, seems to hold that self-esteem depends on others from the very beginning; we do not need to be trained in this direction. Over and over Rawls stresses how our self-esteem depends upon others' admiration of our life plan: "For while it is true that unless our endeavors are appreciated by our associates it is impossible for us to maintain the conviction that they are worthwhile, it is also true that others tend to value them only if what we do elicits their admiration or gives them pleasure."[22] Self-esteem, it seems, is a fragile good, almost wholly dependent upon the admiration of others, which depends in turn upon whether we please or entertain them. Consider the anxiety of the self placed in this position: the self as perpetual salesperson or entertainer. No wonder the guarantees of minimal (maximin) self-respect inherent in the original position are so important.

Like Locke, Rawls would make the dependence on one's self-esteem upon the admiration of others the glue that organizes society. But unlike Locke, he better appreciates how fearfully vulnerable this makes one to one's fellows: thus, the guarantees of the original position. Or rather, Rawls appreciates that when self-esteem is too dependent upon the opinions of others, it becomes not a social glue but an explosive. Preemptive attack and other private strategies against narcissistic injury become the norm, as Hobbes grasped so clearly. Against Locke, who would train people to depend upon the admiration of others, Rawls would set up a system that would set limits—though hardly eliminate—one person's dependence on the esteem of others. But though they start from different ends (Locke from man as self-absorbed narcissist, who must be trained to depend on the esteem of others; Rawls from man as vulnerable narcissist, dependent on the esteem of others and frequently enraged at how vulnerable this makes him), they end up at roughly the same place, each making the dependence of one's self-esteem upon the admiration of others the medium of social coordination. This is for Rawls the standard of justice as well: justice becomes a matter of guaranteeing self-esteem against the onslaughts of others. Only Rawls, it seems, better comes to terms with the fear and aggression associated with such vulnerable self-esteem. That is, he better comes to terms with the fear, rage, and quest for omnipotence associated with vulnerability to narcissistic injury, the way in which these emotions disrupt the well-ordered society.

The way in which Rawls comes to terms with these emotions is not, however, without cost. Approaching them indirectly behind a metaphysical veil leads him to unrealistically idealize the degree to which they can be transcended in the well-ordered society. One sees this unreality in Rawls's developmental psychology—that is, his account of the connection between individual psychological development and the warm fraternal feelings that unite the well-ordered society. Children learn to love their parents when they are treated with love, says Rawls. But by love he means not so much warmth and affection as mirroring the child's ambitions. His ideal parents sound almost exactly like Kohut's ideal parents: empathic selfobjects supporting the child's nascent feelings of self-worth. The child learns to love his parents, says Rawls, because "he connects them with the success and enjoyment that he has had in sustaining his world, and with his sense of his own worth. And this brings about his love for them."[23] As the child develops into a man, similar considerations lead him to love, or at least feel warm and friendly feelings toward a society that protects his self-esteem.

Rawls writes of "the three psychological laws" that connect the love the child receives in the family with the "fellow feeling" that binds a just society.[24] But, there is really only one law: we feel affection toward those who mirror or at least respect and protect our self-esteem. This is why justice as fairness can bind society. It represents more than an agreement to refrain from inflicting narcissistic injury. Or rather, such an agreement leads to affection toward those who adhere to it, for in so doing they respect and value what is most dear to me, me, just as my parents did.

> The effect of these aspects of justice as fairness is to heighten the operation of the reciprocity principle. As we have noted, a more unconditional caring for our good and a clear refusal by others to take advantage of accident and happenstance [including, apparently, of natural talents] must strengthen our self-esteem; and this greater good must in turn lead to a closer affiliation with persons and institutions by way of an answer in kind.[25]

Rawls is correct to make self-esteem important. Indeed, it is striking to recognize how central it is to his account. His sophisticated discussion of shame, which "springs from a feeling of the diminishment of the self," by which he means a loss of excellence, supports these considerations.[26] What is missing, as it is missing in Kohut, is any sense that we might love others independently of their role as mirrors of our esteem. What is missing is what Freud called object love: love of the other qua other. That we might love others for their otherness, care for them first, even before they respect us, care for them even when their life histories prevent them from respecting us—all this finds little place in Rawls's account. It remains a deal, a transaction, a contract: you respect me, and I'll respect you; maybe I'll even feel fond of you for doing so. There are, of course, a lot worse ways to organize society (though one suspects that in a family organized in this fashion children will never know true love). The problem is that in the end Rawls wants more than this. He wants mutual respect and protection to lead to a society in which "the members of a community participate in one another's nature. . . . the self is realized in the activities of many selves." And, he points out, "Different persons with similar or complementary capacities may cooperate so to speak in realizing their common or matching nature."[27] That is, Rawls wants a deep and genuine community, as profound as that idealized by Rousseau in *The Social Contract.*

It does not work, however, not because such an ideal is perforce impossible but because it is too much of a leap, too unconnected to the self that Rawls writes of in the original position. It is idealistic in the psychological sense: a denial of reality, in this case the psychological reality of the self that Rawls constructs. In this respect Sandel is correct. There is something strange about the way that Rawls suddenly moves from the individualistic self to the communal self, a self that wants to share itself with others.[28] There is nothing to connect these selves, nothing in the middle, so to speak. The reason is easy to see. The love and affection that he writes of are narcissistic: I love others to the degree that they mirror, confirm, and respect my self-esteem. Period. Rawls's self is a genuine bipolar self, in which ambition is constrained by the ideal of reciprocity. But, like Kohut's concept of the self, it is not a self that loves and cares for others for their own sake, for the pleasure of loving them. Nor is it a self that loves others for the sake of belonging to them. It loves others, participates in their nature, to the extent that doing so enhances its own self-esteem.

"We appreciate what others do as things we might have done," says Rawls. Or, as Kohut puts it, "One cannot live many different kinds of lives, but one can be empathic with different types of personalities."[29] Because we cannot do and be all that we admire, we vicariously participate in the lives of others who are admirable via the selfobject transference. This is neither pathological nor undesirable. It may even be the beginning of a genuine community. But only the beginning, as it remains so bound to narcissistic goals, as was shown in my analysis of Plato. I vicariously participate in the lives of others not so that I might know them better and hence love them for themselves even more. There is not a hint of this in Rawls, and barely a hint in Kohut. Rather, I vicariously participate in the lives of others for the same reason that I go to the movies: to find distraction from and compensation for the limits of myself and my life by identifying with others. Is this so different from the self manque that Lacan writes of? The problem is not merely that Rawls cannot get genuine community out of his account but that in trying to do so he denies the reality of the self he has created, unrealistically idealizing the potential of guaranteed self-esteem to create community.

One is reminded here of Hobbes's claim, following upon a long account of the supreme transcendent power of the sovereign, that individuals ought not to complain about the sovereign's acts, as "he that complaineth of injury from his Soveraigne, complaineth of that whereof he himselfe is Author."[30] Such an assertion, it was argued, is unrealistic, reflecting an archaic identification with power for its own sake, perhaps as a defense, akin to what Anna Freud calls identification with the aggressor. Rawls is not Hobbes, of course, but the jump from fearful individual to loving, caring community member is similarly unrealistic, suggesting that it too serves a defensive function.

Like Hobbes, Rawls sees society as a mutual-protection association: if you do not inflict narcissistic injury on me, I shall not inflict it on you.[31] Unlike Hobbes, Rawls holds that the force of words is strong enough to hold men and women to *this* covenant, as the security that stems from not being regarded as a means to another's end allows individuals to develop a sense of justice, understood as reciprocity: you respect me, and I'll respect you. This is not a bad arrangement. It is certainly better than the society existing in the United States today, in which even self-respect is a market commodity. What is troubling is Rawls's attempt to sail beyond the society he has created into a community based on love, sharing of selves, and warm fellow feeling. Rawls's concept of the self provides no support for such a move, which is, of course, why he must suddenly jump from one to the other. Here we see the disadvantage of his metaphysical approach to the self most clearly. It encourages the splitting and idealization that leads to such a jump, the topic of the next section.

The Unity of the Abstract Self

In a section titled "The Unity of the Self," Rawls writes of the self in the well-ordered society in terms reminiscent of Aristotle, albeit far more rationalistic: "Now the unity of the person is manifest in the coherence of his [life] plan, this unity being founded on the higher-order desire to follow, in ways consistent with his sense of right and justice, the principles of rational choice."[32] Shortly thereafter Rawls writes that "the essential unity of the self is already provided by the conception of right," by which he seems to mean the unity provided by pursuing a life plan in accord with ideals.[33] His account is not without insight, recognizing the way in which it is the connection between ambitions and ideals that completes the self. Yet his account is so utterly rationalistic, so devoid of any appreciation of how fear and desire might play a role in unifying or fragmenting the self that one cannot help but suspect that reason is serving denial. Rawls's account of the unity of the self is not merely abstract or unrealistic. Rather, abstraction allows him in the name of reason to split off and ignore the fears and desires that fragment and motivate the self, even in the well-ordered society.

Rawls is not wrong to make narcissistic integrity important. What is misleading is the implicit assumption that once this integrity is guaranteed, all else will follow, including love of one's fellows and the beautiful community. In fact, his system does not guarantee narcissistic integrity at all. Like Hobbes's system, it prevents the most brutal assaults on it by others, only Rawls includes as "brutal assaults" others being differentially rewarded for those excellences they fail to place at my disposal! This is not psychologically unrealistic, as Rousseau's account of amour propre reveals. Nevertheless, if the self is anything like Lacan or even Plato says it is, then this will not suffice. The self will always want more. Too much self-esteem is not enough. Mutual protection, mutual respect will never satisfy the self. And a rational life plan will never unify the self (though it may help), because the self is not a unity but a conflicting amalgam of fears and desires, desiring most of all the unity it lacks. This is not to say, I have argued repeatedly, that the self may not be more or less unified, more or less complete. Pace Lacan, it is not an all-or-nothing affair. But this is precisely what Rawls makes it in his account of the unity of the self.

This is unfortunate, for a more realistic approach focusing upon the potential for psychological growth that becomes available when fear of narcissistic injury is mitigated would allow us to begin to fill in the middle ground. How might society foster more mature expressions of self-interest and self-love? How far can reciprocity be carried given the nature of the self that Rawls posits? He does not ignore these questions, of course, but his answers are corrupted by the implicit assumption that once self-esteem is guaranteed, all good things will follow. In one respect, at least, he is like Rousseau. From assumptions of utter individuality he derives complete community, but only by failing to fill in the middle ground. In another respect Rawls is like Plato. For each, "metaphysics" (the quotes apply only to Rawls) serves to split the self, freeing the self from the constraints imposed by the desires each uncovers. Abstraction in the service of denial, I have called it in the case of Rawls.

I long for the time when, freed
from the fetters of the body, I
shall be myself, at one with
myself, no longer torn in two,
when I myself shall suffice for
my own happiness.
—Jean-Jacques Rousseau, *Emile*

CHAPTER EIGHT

Rousseau

Political Theory in
Defense of Self-Esteem

Jean-Jacques Rousseau throughout this book
has been a shadowy presence, sometimes referred to, but never confronted.
Similarly Rousseau shadows Western political thought because he promises
that man need not be split against himself in order to be free and social.
About Rousseau's educational program for Emile, Allan Bloom states, "Its
primary function is to make Emile social while remaining whole."[1] No theorist we have considered has been able to even come close. Does Rousseau?

Robert Nisbet argues that Rousseau would not have taken Rawls seriously,
for Rousseau appreciated as Rawls does not the pure political power, able to
reach into the depths of the psyche, necessary to abolish difference.[2] This,
though, assumes that the elimination of difference means the same thing for
each. It does not. Rawls wishes to eliminate those economic, political, and
social differences that result in differential self-esteem, an idealistic but nonetheless material goal. Rousseau wishes to eliminate difference per se—that
is, the otherness of the other, the existence of other wills. In the end this is
not a political program at all. It is more akin to the desire for absolute presence that Tallis writes of: a psychological-cum-philosophical ideal, in which
the achievement of a self uncorrupted by dependence on others requires the
denial of otherness itself.

It seems impossible to talk about Rousseau's work without talking about his
life, more than in the case of any other social theorist. F. J. C. Hearnshaw
writes that "so intimately . . . were Rousseau's writings associated with his
life that it is impossible to comprehend them without a detailed knowledge of
his curious and remarkable career." English Showalter goes further, arguing
that all of Rousseau's works, not just the *Confessions*, *Reveries*, and other late
writings, are virtual biographies, comprehensible only in this light. "He was
forced to write not just about, but *exclusively* about himself. Few people have
ever so fully transformed their lives into a literary text." Susan Grayson, in
"Rousseau and the Text as Self," goes still further, arguing not merely that

Rousseau's texts are about himself; the texts are themselves Kohutian self-objects, a way to hold the pieces of his fragile self together. [3]

Given that my approach to Rousseau's concept of the self is psycho-analytic, it might seem that it too would stress the linkage of Rousseau's life and work. It does not, in part because this has been done so many times before. But more important, it is unnecessary. A psychoanalytically informed sensitivity to the self in social theory, an approach that sees in the author's use of selfobjects his concept of the self, renders it unnecessary to view Rousseau's concept of the self through the prism of his *Confessions, Reveries,* and *Dialogues.* To be sure, at several points I refer to aspects of Rousseau's life, or rather, conclusions about his life and its relation to his work that schol-ars have come to. This serves primarily as a check on my own conclusions, which correspond in some cases to those of the scholars.

In the end, however, a focus on the relation between his life and work could be misleading. Rousseau takes great pains to stress his difference, his uniqueness from other men. This is how his *Confessions* begins; it is the theme of his biography. Rousseau's *theory* or *concept* of the self, on the other hand, is not unique at all, but shares the concerns of Hobbes, Locke, and Rawls. What is unique is his solution to the problem of reconciling self and society, which rests upon the denial of difference and otherness. To under-stand Rousseau's concept of the self, it is important to make this distinction between self and defense—that is, denial. Lacan suggests that the self *is* the defense. Perhaps it is when we are focusing on individuals, including Rousseau. In his theoretical texts, however, it is useful to make the distinc-tion, and a focus on the virtual identity between his life and texts is not help-ful in this regard. In this respect, at least, Paul de Man has it right in his *Allegories of Reading: Figural Language in Rousseau, Nietzsche, Rilke, and Proust.* [4] The text may not live a life of its own, but it lives a life independent of its author.

The Question of Jean-Jacques Rousseau, as Ernst Cassirer's title has it, con-cerns the unity of his work. How to reconcile the individualistic and commu-nitarian moments? Otherwise expressed, how to reconcile the *Discourse on Inequality,* with its emphasis on the sheer autarky of natural man, with *The Social Contract,* in which man can be forced to be free? Each of the four positions that can be taken in regard to this issue has supporters. Some, such as Emile Faguet, argue that Rousseau is essentially an individualist. "All of

Rousseau," he says, "can be found in the [*Discourse on Inequality*]." Others, such as Ernest Barker, hold that Rousseau is essentially a collectivist, even a totalitarian, albeit a democratic one. Still others hold that Rousseau is simply confused, whereas C. E. Vaughan argues that Rousseau's work must be seen in terms of a journey from individualism to collectivism.[5]

Like Cassirer, I take a unitarian position. But unlike him and other Kantian interpreters such as E. H. Wright, I do not argue that "the idea that man must be perfected by his reason in accordance with his nature runs through all of Rousseau's work and gives it an essential unity."[6] Thus, I do not hold with Cassirer that Kant's interpretation of Rousseau "is the only one which preserves the inner unity of Rousseau's work and which fits *Emile* into the work as a whole without inner break and contradiction."[7]

Wright and Cassirer read Rousseau through Kant by interpreting the "general will" as an act by which man gives the law to himself. By this act of ethical autonomy, man exercises his freedom, demonstrating his independence from natural necessity. On the contrary, I argue below that in accepting the general will, man denies the existence of other wills by equating them with nature. Man willingly succumbs to the naturelike compulsion of the general will in order to avoid human will, quite the opposite interpretation. Rousseau's work need not have an inner unity, and a theory is not to be preferred simply because it preserves a putative unity. The unity of Rousseau's work that I discover is contingent, so to speak: a perspective that illuminates aspects of his project in a way that other perspectives do not.

Emile

Rousseau's *Emile* is the linchpin of the following analysis, in part for reasons suggested by Rousseau himself, who regarded it as the culmination of several tendencies in his thought.[8] *Emile* contains, and explains, the duality that seems to divide the *Discourse on Inequality* from *The Social Contract*. And, as important, Rousseau's fictional account of the education of Emile is written, as he states in the preface, with Locke's *Thoughts concerning Education* in mind.[9] Locke holds that the desire to master others, and so obtain confirmation of the power of one's will, is the problem. He solves it by splitting the self within the pole of ambitions, locating one's esteem in the opinions of others. Rousseau calls this alienation of self-esteem amour propre (as opposed to *amour de soi*, a more benign expression of self-love).[10] His characterization of it reads much like Locke's characterization of the will to mastery: "The desire to command is not extinguished with the need that gave birth to it. Dominion awakens and flatters amour-propre, and habit strengthens it. Thus whim succeeds need."[11] Rousseau's solution is not to exploit amour propre as Locke does but to prevent its emergence by protecting the child from the experience of other wills more powerful than his own, at least until the child is old enough and mature enough that this experience need not divide him in two, splitting self-love into amour de soi and amour propre. As Bloom puts it, "The primary intention of the negative education is to prevent *amour de soi* from turning into *amour-propre*, for this is the true source of man's dividedness. Rousseau's treatment of this all-important theme is . . . introduced by his discussion of the meaning of a baby's tears."[12]

Though tears at first express discomfort, the baby quickly learns that they get adults to do things for him. With this, his concern with his physical needs is transformed into a desire to control the will of adults. His tears become demands, a weapon in a battle of wills. The disposition of adults toward him becomes more important than his physical comfort, and already he is lost to amour propre. Already he is divided, locating himself in the gaze in his parents' eyes (the image in the mirror, as Lacan calls it). For Kohut, this is a sign that the infant is not autistic; he is able to participate in the earliest mirroring selfobject transferences, able to use the parents' admiration of "His Majesty the Baby" (as Freud called it in his paper "On Narcissism") as the nucleus of his self-esteem. Rousseau, though, sees *any* selfobject transference as an alienation of self, a loss of self in the opinion of others—that is, as promoting amour propre. Given this assessment, his solution is straightforward: the child, from infancy on, is not to have genuine object relationships, at least not with people. As Bloom says, "The child must be dependent on things and not on wills. The tutor and his helpers must disappear, as it were, and everything that happens to the child must seem to be an inevitable effect of nature. . . . It is the mediation of human beings in the satisfaction of need that causes the problem."[13]

The solution to the "relative I," as Rousseau calls amour propre, is that the child not have any relatives at all, so to speak, no real relationships. Consider the type of person likely to emerge from such an upbringing: would he or she be even truly human? The melancholy of young Edward Clarke, Locke's educational charge, pales in comparison to the emotional illness Rousseau's regime is likely to inflict. Consider, too, that though Rousseau's educational strategy is precisely the opposite of Locke's, they both define the problem to be solved in virtually identical terms: amour propre, understood as the desire to exhibit mastery over others in various ways and so obtain confirmation of the power of one's will. If Rousseau's solution to the problem of amour propre turns out to be mere idealization and denial, then it will be fair to conclude that his view of the self is continuous (which does not mean identical) with Locke's.

Emile's early education, to about age twelve, is based on a fundamental principle: all obstacles to Emile's will are to appear as natural constraints, not human ones. This involves a number of tricks and deceptions, in which the child is not punished for lying but made to suffer the consequences—for example, living in the drafty room whose window he has broken. Why? Because "all wickedness comes from weakness."[14] If the child does not confront other wills, he will not know he is weak. One does not, suggests Rousseau, feel weak in comparison to nature; nature (for example, the drafty room) simply is. In some respects this is not bad educational psychology. The child does need to be protected from his own weakness, his own vulnerability. Conversely, it is appropriate for parents to confirm the child's narcissistic grandiosity. Rousseau takes an important principle and makes it the only principle.

Consider, for example, how the child is to be taught compassion: by confronting only inferiors in luck and circumstances so that his envy is never evoked. Thus, he is taken to see various people in unhappy and difficult circumstances.[15] The reasoning is straightforward, as Bloom points out: "*Amour-propre* is alienating only if a man sees others whom he can consider happier than himself. It follows that if one wishes to keep a man from developing the mean passions which excite the desire to harm, he must always see men whom he thinks to be unhappier than he is."[16] Later, Emile will read about various heroes in Plutarch's *Lives* and elsewhere. He will not, however, desire to emulate them, for his early education will have inoculated him against not merely envy but admiration of others. Rather, he will feel compassion for their vanity and tragic failings.[17]

Rousseau's insight into the need to protect Emile from narcissistic injury has become obsession. Strength, autonomy, and self-sufficiency are achieved only by avoiding all relationships of dependence, including interdependence, with others (except the tutor, a point discussed shortly). In fact, the avoidance of such relationships does not prevent narcissistic injury. It can only "prevent" transmuting internalization, in which the good attributes of others become one's own. Avoiding selfobject relationships with others does not avoid narcissistic injury. It is a *sign* of narcissistic injury, in which the self feels so vulnerable and fragile, so intensely needy, that it withdraws into a world of internal object relationships, lest it be obliterated in the selfobject transference. Does this mean that Emile has a narcissistic personality disorder? Not at all. Emile is a literary creation, and an especially artificial, one-dimensional one at that. (This is no criticism of Rousseau's literary talents; unlike *Nouvelle Héloise, Emile* is not a novel.) It means that Rousseau's program of education is impossible. Amour propre lies so close to the surface and is so easily evoked by the slightest comparison that the child must be raised in a virtual Skinner box in order to avoid its eruption. He may not even have heroes. Otherwise expressed, the chains that Rousseau would free man from are not merely the chains of tyranny. They are the chains of all interdependence, including that of friends and family.[18] Only in the absence of all human ties can amour propre be avoided—that is, only when humans are no longer recognizably human. Is this not the lesson of the *Discourse on Inequality* as well? What does it mean—or matter—if man is born good if he is corrupted by human relations, which are naturally characterized by interdependence? This is like saying humans are good as long as they are not human.

The state of nature, it will be recalled, is best seen as an account of human nature. Rousseau argues in the *Discourse on Inequality* that other philosophers have not gone back far enough into nature, which means that they have not looked deeply enough into human nature.[19] Rousseau looks deeply, and what does he find? That natural man is insane, though of course he does not put it that way. Natural man is insane because he has no language, no relationships, and no needs other than purely physical ones.[20] In a word, he is autistic. Why? Because this is the only alternative to amour propre, the view of human nature found in Hobbes, Locke, and Rawls. Insanity or dependence on others and with it amour propre: these are the two choices. What about the general will? Is it not the cure, so to speak, on the large scale that *Emile* is on the small, both instituting a regime in which the individual is freed from dependence on particular wills? It will be argued below that the general will is not so much cure as defense, seeking to recreate the illusion of utter autonomy in a world of constraint: the chains of relationships. But, it might be argued in response, natural man is neither history nor psychology; he is metaphor for a state of innocence that once lost can never be recovered. Absolutely; this is my point. Rousseau's ideal of innocence ("Que la nature a fait l'homme heureux et bon, mais que la société le déprave et le rend misérable")[21] defends man against the evil within—amour propre—only by making him inhuman, insane. Rousseau's argument deconstructs itself. Or rather, it avoids this fate only by confounding freedom and sovereignty in the general will, a point discussed shortly.

The last book (actually, last book and a half) of *Emile* seems to follow a different pattern, in which Emile is introduced to love. He has, it seems, a genuine relationship with Sophie, just as he does with his tutor. Yet though the relationship and affection are real, the pattern is the same. She must not oppose her will to his, at least not directly. She will work her will only by making it appear to Emile as if it is his own. This, of course, is an ideal that is hardly unique to Rousseau, being the subject of countless jokes, sayings, and stories. More characteristic is the overall tone of Emile's relationship to Sophie, which reminds one (as it apparently reminds Allan Bloom) of the ideal Platonic relationship, in which one separates attributes and persons so that one might partake of the attributes while avoiding dependence on the person. Or as Bloom puts it, "It is not quite precise to say that [Emile] loves an 'other' for he will not be making himself hostage to an alien will and thus engaging in a struggle for mastery. This woman will, to use Platonic language, participate in the *idea* he has of her."[22] Here is the only safe relationship, the only one that does not evoke amour propre: one that does not involve real relationships either.

I promised not to confuse Rousseau's life and work. Nevertheless, Casanova tells a story about Rousseau so appropriate that I must recount it here. The prince of Conti makes a special visit to dine with Rousseau. After talking for several hours, Rousseau sends the prince away in order to prepare a special dinner. When the prince returns, he sees three places set. Who, he asks, is the third person? "The third person, Monseigneur, is another myself. It is a being who is neither my wife nor my mistress nor my servant nor my mother nor my daughter; she is all of these." The prince replies that since he came to dine only with Rousseau, he will leave Rousseau to dine with his other selves. Casanova concludes that unless one is truly remarkable, the attempt to be seen as such becomes merely eccentric. We may, however, draw a second moral. A being who is all these things to Rousseau would seem to have no independent reality for him at all. She is not merely, but only, the container of his ideas—not Platonic ideas, as Bloom would have it, but the projection of internal objects: images of desire. The woman, Casanova tells us, was Mademoiselle Le Vasseur, the famous Thérèse, "whom he had honored with his name, except for one letter of it, under the mask of an anagram."[23] They go together, it appears: the experience of other as mere container of one's desires is the counterpart of the refusal to appreciate the uniqueness of the other.

What about Emile's tutor? Certainly Emile has a close relationship with him. Indeed, it is the only genuine selfobject relationship that Emile participates in. Furthermore, it is a remarkably intense relationship. The tutor is with him constantly. "Do not leave him alone, day or night. At the very least, sleep in his room." Ostensibly designed to prevent masturbation (for which Rousseau uses the term *supplement* [*supplément*], the same term he employs to characterize Thérèse),[24] this closeness is designed to promote a profound transmuting internalization, in which the tutor's sense of right and wrong will become Emile's own. Yet if this is so, why does *this* relationship not overwhelm Emile's vulnerable self, evoking the "relative I," envy, and all the rest? In part because the tutor disguises his will as nature when Emile is young (but perhaps all children experience their parents' wills in this fashion). In part too because the tutor is of lower social status, much like a valet or social secretary (positions Rousseau was familiar with).

The discrepancy in social status is seen in a story Rousseau tells at the conclusion of book 2, where Lord Hyde accompanies a friend on a visit to his friend's son and his tutor. The son seems to have learned well, and the tutor is rewarded by the father with "the title to a lifetime pension in addition to his salary."[25] To be sure, Rousseau notes earlier that it is important that the tutor not be for sale, "otherwise what you are giving him is not even a master but a valet."[26] But this is not the issue as far as the son is concerned. The issue is social distance. Emile's situation is like that of the sons of wealthy men at prestigious private schools, who, while under the complete control of their masters, know that one day they will exceed their masters in wealth and power. It is this that makes their subservience both more galling and more tolerable—more galling because it is administered by social inferiors and more tolerable for the same reason. Emile's attitude toward his tutor is not identical; he is never galled (except, perhaps, when the tutor orders him to leave Sophie for two years). But can all his tutor's attempts to prevent Emile from confronting those whose power and good fortune might make him envious not apply to the tutor himself?

The Social Contract

The problem posed by *The Social Contract*, especially when seen in light of Rousseau's *Discourse on Inequality*, is the problem of how to reconcile humanity's natural freedom, which means to live without a superior on earth, with society. This is similar to the problem addressed by this book: how to render the self autonomous, integrated, whole, and social? *Emile* reveals Rousseau's answer. All opposing wills are to be rendered tantamount to the unchanging given-ness of nature. The general will of *The Social Contract* is like the tutor's fiction: will in the disguise of nature. Ernst Cassirer sees this clearly. Rousseau, he says, teaches that we should learn to submit to the law of the community "just as we submit to the law of nature; we are not to acquiesce in it as an alien dictate but must follow it because we recognize its necessity . . . and can absorb this meaning into our own will."[27] Cassirer is not troubled by this; he does not see it as the reification of will as nature because, as noted previously, he interprets Rousseau as a Kantian, so that the general will becomes tantamount to the categorical imperative: will for yourself only that which you could will should it become a universal law.

Although this is not the place to go into the errors of such an interpretation, one point stands out. The general will, when it is legitimate, may be general, but it is hardly universal. Rousseau frequently points out that it reflects the consensus of the community, the "civil religion" as he sometimes calls it—that is, the community's interpretation of its culture and tradition, which may vary considerably from community to community.[28] To equate this consensus with the universal law of nature is the worst type of reification. Yet Cassirer is not mistaken in detecting that this is Rousseau's intent. Like the tutor in *Emile*, the general will disguises will and constraint as objective givens and so makes constraint and the opposition of other wills more acceptable, less of an insult to the self, less likely to evoke narcissistic injury and with it amour propre. Today the demands of science and technology ("you can't stop progress") seem to perform a similar function, concealing the will and choice behind the constraint. "Science and Technology as 'Ideology,'" Jürgen Habermas calls it. This is probably true. It is insightful psychology on Rousseau's part. But it remains insightful psychology into the operation of the defenses of the self and should not be confused with insight into freedom.

It is no coincidence that Rousseau's most notorious statement about freedom is one that denies the otherness and difference inherent in constraint by identifying dependency, not force, as the alternative to freedom: "Whoever refuses to obey the general will shall be constrained to do so by the whole body; which means nothing else than that he shall be forced to be free; for such is the condition which, uniting every Citizen in his Homeland, guarantees him from all personal dependency."[29] As long as the constraint is not an identifiable other will, it is not really constraint at all. This is why Jean Starobinski, in *Jean-Jacques Rousseau: Transparency and Obstruction*, argues that freedom for Rousseau is "not freedom to act but freedom for self-presence; it is mere feeling." Freedom is "defined essentially as freedom from difference or otherness."[30] Freedom for Rousseau is akin to the ideal of absolute presence discussed in chapter 2: Rilke's angel, a being in whom "thought and action . . . will and capability, the actual and ideal" are one. Rousseau's psychological insight is profound: the desire for absolute presence reflects a real need. But it is a psychological insight that plays havoc with political freedom if the two are ever confused. And perhaps it is some of Rousseau's readers and followers who are more confused on this point than he was. Rousseau knew what he was doing—protecting people at any cost from narcissistic injury and so preventing the emergence of amour propre. Do they?

As the preceding paragraph suggests, Rousseau's transformation of will into objectivity is part of his larger project: his rejection of otherness, of difference. When the general will is legitimate, according to Rousseau, there can be no real conflict between self and other. This is why the individual can be "forced to be free," why "the general will is always right," so that in obeying the "general will," individuals "obey no one, but simply their own will."[31] Consider for a moment a personal relationship in which the other genuinely has your interests in mind: a good friendship or a good marriage, for example. No matter how much each wills only the best for the couple, there will always be otherness, always difference, even about the most general things. Often this is what gives the relationship spice.

To be sure, *The Social Contract* represents an ideal, a norm. It is not a utopian program to be instituted but a standard of evaluation. But it is just this ideal standard that must be criticized, as it idealizes what is not ideal: dedifferentiation, the denial of otherness and difference. As Starobinski points out, there are two ways to deny otherness: utter unity, in which difference itself is denied, and complete autonomy, autarky, in which any dependence on the other is denied.[32] Usually seen as opposites, from the perspective of denying otherness, unity and autarky are identical. Here is the solution to the riddle of Rousseau's work, in which the autarky of natural man in the *Discourse on Inequality* becomes the unity of the social contract. From the perspective of Rousseau's program these are not opposites at all, but two sides of the same coin, the coin that denies difference. Why is the denial of difference so important? It is difference, particularly the difference of wills other than our own, that inflicts narcissistic injury and evokes envy, and with it amour propre: the emotion that Plato (Bloom compares amour propre to thumos, but it seems just as much an attribute of Platonic desire),[33] Hobbes, Locke, and Rawls all worry about, dividing the self to contain it. Rousseau would avoid dividing the self, but he succeeds only by denying difference—the reality of separate and interdependent selves.

Narcissism as Defense against Amour Propre

Denial of difference, confusion of the self's power with another's, of freedom and dependence, of self and other: these are the defining characteristics of primary narcissism, understood as a state of predifferentiation and lack of separation between self and other, so that the other's power and interests are seen as an extension of one's own. Narcissism is the first stage of emotional development, characterized by what might be called a confused self-centeredness, in which the self one is centered on includes the other.[34] Several authors have suggested that both Rousseau and his theory are narcissistic to the core, and considerations like these seem to support this conclusion.[35] This, however, is not my conclusion, at least not when put so simply. To be sure, Rousseau himself was probably profoundly narcissistic. It is in this vein that Starobinski, formerly a psychiatrist, argues that Rousseau's use of the term *supplement* to characterize both his practice of masturbation and his relationship to Thérèse shows that his choice of object had regressed to the self, which is how narcissism is defined.[36] But the self that Rousseau writes of in his texts does not seem narcissistic in quite the same way. In this case narcissism is not so much a worldview as a defense, and not against difference but against amour propre.

Denial of difference, which is necessary if amour propre is to be avoided, serves the "great principle" around which Rousseau's work is organized, according to both Gustav Lanson and Starobinski: that "evil originates outside the self and remains external to it."[37] Many of the most narcissistic aspects of Rousseau's concept of the self stem neither from its inability to distinguish itself from others nor from Rousseau's inability to draw subtle distinctions between the needs of one's self and those of another. Quite the contrary, his work is filled with such distinctions. They constitute the best part of *The Social Contract*, in which Rousseau is always careful to distinguish between a legitimate and a merely empirical agreement, for example, or between governors and sovereignty.[38] Rather, the narcissism of Rousseau's concept of the self is a higher-order narcissism, so to speak: a defense in the service of an already differentiated self that does not wish to recognize the evil within. Evil (understood as amour propre), not narcissistic dedifferentiation, is the fundamental issue; the latter serves as defense to avoid confronting the former.

One sees the secondary, or defensive character of Rousseau's narcissistic concept of the self (that is, how it defends a self that has developed beyond the stage of primary narcissism) in his refusal to idealize power and ambition for its own sake. In this respect, Hobbes's concept of the self is more primitive, as his self makes no distinction between power and goodness. Rousseau's does. Nisbet argues that Rousseau displays "an almost mystic dedication to omnipotence," whether in the person of legislator, tutor, or general will. But Nisbet goes on to add that this "dedication" is only to "legitimate" power.[39] This adjective, though, makes all the difference, for it reveals that Rousseau is not infatuated with power for its own sake but as it serves as an instrument by which to realize ideals. Power, in Rousseau's account, remains bound to ideals, the key sign of a mature self.

Rousseau's great contribution to political theory is in the area of legitimate power: his redefinition of sovereignty. Previously, as James Miller points out in *Rousseau: Dreamer of Democracy*, sovereignty meant power. Hobbes took this definition to its limit, but his view was not unique. "When Hobbes transported his own Latin concept of *summum imperium* in English under the rubric of the 'sovereign,' he defined the word to carry all the implications of unrivaled power conveyed by the original Latin. Most modern writings shared this understanding of the term."[40] Rousseau, on the other hand, joins sovereignty to legitimacy, so that "the synonym for sovereignty was no longer *empire*, but *volonté*."[41] Never again could it be simply assumed that sovereignty and power were one. The question of what constituted legitimate power, justified power, would have to be addressed. In this way Rousseau transformed the world of republican discourse forever, no mean achievement.[42]

Rousseau's fateful error lies elsewhere, in his attempt to deny that legitimate sovereign power might constrain the freedom of the self. One cannot have all of every good thing. Legitimate power and individual freedom frequently conflict, and political theory—especially democratic political theory—is the story of the compromises reached between them. I have tried to tell one chapter in this story, about the compromises that several political theorists are willing to accept in the integrity and *muendigkeit* of the self in order to make it compatible with social order. That it is a democratic social order that Rousseau is concerned with obviates not at all the need for such compromises. It may make the need for compromise more poignant, but this is a different story, one that Rousseau mistakenly suggests need not be told. In fact, it is this painful story that is the most important story of all, precisely because it concerns the compromises necessary between two esteemed goods.

Conclusion: The Costs of a Political Theory as Defense of the Self

Sympathetic critics of Rousseau, such as Peter Gay, usually distinguish between Rousseau as a theorist of the democratic ideal and Rousseau as a theorist of the democratic state, his contribution being to the former, not the latter.[43] Something like this is probably valid, as the preceding comments on his contribution to the theory of legitimate sovereignty suggest. Nevertheless, it is easy to make too much of this distinction, and not only because of Rousseau's reluctance to recognize that even legitimate sovereignty may constrain freedom. His denial of difference, his equation of unity and autonomy, cannot help but influence his democratic ideal as well. Frequently commented upon are his dramatic remarks, such as that the individual may be "forced to be free." It may be useful to focus upon a less dramatic, but no less important aspect of his democratic theory, an aspect identified by Judith Shklar.

Many, such as Benjamin Barber, see Rousseau as the theorist of vigorous public discussion and debate, an impression encouraged by Rousseau himself in his praise of Geneva (actually an oligarchy run by the "Small Council"),[44] yeoman farmers deciding their affairs under a tree, and so forth.[45] In fact, there is little public discussion of affairs in Rousseau's account and no organized public realm or *Oeffentlichkeit* at all. The reason is apparent: such discussion can only reveal difference and dissent. It would not be inaccurate to call Rousseau the theorist of the New England town meeting, but only after we understand what town meetings were really about in the late 1700s.

New England town meetings in the eighteenth century were also meant to achieve consensus. Differences were generally called unhappy, and the primacy of peace rendered discord [and] argument . . . unacceptable. The meetings were not presented with a choice of competing interests or opinions. They met to reassert the unity of townsmen. . . . Neither the defense of private interests nor the projection of personal ideas was welcome.[46]

Not only is Rousseau not a theorist of public discussion; he is not a theorist of *political* community either. There are lots of festivals, games, and so forth in his good society, serving to promote ties of esteem and affection among the citizens. Beyond this, their function is strictly private, serving to arrange marriages and so forth. For Rousseau, the Swiss mountain cantons were well suited for democracy because their citizens were kept indoors and apart by the weather for almost half the year. This minimized the promotion of parties and faction, each member of the assembly isolating himself before voting in order to know only his own heart.[47]

Not merely the ideal of the general will, but political life in general evinces the strange mix of unity and autarky in Rousseau's work. Each citizen is part of the whole, but the parts of the whole—the citizens—rarely confront or debate each other over issues. Why? Confrontation and debate—public discussion of the issues—can only accentuate difference and so draw out amour propre, which stems, Rousseau tells us in *Emile*, from comparative weakness. Shklar puts it this way. The primacy of isolation in Rousseau's work

> expresses a profound sense of weakness and inadequacy. In solitude one is at last safe from the domination of others. This is not the solitude of Prometheus but the self-protective flight of the incredibly weak who are afraid of being bossed. Mutuality is achieved by avoiding face-to-face relationships, and the impersonality of legal relationships becomes a substitute for politics. That . . . may have an obvious advantage for those whose chief hope is to escape subjugation, especially in the form of personal dependence.[48]

It is not surprising that a theorist so dedicated to protecting the self from the depredations of other wills constructs a political ideal in which such wills never meet. The question that must be asked, of course, is whether such an ideal has anything to do at all with democratic politics. Rousseau remains a theorist of community and its healing powers.[49] But it is no political community, and they should not be confused.

In the end, Rousseau's view of the self is unexceptional, concerned with much the same issues as Plato, Hobbes, Locke, and Rawls: the problem is the self's anxious desire to master others and so avoid insult and injury to its self-esteem. What is unique is Rousseau's solution, the denial of difference, rather, his elaboration of defense against difference into a political theory. Casanova concluded that in his person Rousseau was not exceptional, merely eccentric. Applied to the entirety of his political theory, such a conclusion would be too harsh, for he makes a genuine contribution to the theory of democratic sovereignty. What is eccentric about his political theory is its organization around the denial of difference, so that almost all its central aspects serve or depend upon this denial. Why?

One could speculate about the connection between this denial and Rousseau's personal life, as he clearly wants us to do. Indeed, from this perspective, his *Confessions*, *Reveries*, and so forth are rhetoric, functioning like the magician who calls attention to his left hand so that we will ignore the right. Intended or not, Rousseau's confessions distract us from the fundamental issue: the plausibility of his argument that the self emerges good and whole, and society need not make it otherwise, even as it always has. In order to support this argument, this possibility, Rousseau must deny to the civilized self the perception of difference, the good society being one that supports this denial. Society itself becomes the veil of ignorance. That this is necessary tells us something not just about Rousseau but also about the plausibility of his argument about the self's innate goodness.

The fully developed state will
. . . unite somehow the radical
moral autonomy of Kant
and the expressive unity
of the Greek Polis.
—Charles Taylor, *Hegel*

CHAPTER NINE

The Self and Its Discontents

Contrary to Hegel's ideal, my considerations suggest how difficult it is to do even half the job right. Not the combination of autonomy and expressive unity but the combination of autonomy and civilized society is the ideal that seems to elude Plato, Hobbes, Locke, and Rawls. All split the self in some way, sacrificing its autonomy in order to make it social. Rousseau does not, but only by denying difference—not the difference of individuality but the differences among individuals that make *community* possible and real. This renders his solution untenable: a denial, not an answer.

The Discontent of the Self

Plato splits the self in the name of reason so that reason might soothe its pain in an archaic selfobject transference with Beings. Locke splits the self within the pole of ambitions, encouraging an archaic selfobject transference, so that self-esteem might be made dependent upon others and in this way the self made safe for society. Rawls sees the risks in such an arrangement but in the end denies the inner reality of the self whose esteem he would protect, like Plato turning to philosophy as a defense against the disunity of the self and the intensity of its needs and fears. Hobbes refrains from such strategies of division, but only because he is content to begin and end with a stunted self. Such strategies, it must be emphasized, do more than sacrifice the romantic dimension of the self, its concern with authentic inner experience and the like. They threaten the very self that liberalism claims to protect, weakening the psychic sources of what Kant calls Mündigkeit: mature autonomy. Or, as Frithjof Bergmann has written, "an act is free if the agent identifies with the elements from which it flows; it is coerced if the agent dissociates himself from the element which generates or prompts the action. . . . The primary condition of freedom is the possession of an identity, or of a self—freedom is the acting out of this identity."[1] Weaken the self, and one weakens the sources of freedom, including the moral freedom to choose rightly—or wrongly.

What about Plato, who clearly did not seek to protect the liberal self? One reason so much attention has been devoted to Plato is to demonstrate that this is not a problem that can be solved by simply returning to the classical concept of the psyche and its correlate, objective reason. Plato does not merely enrich self-consciousness with self-knowledge. He sacrifices the former for the latter, perhaps a defensible choice, but not an appealing one even to many critics of liberalism. At least not when stated so baldly.

None of the theorists considered here really comes to terms with the self, sacrificing at least some of the self each sets out to protect. This is not, one suspects, because they are not smart enough or because they lack the latest psychological theory. Rather, they are confronting an insoluble dilemma. Generally couched in terms of the conflict between self and society, this phraseology actually conceals the problem insofar as it suggests that the conflict is between individual freedom and society's needs. In fact, these theorists recognize that the self desires not merely to be free but to affirm its freedom—actually its narcissistic integrity—by bending others to its will. Amour propre, Rousseau calls it. It is this that makes the self so difficult for society. The archaic, untutored self does not desire simply to be left alone to do what it will; it desires to impose its will on others. On this point Plato (for whom, it will be recalled, it is the tyrant who epitomizes desire), Hobbes, Locke, and Rawls agree. Rousseau in effect agrees, as his solution would render man inhuman, or insane, in order to overcome amour propre. They agree too, I have argued, that the mature self cannot be counted on to contain its archaic desires, at least not in large enough numbers to make society possible. Thus it is necessary to organize society around split selves, compacts by which all agree not to inflict narcissistic injury, and so forth.

In *Another Liberalism*, Nancy Rosenblum makes the simple but powerful point that the "romantic flirtation with death shatters assumptions about the universal desire for security."[2] If only Hobbes were correct, it would be so much easier (or rather, if only a particular one-dimensional reading of Hobbes were correct). If only, that is, people sought security above all else, then social order would be easy, or easier in any case. In fact, what the individual so often seeks is to master others and so obtain confirmation of the power of his or her will. Locke comes closest to the mark in this regard: individuals seek to master others not merely out of fear but out of the satisfaction that it brings. What kind of satisfaction? Narcissistic satisfaction. Simply *being* free is not enough because the self is not enough. This freedom must be confirmed by others, generally via their subordination. This is, of course, a sign of a weakness in the self, not a strength. To be unable merely to *be* free, to require its constant confirmation, is a sign of narcissistic anxiety, it might be called: the fear that the self is not enough. In the language of Lacan, the ego defends against the subject by dominating it. Only it is not merely its own subjectivity that the ego dominates but that of others as well.

There is some truth to Wolin's suggestion that liberalism is first and foremost about fear. It is, however, not only fear of loss of possessions and status that liberal theorists fear. They fear the self, the intensity of its fear, desire, and rage. So did Plato. This is why their solutions do not better respect the self they are seeking to protect: they fear it still more. Often these theorists confront this fear; this is what makes them great. Generally they do not transform fear, desire, and rage into "interest" in order to rationalize it or buy it off with social goods (Locke, of course, comes closest to this strategy in his treatment of property). Nor do they transform powerful fears and desires into lukewarm sentiments, as Adam Smith does.[3] None is a "psychometaphysician" (at least not when the works of each are considered as a whole), to use Amelie Rorty's term, in which abstract analysis of what is required to hold experience together substitutes for an analysis of real selves.[4] Often the theorists considered come right out and state their fears and concerns about the self. But not always. Sometimes one must search for it, in Rawls's case behind the metaphysical veil.

One thing all the authors agree upon, including Plato, Kohut, and Lacan, is that desire cannot be left to ideals. Ideals are too weak to constrain unintegrated desire, the self too likely to transform ideals into the image of desire. Ideals cannot take the place of self-control, nor can they perform the function of self-control. Noble ideals that define and limit the self are themselves an outgrowth of the mature self, a modification of its ambitions as Kohut sees it, not an alternative to maturity nor a substitute for self-control. Any adequate social theory must first deal with the problem of desire, and it cannot do so merely by positing beautiful ideals. Here is another reason these authors are so harsh on the self. They understand that there is no alternative to self-control, even if the self must be divided against itself in order to achieve it.

It will no doubt be recognized that this thesis is not original. It is a self-psychological version of Freud's in *Civilization and Its Discontents*. In the place of libido and aggression (eros and thanatos), I have put the needs and fears of the self. My formulation has an advantage, however. Conceptualizing libido and aggression in terms of what was essentially a hydraulic model, Freud saw the issue strictly in terms of the degree of repression necessary to maintain civilized society. Society might be rendered a little less repressive or a little more so. These were the only options, a framework so overarching that the details, such as whether this repression was imposed by democratic or authoritarian means, hardly mattered.[5] A self-psychological perspective is not necessarily more optimistic, but it is more complex, revealing that there are lots of ways to come to terms with the self, to make it safe for society. Put more cynically, there are lots of ways to divide the self against the self, to weaken it in the name of social tranquility.

All that I have examined involve sacrificing the self in some way, splitting off or denying the very needs and fears of the self that the author set out to come to terms with (or, in Rousseau's case, denying otherness and difference). In response it might be argued that this is really not weakening the self at all but strengthening it, quelling those base and unacceptable impulses that must in the end destroy it or at least make it less eudaimon. As Bergmann puts it, "parts of my self or of my nature are bound to be unappealing or mean or retrograde or evil. . . . Expressing these would not just be a slight and easily outweighed advantage, but would be a straight detriment. It is the hindrance or the extirpation of these impulses that represents the immediate gain. So freedom needs to be limited not only for the sake of others."[6]

Surely such an insight is generally correct: the self who is a slave to its desires is not a happy self. This is the thesis of *The Republic*. It is, however, the thesis of this book that *how* one seeks the "hindrance or the extirpation of these impulses" is crucial and likely to be not so much overlooked as disguised by abstract talk about moral freedom, educating the passions, and the like. Rather, we must talk about real selves.

The Self is Not Constructed Like Our Concepts of It

It is not for reasons of methodological individualism that we should focus on the self. It is not because we must assume, as good empiricists, that only individuals are real. Freud speculates that group psychology precedes individual psychology, and Kohut and Lacan both suggest that it is the self's relationships that are prior to the self. It is actually Rousseau who is the great methodological individualist. Rather, we should focus on the self for reasons of value, which is not to say that we must value the self for itself most of all. Nevertheless, all other values have value only in reference to this self. Therefore it is appropriate to be clear about how one is parsing the self, so to speak, in order to realize these values.

All the political theorists studied in this book are clear on this point, even if one has to search for it a bit. This is what makes them great. This is what the "Great Conversation" in political theory is about: what about the self is most valuable, and how can it be protected, *particularly against other aspects of the self*? One sees this over and over in the theorists studied. Each values the self (Hobbes may be the exception), but ends up doing horrid things to it—and not merely to make it safe for society but to save it from itself, usually from its archaic desires.

The problem, seen most clearly in the discussion of Plato, is that the self is not built like our concepts of it assume. There is no part of the self, the good part, that can be separated out and protected from the bad part without doing damage to the entire self. The operation required is much more crude, a virtual lobotomy, usually sacrificing much of what it is that the theorist values about the self. Amour propre cannot be separated from amour de soi without obliterating the "soi." (To be sure, Rousseau seeks to return to a time before they are separated, but this turns out to be a time prior to self-other differentiation as well.) Here is where the psychology of the self comes in, laying out the costs of dividing the self against the self in various ways while reminding us that there is no alternative except denial.

Here is the troublesome reality of the self. It is not constructed like our philosophical concepts but stubbornly joins what our concepts would separate, such as reason and desire. This is why the ideal solution is impossible: to split off only the bad stuff, leaving all the good stuff, so that splitting is actually an enrichment of the self along the lines suggested by Bergmann in his discussion of freedom. Splitting is far too crude, too global, for this. Even were it not, culture and society function far too imprecisely to do it right. It is the task of political theory—what political theory is properly about—to go back and forth between concept and self, taking both concept and self seriously, neither reducing self to concept nor pretending that the self can be parsed as though it were a sentence. One can hardly do this if one's model of the self is a mere reflection of the concept, be it the concept of community or the concept of justice.

Sandel is hardly the only theorist to see the self in the mirror of a single concept. His is only the most ironic version of this tendency, as he organizes his argument around a criticism of Rawls for doing precisely this. Macpherson, too, sees the self in this fashion, assuming that the Hobbesian self is but a reflection of competitive market societies. Eliminate the economic need to appropriate and invade others, and Hobbes's account of human nature is void. Is the self void, too, waiting for another ideological abstraction to bring it to life? Although Macpherson presumably does not believe that it is, nothing he says supports the contrary. Rejecting this mirror-image view of the self does not, of course, require the assumption that the self is everywhere the same or that capitalism does not bring out some of its less attractive aspects. Indeed, it is such either-or thinking that is the problem.

Here is the real danger, and often a quite subtle one: constructing our social theories so that the self does not really exist in them, so that we need not confront the hard choices and the limits of utopia. For such defensive purposes, abstract metaphysical selves, such as the ghostly self that Sandel (mistakenly) attributes to Rawls, function just as well as the selves of the mirror-modelers. Although not always confronting all the hard choices, the authors I have considered write about real selves. This is their great virtue. Anyone can come up with a beautiful theory of society simply by treating the self as the dependent variable, so to speak. This, too, is treating the self as a means, not an end. The real trick is to take the desires and fears of the self seriously and still come up with a decent society. Doing so also shows more respect for the real self. One cannot respect what one will not even see.

To argue that the self exists and that it is not a mirror of its environment is, of course, not the same thing as arguing that the individual is prior to society, whatever that might mean. Indeed, one reason that Kohut is useful is because he reveals how pointless this whole debate really is. He does so by drawing attention away from such an abstract and fruitless formulation of the issue to a more precise one. Of course, the self is fundamentally social, constituted by its relationships with others. Not the self but the selfobject transference comes first. The important question is the quality of the self's relationships, particularly whether its selfobject transferences are archaic or mature. To answer this question requires that the theorist posit a model of the self in the first place. The self that fades into the background, be it social or philosophical, is not a self that is constituted by its relationships. It is no self at all.

I-Selves, We-Selves, Real Selves

This is such a difficult and contentious issue that it is worthwhile trying to make this point in another way. No matter how many times it is denied, a call to focus on the self is likely to be interpreted as a backhanded way of valorizing the assertive, acquisitive, liberal self. This is especially the case within the framework of an argument that sees in Rousseau's solution no solution at all (though it should not be overlooked that in important respects Rousseau's is the most individualistic self of all). For this reason it may be useful to consider an account of the communal self that fulfills all the requirements laid out above. It takes the self seriously while in effect arguing for the superiority of the communal self, or at least its moral equivalence.

The vehicle is not a work in political theory, or at least not in what is usually called political theory. It is a work in political psychology, *In Search of Self in India and Japan*, by Alan Roland.[7] Drawing heavily upon Kohut, Roland focuses upon what is often called the cultural or group self, a frequent topic of psychoanalytic anthropologists. In general I have eschewed this approach, focusing instead on the nuclear or individual self. One reason is that mixing sociology and psychology always risks (even if it need not succumb to, as it does not in Roland's case) trivializing both. Theodor Adorno's by now classic statement still holds. In analyzing the conflicts of individuals, he says,

> psychoanalysis carries specific conviction; the further it removes itself from that sphere, the more its theses are threatened alternately with shallowness or wild over-systematization. . . . The further it departs from [that sphere] the more tyrannically it has to proceed and the more it has to drag what belongs to the dimension of outer reality into the shades of psychic immanence. Its delusion in so doing is not dissimilar from that "omnipotence of thought" which it itself criticized as infantile.[8]

A second reason that I have focused on the individual rather than the cultural self is that doing so better lends itself to developing a psychoanalytic approach to reading texts about the self. To be sure, the individual and the cultural self are hardly distinct entities; the individual self contains the cultural self, and vice versa. It is primarily a question of perspective. And from my perspective here, Roland's work is most useful in demonstrating that putting the self at the analytic center is distinct from praising political individualism. For Roland quite successfully puts what he calls the nonliberal "we-self" at the center of his analysis.

Roland distinguishes among three aspects of the self: the familial self (the we-self), individualized self (the I-self), and the spiritual self. All selves have all three components. It is the relative balance and emphasis among the three that shifts across cultures, as well as among individuals within cultures. The familial, or we-self is the dominant component of the self in India and Japan, according to Roland. He defines it in terms of the following three categories. *Symbiosis-reciprocity* is an orientation "that involves intensely emotional intimacy relationships, with their emotional connectedness and interdependence, in relationship-centered cultures where there is a constant affective exchange through permeable outer ego boundaries, where a highly private self is maintained, where high levels of empathy and receptivity to others are cultivated."[9] *Narcissistic configurations of we-self regard*, the second category, means that a person's self-esteem depends heavily upon the reputation and honor of the family and other groups to which he belongs. A *socially contextual ego-ideal*, the third category, is one that carefully observes traditionally defined reciprocal responsibilities and obligations. Persons and traditions, rather than abstract universal values, characterize such an ego ideal.

The individualized, or I-self is defined by Roland in terms of relatively self-contained outer ego boundaries, sharp differentiation between inner images of self and other, individualistic narcissistic structures that depend less on the achievements and status of the group, and a superego organized around relatively abstract principles of behavior. It is the "predominant inner psychological organization of Americans, enabling them to function in a highly mobile society where considerable autonomy is granted if not imposed on the individual."[10]

The spiritual self, especially in India, is in some ways the opposite of the we-self without becoming more like the I-self. Its ideal is the holy man, with no ties to anyone or anything, who seeks to transform and generally transcend the self to a realm of pure being. Such a self is usually unconnected to society. In the West, on the other hand, the spiritual self is more akin to the artistic self, the Promethean self who creates the self out of nothing and in so doing challenges society.

In Western psychoanalysis, says Roland, it is assumed that individuation goes hand in hand with gradual separation from mother, leading to firm ego boundaries and a sharp differentiation between inner images of self and other. "These developmental lines in American children are viewed as so intrinsically interrelated that [Margaret] Mahler has hyphenated this process as separation-individuation, and of course has assumed it to be universal."[11] In fact, says Roland, there is no intrinsic connection between separation and individuation. One can get the former without the latter. This is the mark of the we-self. In the I-self, inner and outer ego boundaries are virtually identical. In contrast, the we-self often maintains a private inner self, coupled with permeable outer ego boundaries.

In a Westerner, such a private inner self (what the psychoanalyst Harry Guntrip calls the "true self," the "lost heart" of the personal self) would usually be a sign of emotional illness, as it would likely be as alienated from the individual as from others. This is an implication of the virtual coincidence of inner and outer boundaries. In the we-self, however, the inner self is usually quite accessible and frequently quite rich. In the Indian self, particularly, Roland found real depths of fantasy, sensuality, and spirituality.

> I have found in psychoanalytic therapy that once one gets by the delib-
> erate caution and circumspection involved in proper behavior by estab-
> lishing a relationship of confidentiality and trust, Indian patients tend to
> be much more in touch with the intense feelings and fantasies of their
> inner world. . . . Individuality . . . is richly developed in certain ways
> in Indians. Their individuality is first fostered by the prolonged sym-
> biotic, nurturing maternal relationships. Where close affectional ties
> and emotional responsiveness are present, and strong identification
> processes are at work, rich individuality usually develops. Moreover,
> Hindu culture not only recognizes the particular proclivities of a per-
> son, but also accords a remarkable degree of freedom in feeling, think-
> ing, and maintaining a private self, while greatly encouraging the culti-
> vation of one's inner life, in counterpoint to the considerable constraints
> in behavior in the social hierarchy.[12]

The we-self, it seems, may be just as rich, perhaps richer, than the I-self. Competitive liberal individualism may, as Roland suggests, require far more repression of one's inner life—the single most important resource to the self, the single most important resource for genuine individuality.[13] Indeed, Kohut, along with a number of other psychoanalysts such as Joan Riviere, is concerned that the self in Western culture is becoming impoverished as achievement in the outer world takes the place of development in the inner world. It may well be that the we-self, free of some of these competitive pressures and secure in its understanding of itself in terms of its relation to tradition and hierarchy (for the we-self, one is "*always* located in relationship to others"), is in a far better position to develop its inner world, its inner life.[14] Arguably this is a better measure of self-development and cultivation than individuation (though they need not, of course, be alternatives). To be sure, the we-self is not always characterized by a rich inner life. In Japan, Roland finds so much pressure applied so early on the self to achieve in the name of the group ("narcissistic configurations of we-self regard") that the development of an inner life seems thwarted. The point is not that the we-self is automatically richer but that individuation and richness, understood as being in touch with one's inner life, do not automatically go together.

The we-self requires more frequent and constant mirroring than the I-self, depending much more than the I-self upon the actual presence of responsive others. Conversely, the we-self does not internalize others (transmuting internalization) as thoroughly as the I-self. It is this attribute of the we-self that frequently inclines Westerners to regard it as less mature. Yet once again the situation is not so simple. Kohut argues that "autonomy is impossible." We constantly require the presence of responsive selfobjects, even if this presence is internalized. From this perspective, the need for selfobjects is not the question, but rather how we use them—in an archaic or a mature fashion. Nothing in Roland's account suggests that the we-self is involved in more *archaic* relationships with its external selfobjects, just more frequent ones. It is the isolated, alienated self, separated from others by the perpetual struggle for existence, who is more likely to depend more upon archaic selfobject relationships, in which fantasies (often unconscious) of total dependence on or total control of others predominate. Certainly such fantasies fill the mass media in the United States. This is what a *Culture of Narcissism* is about.

It is apparent that the we-self is just as worthy of being the center of our analysis as the I-self—if, that is, we value the we-self qua self, not merely as concept, defense, or ideal. Indeed, if we measure the self by the richness of its inner life, we may find the we-self more worthy. Nothing in my argument about the importance of putting the self at the center of our studies requires or implies that it be the I-self, the competitive, individualistic self. To analytically privilege the self by always asking questions such as "Is this regime or way of life good for the self?" has nothing to do with privileging a particular type of self. To analytically privilege the self is, however, more than a methodological act. It is also a moral act, insofar as it says that the self is an important entity. To be sure, one could methodologically and conceptually focus upon the self while holding that it is a pernicious entity, one that must be studied in order to contain it. Indeed, this attitude is not alien to the theorists I examine. One could not, however, really do the opposite: ignore the real self, derive it from metaphysical, philosophical, and other assumptions, while truly holding that the self is valuable and worthy of care, protection, and so on.

Seen in this light, the real enemies of the self are not the deconstructionists such as Lacan who seek to show that the self is a neurotic symptom. The real enemies of the self are those who write of a need for a socially constituted self, as though this answered anything or meant anything other than the obliteration of the self. To write of the socially constituted self addresses none of the questions about the self that we want to answer, such as how we can protect and foster a rich inner life while overcoming the isolation and fear that leads monadic individuals to substitute wild self-assertion for self-cultivation. To write of the contribution to self-development achieved through meaningful political participation, identifying with the group, and so on is, in this context, not so much wrong as meaningless.

Consider, for example, Roland's analysis of how a strong we-self is developed in India and Japan. Prolonged, intense mother-child emotional involvement is common, with the child sleeping with the mother far longer than in most Western societies. The child is picked up more frequently, weaned later, toilet-trained later, and in general gratified more freely. The result, says Roland, is a child who has much less need for what psychoanalysts call "transitional objects," such as the special blanket or teddy bear, that represent mother in her absence.

Instead, this intense mothering creates an inner core of well-being, and a profound sense of protection, with the expectation that others will somehow come through for you, inuring the person against great struggles and frustration. Simultaneously, there is a subtle inhibition of too great self-other differentiation and separation through the amount of gratification and closeness an Indian child experiences. This decidedly contrasts with the "optimal" frustrations of the Western child, which foster the inner separation process of the child from the mother.[15]

After this prolonged period of early childhood gratification, there is a crackdown at about the age of five through adolescence, during which it is demanded that the child behave properly in hierarchical relationships. It is this combination of gratification and crackdown that fosters the we-self, or at least that version of the we-self characterized by an intense and rich inner life.

Roland's analysis is not necessarily correct, of course, but that is not the point. The point is that it is this level of analysis of the self that is necessary if one is to say anything meaningful about it, one that appreciates the *interaction* of inner self and outer world. One finds this level of analysis in Plato's discussion of the relation between regime and character (*Republic*, books 8 and 9) and Locke's *Some Thoughts concerning Education*. It is also present in Rousseau and to a lesser degree in Hobbes and Rawls. Roland's analysis also suggests the futility of regarding the self as a mirror of its culture. The we-self is not created by living in a pure we-world (that is, the group, the commune, or whatever). But neither is it created by pretending that other wills do not exist. Roland suggests not only that Rousseau has it wrong but that he has it backward. The we-self is fostered by an environment in which emotional intimacy and intense gratification are coupled demands for appropriate behavior. We-selves (or at least we-selves with a rich inner life) stem from intense emotional relationships, not a Skinner box.

This claim is supported by Bruno Bettelheim's controversial study of child rearing in the Israeli kibbutz, *The Children of the Dream*. Writing of the first generation of these children, who were separated from their parents at birth, Bettelheim says that though they showed no loss of basic security, they were less morally autonomous, less able to resist the group. They were also less able to identify imaginatively with others and so feel empathy with outsiders, who were different from themselves. Bettelheim speculates that this stems from a "moderately impoverished" inner life, the consequence of the child's never having to introject (internalize as part of himself) an image of his parents in order to protect himself from their loss, as he is never so dependent upon them in the first place. Not an internal parent but the actual peer group is central to the child's psychic life. It is as though the child never needs to engage in transmuting internalization in order to make the parent his own, for the peer group is always with him.[16] Bettelheim's observations are by no means universally accepted, although some who reject his conclusions have made similar observations about the lack of moral autonomy and imagination among the first generation of kibbutz-raised children.[17] But, as with Roland, this is not really the point. The point is once again that the self is not a mirror. External influences are transformed by the self in subtle and important ways that political theorists, interested in the good society, can hardly ignore, lest they idealize a parody of community—or autonomy.

No matter what one's concept of the ideal self, it is this type of analysis, always moving back and forth among infancy, childhood, and adulthood, and thus between the archaic and mature sectors of the self, that is necessary. It is not the task of political theory to mimic Roland's comparative study. His is empirical research, albeit research informed by an ideal, even by a concept. It is the task of political theory—or rather, of ambitious political theory that seeks to be a part of the "Great Conversation"—to go back and forth between insights such as Roland's and its concepts and ideals. This is, in effect, what Plato, Hobbes, Locke, Rawls, and Rousseau do. To ignore the inner world of the self on the ground, not always explicitly stated, that one is really interested in the public self, metaphysical self, political self, or whatever leads not only to an inadequate conceptualization of the self. It also risks impoverishing the self, treating it as though it had no inner life or could be harmlessly divided to fit one's concepts.

Conclusion: Myths of Wholeness, Constructed Selves, and Noble Lies

The reader will undoubtedly have noticed that Roland's view of the self is brighter than the eclectic mix of Kohut and Lacan that informs my account. This is, I believe, because Roland does not probe as deeply, a limitation of the cultural self approach. It was not necessary for him to probe as deeply, as he did not set out to explain the equally dark views of Plato, Hobbes, Locke, Rawls, and Rousseau. That is, he did not set out to explain the desire, rage, and fear that lie at the center of these theorists' accounts. Indeed, this is why I turned to Lacan. Kohut's account of the self is really too bright to illuminate the dark corners of the self that these theorists take so seriously. In this regard, it must be emphasized that the we-self is not a way of avoiding the trade-offs discussed above. Rather, it is simply one more way of making them. Or rather, it contains a hint as to how these trade-offs would be made, whereas contemporary political theorists who write about the *moi commun*, as Rousseau calls it, frequently provide no clues at all.

There are no ideal solutions, only more cautions than guidelines. A particularly important caution is that strategies that would create community by extending the boundaries of the self should be regarded with suspicion. They are likely to be either exaggerated versions of Locke's strategy of splitting the self so as to locate self-esteem in others or of Rawls's tendency to idealize communal feelings that lack a secure foundation in the self. To extend the self in this way is, of course, no improvement on liberalism but simply an exaggeration of its worst features.

If the strategy of creating community by extending the self is problematic, so too are solutions that recognize the intensity of the self's desires, counting on the public-private distinction associated with liberalism to keep them in check while providing a haven for self-realization. Rosenblum states that

> liberalism cannot entirely prevent . . . the return of the repressed. Benjamin Constant is one of the few liberals able to endure this idea. He is willing to place narcissism and nihilism at the center of his argument for private life. . . . In fact, Constant turns the existence of the dark side of personal life into an argument in defense of liberalism. The question for him is not whether people will withdraw and turn inward and whether impulses will then be expressed (they will), but whether passionate expression is available for political exploitation. Liberalism offers security against this. Separation of spheres and guarantees of undisturbed privacy can set bounds to narcissism and nihilism. The personal can be excluded from the formal, impersonal domain of society and contained in private.[18]

In short, the distinction between public and private protects the former as much as the latter.

None of the theorists considered here lends much support to this strategy. Each sees the self as so demanding in its fears and desires that it will never stay in its place unless it is divided against itself in some way, made subject to an absolute sovereign, or publicly guaranteed not merely its privacy and freedom but its narcissistic integrity as well. None of these strategies respects the public-private distinction, arguments about Hobbes being a liberal notwithstanding. As these last comments suggest, it is not merely the self that exerts pressure on the public-private distinction. Today neither politicians nor bureaucrats nor corporate spokespersons nor the mass media nor popular culture nor advertisers remain on their side of the line either, if the public-private distinction even makes sense in a world dominated by such entities. It is Constant who also said that modern despotism "pursues the vanquished into the interior of their existence; it maims them spiritually in order to force them to conform." Although Rosenblum appreciates Constant's concern as it pertains to "passionate politics," she does not seem as sensitive as Constant to how this hostile pursuit of the self may become a characteristic of routine liberal bureaucratic politics as well.[19]

Myths of wholeness (albeit in this case a wholeness restricted to the private sphere) are not the sole property of communitarians such as Rousseau, if he is indeed a communitarian. Rosenblum suggests that romanticism has closer links to liberalism than it does to communitarianism. This is because romanticism is often profoundly individualistic, concerned with the integrity and authenticity of inner experience, the inner temple of the self. Thus she argues that "romanticism can come home to liberalism," enriching liberalism while tempering the extremes of romantic individualism, which risks abandoning society.[20] Important here is not so much Rosenblum's thesis as her attempt to combine the two traditions via a normative psychology, which tells us, for example, the best balance between the search for authentic inner experience and social belonging. Rosenblum employs the life-cycle psychologies of Erik Erikson and Daniel Levinson, arguing that they reveal how the balance may shift over the course of a lifetime in order to meet the needs of the maturing, changing self. Liberalism is desirable because it provides a rich menu for the developing self to choose from.

> Life-cycle theory proposes something more extravagant than successful socialization, ego development or autonomy: *a genuine myth of wholeness.* . . . With the claim that heterogeneous spheres are not just scenes of self-cultivation but ingredients of personal development, life-cycle theory proposes a new experience of liberalism. An objective structural correspondence between pluralism and identity-formation converses with a subjective feeling of being at home in a complex and differentiated society.[21]

Rosenblum is too sanguine. We should be suspicious even of myths of wholeness. Like the metaphysical self Sandel attributes to Rawls, such myths generally serve to split off and deny all that stands in the way of wholeness. In so doing, these myths distort inner experience rather than serve it, rendering the self even less whole by rounding off its corners, as it were. The myth of wholeness is the myth of the ego, not the subject.

It is important to draw the right lesson from these considerations, lest we end up like Lacan, concluding that because wholeness is a myth, so too is the self. Indeed, beyond analyzing the concept of the self held by various authors, this has been my primary concern: to challenge the all-or-nothing perspective on the self, a perspective that appears in several guises.

Ann Hartle, in *The Modern Self*, compares Rousseau's *Confessions* with those of Saint Augustine. For Augustine, the self knows itself only in terms of its relationship to God. "Man does not make himself and thus he does not know himself. He is understandable only in terms of God's providential intention and this he sees only through a glass darkly. One's recollection of oneself is radically and essentially incomplete."[22] Rousseau, on the other hand, constructs himself out of his imaginative re-creation of his recollections. In what he calls his reveries, he puts his experiences together in a meaningful pattern in order to create a self. Here are the two options, the two extremes to which there is no middle: to understand oneself in terms of one's place in a meaningful cosmological hierarchy or to create oneself out of one's own experiences and so in effect supplant God. Says Hartle, "The inner, natural self, which, for Rousseau, underlies the imaginative construction of the . . . self, is a self without God. It is, at the same time, a self which replaces God: it possesses what, for Augustine, are divine attributes."[23] Prime among these attributes is self-sufficiency.

In book 8 of his *Confessions*, Rousseau tells the story of his friend Mussard, who retires from business in order to devote himself to rest, enjoyment, and practical philosophy. One day Mussard is digging in his garden when he comes across a great number of fossil shells. Mussard is so fascinated by the shells that he develops an entire cosmology based on them, in which everything is composed of shells, everything explained in terms of shells. Rousseau calls this "conchyliomania," the result of the creative imagination (the same creative imagination that creates the self) run amok, so that everything is connected with everything else, gaining its meaning only from its relation to shells. "Conchyliomania" is paranoid thinking (paranoia need not involve delusions of persecution; it is defined by the utterly systematic character of the delusions, in which everything is meaningfully connected to everything else).[24] This is the same thinking that characterizes much of the second part of Rousseau's *Confessions* regarding the Great Plot mounted by Diderot and others against him. Here is the flaw in the project of the modern self, suggests Hartle.[25] The imaginative reconstruction of the self ends up being little more than a paranoid projection, in which everything is connected to the self but only to defend the self against the chaos within: the fear that it is not connected to anything; indeed, the pieces of the self are not even connected to each other.

Hartle makes a powerful point, more powerful than she knows. It applies to the self of Rousseau, but it applies equally well to that of Augustine. What else is the Great Chain of Being, a hierarchy that connects God with the lowest animal so that every being has its proper place, but a paranoid projection?[26] This means not that Neoplatonism is a form of insanity but that it too is an act of creative imagination, designed to stave off the chaos within, not just without. But unlike Rousseau's creative imagination, Neoplatonism does not know itself to be imagination, believing itself to be insight into an objective order. If, however, we hold that it is not (or perhaps even if we hold that it is, as long as we are concerned with the self-psychological function of such a belief), then it is apparent that Neoplatonism is no alternative to Rousseau's creative imagination, but simply another version of it. It is a version sanctified by tradition and reinforced until recently by the most important institutions in society, but it remains a defense constructed by the cultural ego against the subject's fear of its own dissolution, experienced as a lack of connection to itself and to the world. It is, I argued, into a world in which this cultural defense was coming completely unglued that Hobbes stepped.

One might conclude from all this, as Lacan does (or rather, as one strand of Lacan's thought does), that the self does not exist. But why? This is the intellectually and morally honest choice only when the alternative is an act of "wild self-assertion" as Theodor Adorno calls it: aggression and rage, narcissistic rage, in response to the lack in the self. But it has been the point of this book to show that these are not the only two alternatives. To construct the unity of the self by an act of imagination (or by countless acts of imagination stretching over many years) that connects in a realistic way who one is with how one wants to be—an account that Kohut explains in terms of the bipolar self—need not be an act of the ego against the subject. Not if this account is constructed in full awareness that it is partial, provisional, serving to give the illusion of unity to what is actually a fragmented subject.

But perhaps this puts it too harshly. What else *could* the self be but this? A provisional partial unity created out of the imaginative integration of the events of one's life, events that may be categorized in terms of ambitions, talents, ideals, and so forth. Is this unity really an illusion? One must ask what illusion means here. If it is constructed with will and consciousness, in full awareness of the risks identified by Lacan, so that it is not merely a structuralization of the ego's defenses, then it is not clear that illusion is the appropriate term. That it is constructed, and in this sense artificial (that is, not God-given), as well as fragile, does not automatically make it an illusion. Indeed, the real illusion would seem to be the view of the self for which Bloom and Hartle seem so nostalgic: one that understands itself as a link in the Great Chain of Being, but only because it fails to understand that it has created this order out of its own subjective need, or rather, out of the need of the ego to defend against the chaotic, disconnected desires of the subject.

Furthermore, some such as Bloom seem to understand this objective order to which the self corresponds as a virtual "noble lie": literally false, but functional if all, including the guardians, believe it. Perhaps, but if the highest value is neither civil concord nor psychological harmony, but truth, then Lacan would seem to come closer to the mark—if, that is, he is read in the Faustian spirit recommended earlier, not as a raging, disappointed Platonist who will have no self if he cannot have a perfect one. Seen from this perspective, the problematic of the modern self offers possibilities for both good and evil. It may be more authentic than the Neoplatonic self, for it knows the constructed character of its selfhood. This knowledge, though, may send it into narcissistic retreat, particularly if the culture provides insufficient material out of which to construct a meaningful self, what MacIntyre calls the narrative unity of the self. Today this seems to be the case in much of the Western world, especially the United States. It is a catastrophe, but this cultural catastrophe should not be confused with the project of the modern self per se. This project retains the potential to be liberating.

Although Bloom's version of the noble lie is troublesome, others are less so, such as MacIntyre's narrative unity of the self. The danger of any such lie is that it serves as a weapon of the ego against the subject, splitting off and denying all those aspects of the self that contradict the ideal of unity. In the end, such lies only strengthen the archaic forces of the self. If, however, such a lie is told with will and consciousness—which means that the unity that it represents is understood to be a utopian ideal, true only in the sense that utopia is true: it exists nowhere—then it can be salutary. As Plato recognized, it is sometimes permissible to tell noble lies precisely because there is a truth of the matter. Because there is a truth we can distinguish noble lies from base lies from mere lies. It is only because there is a truth of the matter that it is possible to tell lies with will and consciousness. First, though, one must tell the truth.

The truth is that the constructed self is real, albeit so lacking in unity that it is generally in a state of desire for itself—for the unity it lacks. Frequently it seeks to bend others to its will in order to achieve evidence of its power, as though power over others could confer unity. It never does, at least not for long, and the self is forced once again to confront its own lack—or to escape from it. Virtuous noble lies, as they might be called, should encourage the self in this confrontation. One way they can do so is by valuing the Faustian will to truth about the self, finding worth in the search as well as the willingness to accept what is found. Stuart Schneiderman subtitles his study of Jacques Lacan *The Death of an Intellectual Hero*.[27] In so doing he reveals the narrative unity to such a life, including its tragic character. Another way the noble lie can encourage the self to confront itself is almost the opposite. It can render meaningful, even heroic, those everyday achievements of self-discovery and self-acceptance that often go unnoticed—all those things we do that signify an acceptance of ourselves as imperfect, incomplete, lacking, that is, all the things we do that acknowledge rather than seek to escape from the lack in being that is ourselves. Consider, for example, the wry smile to oneself when one becomes aware of a long-held fantasy of desire that one suddenly recognizes will never be (and perhaps never could be) fulfilled.

Although such virtuous noble lies will vary enormously, they will all have several features in common. First, they will not be built on narcissistic rage and resentment, in which the only alternatives are perfect selves or no selves. Nietzsche's "Übermensch" obviously fails this test; so too does the self that Lacan writes of (as distinct from Lacan's own practice). Instead, virtuous noble lies will create a space between ideal and real that may be filled by various approximations, tendencies, experiments, and so forth. Not merely the hero who daily strives to lessen the distance between ideal and real (if only by calling the real by its right name) but the man or woman who daily lives with the lack, finding in its acceptance a certain freedom and even joy, both belong in this space. Second, virtuous noble lies will not be myths of unity that can only defend ego against subject. This means that they will remind us at almost every turn that they are utopian: about nowhere. The lie itself has a playful quality, telling us not to take it too seriously. What Adorno says of philosophy applies also to the virtuous noble lie. It is the most serious of things, but then again it is not all that serious.

Third, and most important, virtuous noble lies will put the subject first. What this means is best explained by contrasting the virtuous noble lie with the mere lie that Nichols writes of in *Socrates and the Political Community*: "The city pretends that man is simple enough that he can live merely as a citizen. It pretends that it is the whole that satisfies or completes man. By insisting that it fulfills man's eros, it destroys man's eros." [28] There may be a purpose to such lies (the purpose of social order), but they should not be confused with the virtuous noble lie that I am proposing, the lie about the narrative unity of the self. The purpose of this lie is to protect and defend the self, to be its paladin, its champion. Putting the subject first does not mean, it has been argued at length, setting the individual against the world. It does mean that the interests of the subject come first, be it an I-self or a we-self.

Too often social theory has forgotten that it has a subject: the subject. Representing society and social order against the subject may still serve some of the interests of the subject, preventing his destruction at the hands of other desiring subjects, for example. But this should not be confused with representing the subject per se. Indeed, this confusion is such an enormous problem and temptation that perhaps it is best to turn Plato on his head here and restrict the noble lie to accounts that put the subject first. And what should we call all those accounts that put society first? We should call them the truth if in fact they are. The truth is that the subject must compromise, and be compromised, for the sake of the social order, and perhaps even for the sake of the subject. There is no alternative. Or rather, the alternative is to do what all the theorists considered (except Hobbes) do, Rousseau most of all. Represent this compromise as though it were actually the realization of true selfhood and the like—that is, tell the lie.

In response it might be argued that it is not the job of social theory to champion the subject, but rather, to seek the compromises just discussed. It is the job of the artist to champion the subject. Perhaps. What I am recommending with the virtuous noble lie is that the social theorist take over this artistic task. The virtuous noble lie *is* this artistic championing of the self, done with will and consciousness. To the social *scientist*, who sees in this program only the confusion of myth and reality, I have but two responses. First, in abandoning such virtuous noble lies, be careful that you are not abandoning more of the Western tradition than you recognize. As pointed out in chapter 1, a concern with the self as a center of value in its own right may be the last thread holding this tradition together. Second, be sure to tell only the truth: that the regimes you recommend generally serve the interests of social order against the subject. Hobbes came closest to this truth, and it is not pretty.

Notes

Chapter 1 Metaphysical Selves, Real Selves

1. James Walkup, "Introduction," *Social Research* 54, no. 1 (Spring 1987): 3–9, p. 5.

2. Michael Sandel, *Liberalism and the Limits of Justice*, p. 95.

3. For a discussion of the casual sense in which the term *metaphysics* is used in this manuscript, see chap. 7, p. 142.

4. Amy Gutmann, "Communitarian Critics of Liberalism," *Philosophy and Public Affairs* 14, no. 3 (1985): 308–322, p. 317.

5. Amelie Oksenberg Rorty, "Persons as Rhetorical Categories," *Social Research* 54, no. 1 (Spring 1987): 55–72.

6. Alfonso Damico made this argument to me.

7. Thomas Schelling, *The Strategy of Conflict*. Max Weber, *The Theory of Social and Economic Organization*.

8. Hume, *A Treatise of Human Nature*, Bks. I and II, 2 vols., ed. L. A. Selby Bigge, bk. I, pt. 4, sec. 6.

9. Kant, *Critique of Pure Reason*, trans. N. Kemp Smith, pp. 136–137 (pp. A 107–108 in the German first edition).

10. From entry titled "Self" in *The Compact Edition of the Oxford English Dictionary*.

11. C. H. Cooley, *Human Nature and the Social Order*, pp. 182–185. George McCall, "The Social Looking Glass: A Sociological Perspective on Self-Development," in *The Self: Psychological and Philosophical Issues*, ed. Theodore Mischel, 274–287, p. 274. I follow McCall closely on this topic.

12. Robert E. Park, "Human Nature and Collective Behavior," *American Journal of Sociology* 32 (1927): 733–741, p. 738. Quoted in McCall, "Social Looking Glass," p. 275.

13. Erving Goffman, *The Presentation of Self in Everyday Life*.

14. T. Mischel, Introduction to *The Self: Psychological and Philosophical Issues*, ed. T. Mischel, 3–30, pp. 23–24.

15. Charles Taylor, "What Is Human Agency?" in *Human Agency and Language, Philosophical Papers*, vol. 1, 15–44, pp. 23–24; quote from pp. 42–43. See also p. 34.

16. Alasdair MacIntyre, *After Virtue*, pp. 203–206. Allan Bloom, *The Closing of the American Mind*, pp. 173–179.

17. John Passmore, in *Times Literary Supplement*, May 26–June 1, 1989, pp. 567–568.

18. Taylor, "What Is Human Agency?" p. 44.

19. From a blurb by Taylor on the back cover of the Cambridge paperback edition (the one cited here) of *Liberalism and the Limits of Justice*.

20. Sandel, *Liberalism*, p. 95.

21. Ibid., pp. 62–63.

22. Norman O. Brown, *Love's Body*, pp. 146–147.

23. Sandel, *Liberalism*, pp. 148–152.

24. Ibid., p. 160.

25. Taylor, "What Is Human Agency?" pp. 21–26.

26. Sandel, *Liberalism*, p. 57.

27. Stephen Toulmin, "Self-Knowledge and Knowledge of the 'Self,'" in *The Self: Psychological and Philosophical Issues*, ed. Theodore Mischel, 291–317, pp. 311–312.

28. Sandel, *Liberalism*, pp. 78–81.

29. Taylor, "The Concept of a Person," in *Human Agency and Language, Philosophical Papers*, vol. 1, 97–114, pp. 109–114.

30. Said as quoted by Raymond Tallis, *Not Saussure: A Critique of Post-Saussurean Literary Theory*, p. 48.

31. Gutmann, "Communitarian Critics of Liberalism," pp. 308–309.

32. Roberto Unger, *Knowledge and Politics*, p. 228.

33. Freud, *Totem and Taboo*, p. 106.

34. Thomas Nagel, in *Times Literary Supplement*, July 8–14, 1988, pp. 747–748.

35. MacIntyre, *After Virtue*, p. 191.

36. MacIntyre, *Whose Justice? Whose Rationality?* p. 393.

37. MacIntyre, *After Virtue*, p. 205. Quoted by Emily Gill, "Goods, Virtues, and the Constitution of the Self," in *Liberals on Liberalism*, ed. Alfonso Damico, 111–128, pp. 120–121.

38. MacIntyre, "Moral Rationality, Tradition, and Aristotle," *Inquiry* 26, no. 4 (December 1983): 447–466, p. 451.

39. MacIntyre, *After Virtue*, p. 153. Gill, "Goods, Virtues," p. 121.

40. MacIntyre, *Whose Justice?* pp. 337–338, 346–347.

41. Alford, *Narcissism*, pp. 9–17.

42. Hume, *A Treatise of Human Nature*, bk. II, pt. 3, sec. 3.

43. Thomas Spragens, Jr., "Reconstructing Liberal Theory: Reason and Liberal Culture," in *Liberals on Liberalism*, ed. Damico, 34–53, p. 41.

44. Nancy Rosenblum, *Another Liberalism: Romanticism and the Reconstruction of Liberal Thought*, pp. 129–135.

45. Martha Nussbaum, *The Fragility of Goodness: Luck and Ethics in Greek Tragedy and Philosophy*, pp. 371, 357.

46. In "Technologies of the Self," in *Technologies of the Self: A Seminar with Michel Foucault*, ed. Luther Martin, Huck Gutman, and Patrick Hutton, pp. 16–49, Foucault seeks to separate the Delphic *gnothi sauton* (Know yourself) from the program he finds announced in *Alcibiades I*, 127d: *epimelesthai sautou* (to take care of yourself). Though Foucault had barely begun this project (the third volume of his *History of Sexuality*, titled *Care of the Self*, trans. Robert Hurley, is very narrowly focused) and thus its success cannot be evaluated, he clearly saw the risk involved. To care for oneself in the absence of self-knowledge promotes a hypochondriacal concern with the self as body (p. 29). Though I too question Plato's interpretation of *gnothi sauton*, my prescription is to draw a distinction between self-knowledge and self-consciousness, thus avoiding the problem—or

rather, the ironic and ludicrous circumstance—of a being caring for itself in the absence of both.

47. Charles Taylor, *Sources of the Self: The Making of the Modern Identity.*

48. Ibid., pp. 515–521. Martha Nussbaum, "Review of *Sources of the Self,*" in *The New Republic* (April 4, 1990): 27–34, p. 31. In fact, I make much the same argument as Nussbaum in my *Melanie Klein and Critical Social Theory: An Account of Politics, Art and Reason Based on Her Psychoanalytic Theory.*

49. Taylor, *Sources of the Self,* pp. 516–517.

Chapter 2 A Psychoanalytic Account of the Self: Kohut as Decentered by Lacan

1. Kohut holds to what he calls his "complementarity principle," according to which Freud's drive theory is best suited to explaining the oedipal neuroses, whereas self psychology is best suited to explaining the increasingly common and largely preoedipal disorders of the self. See *The Restoration of the Self,* pp. 77–78. It does not work. If driven behavior is the result of a breakdown of the self, as Kohut says it is, then does not a theory that views drives as primary miss the point? As Jay Greenberg and Stephen Mitchell put it in *Object Relations in Psychoanalytic Theory,* "The 'principle of complementarity' seems less designed to integrate two compatible and mutually enriching perspectives than to preserve an older framework that is conceptually incompatible with a newer one" (pp. 363–364). My attempt to blend Kohut and Lacan is sensitive to this problem.

2. J. Laplanche and J.-B. Pontalis, *The Language of Psycho-Analysis,* trans. Donald Nicholson-Smith, pp. 455–462 (entry on "Transference").

3. On this point, see Alford, *Narcissism,* pp. 53–71.

4. Kohut, *The Kohut Seminars,* ed. Miriam Elson, pp. 78–79; also pp. 297–307.

5. Ibid., pp. 78–79, 303–305; also pp. 40–42.

6. In his later work, Kohut posits a third selfobject transference, called the twinship or alterego transference. It is far less important and is never theoretically integrated (e.g., never given a pole of its own). See *Restoration of the Self,* p. 44. Kohut, *How Does Analysis Cure?* ed. Arnold Goldberg, pp. 193–199.

7. Kohut, *Restoration of the Self,* pp. 171–219.

8. Ibid., pp. 3–4. Kohut argues that a successful analysis may focus far more heavily on one pole than on the other; both need not be restored to health. How this fits with his argument that the fully developed self functions in a sectorial fashion, in which ambitions are connected to ideals via the tension arc, is not entirely clear, as it seems for this to happen both poles must be in good order.

9. Kohut, *Seminars,* p. 95. *Restoration of the Self,* pp. 30–33.

10. Ernest S. Wolf, "On the Developmental Line of Selfobject Relations," in *Advances in Self Psychology,* ed. Arnold Goldberg, 117–130, p. 130.

11. Greenberg and Mitchell, *Object Relations in Psychoanalytic Theory,* p. 369.

12. Kohut, *Seminars,* p. 29.

13. Kohut, *How Does Analysis Cure?* pp. 185, 208.

14. Wolf, "On the Developmental Line," p. 130.

15. Greenberg and Mitchell, *Object Relations in Psychoanalytic Theory*, pp. 371–372.

16. Kohut, "Thoughts on Narcissism and Narcissistic Rage," *Psychoanalytic Study of the Child* 27 (1973): 360–400. Reprinted in *Self Psychology and the Humanities*, ed. Charles Strozier, pp. 124–160.

17. Ibid., p. 386.

18. Ibid., p. 379.

19. Ibid., pp. 362, 382.

20. Laplanche and Pontalis, *Language of Psycho-Analysis*, pp. 427–430 (entries "Splitting of the Ego," "Splitting of the Object").

21. Sigmund Freud, "Splitting of the Ego in the Process of Defence" (1940), in *The Standard Edition of the Complete Psychological Works of Sigmund Freud*, 24 vols., ed. James Strachey, vol. 23, pp. 271–278.

22. Marian Tolpin, "Discussion of 'Psychoanalytic Developmental Theories of the Self: An Integration,'" in *Advances in Self Psychology*, 47–69, pp. 57–59.

23. This claim stems from an analysis of all the cases listed in the "Concordance of Cases," in *Restoration of the Self*, p. 329.

24. Otto Kernberg, *Borderline Conditions and Pathological Narcissism*, pp. 308–310.

25. Kohut is weak on this distinction. See *Seminars*, pp. 222–259.

26. Projective identification emphasizes the way in which our fears and desires make the environment. Kohut, on the other hand, pays more attention to the effect of the environment on the self. It is thus understandable why he would ignore the phenomenon, though the concept of projective identification is hardly incompatible with a Kohutian perspective. The concept of projective identification was developed by Melanie Klein, but has been used by a number of non-Kleinians. On this point, see R. D. Hinshelwood, *A Dictionary of Kleinian Thought*, esp. p. 182. See also Alford, *Melanie Klein and Critical Social Theory*, pp. 30–31, 65.

27. Kohut, *Self Psychology and the Humanities*, p. 235.

28. Kohut, *Restoration of the Self*, pp. 251–253.

29. Susan Grayson, "Rousseau and the Text as Self," in *Narcissism and the Text*, ed. Lynne Layton and Barbara Shapiro, pp. 78–96.

30. Martha Evans, "Introduction to Jacques Lacan's Lecture: The Neurotic's Individual Myth," *Psychoanalytic Quarterly* 48 (1979): 386–404.

31. Anthony Wilden, Translator's Introduction to *Speech and Language in Psychoanalysis*, by Jacques Lacan, trans. Wilden, pp. vii–xix.

32. Daniel Stern, *The Interpersonal World of the Infant: A View from Psychoanalysis and Developmental Psychology*, pp. 82–89.

33. Jacques Lacan, "The Mirror Stage as Formative of the Function of the I," *Ecrits*, trans. Alan Sheridan, pp. 1–7. (Hereafter the page numbers in *Ecrits* shall be cited, not the essay titles.)

34. Bice Benvenuto and Roger Kennedy, *The Works of Jacques Lacan*, p. 55. I follow Benvenuto and Kennedy closely at several points; they are remarkably clear.

35. *Ecrits*, pp. 6, 12. *Works of Jacques Lacan*, p. 57. Cf. Kohut, "Narcissistic Rage," pp. 384–385.

36. *Works of Jacques Lacan*, p. 207.

37. Lacan, "Some Reflections on the Ego," *International Journal of Psycho-Analysis* 34 (1953): 11–17, pp. 11–12. Quoted in John P. Muller, "Ego and Subject in Lacan," *Psychoanalytic Review* 69, no. 2 (1982): 234–240, p. 234.

38. *Works of Jacques Lacan*, p. 116.

39. *Ecrits*, p. 86. Louis A. Sass, "The Self and Its Vicissitudes: An 'Archaeological' Study of the Psychoanalytic Avant-Garde," *Social Research* 55 (Winter 1988): 551–608, pp. 600–601. I follow Sass closely in the first half of this paragraph.

40. Kohut, *Restoration of the Self*, p. 303.

41. Sass, "The Self and Its Vicissitudes," p. 604.

42. Ibid., p. 601, internal quote from Lacan, *Le séminaire*, vol. 1, p. 22 (translated by Muller, "Ego and Subject in Lacan," p. 240).

43. *Ecrits*, p. 300.

44. Sass, "The Self and Its Vicissitudes," p. 602.

45. Muller, "Ego and Subject in Lacan," p. 237.

46. Tallis, *Not Saussure*, p. 231. Internal quote from J. B. Leishmann's introduction to his translation of Rilke's *The Duino Elegies* (London: Hogarth Press, 1967).

47. Tallis, *Not Saussure*, p. 205.

48. Ibid., pp. 226–229; quote p. 229.

49. Evans, "Introduction to Jacques Lacan's Lecture," p. 393, gives the sources for these characterizations.

50. Muller, "Ego and Subject in Lacan," p. 240; emphasis mine.

51. *Self Psychology and the Humanities*, p. 22.

52. *Works of Jacques Lacan*, p. 61.

53. Nussbaum, *Fragility of Goodness*, p. 75.

54. Nietzsche, *Will to Power*, trans. W. Kaufmann and R. J. Hollingdale, p. 519, cf. p. 576. Quoted in Nussbaum, *Fragility of Goodness*, p. 161.

55. Theodor Adorno, *Negative Dialectics*, trans. E. B. Ashton, pp. 22–24.

Chapter 3 The Prehistory of the Self: The Psyche from Homer to Plato's *Gorgias*

1. *Psyche* is a standard transliteration of the Greek ψυχή. The upsilon is commonly rendered as a "y" when there is no diphthong. It will be noted when Plato is using the pronoun instead of the noun.

2. Leo Strauss, *The Political Philosophy of Hobbes*, trans. Elsa Sinclair, p. 128.

3. George Devereux, "Greek Pseudo-Homosexuality and the 'Greek Miracle,'" *Symbolae Osloenses* 42 (1967): 69–92.

4. Hans Kelsen, "Platonic Love," trans. George Wilbur, *American Imago* 3 (April 1942): 3–110, pp. 4–50.

5. Sigmund Freud, *Three Essays on the Theory of Sexuality*, trans. James Strachey, preface to the 4th ed., p. xviii. See also *Group Psychology and the Analysis of the Ego*, in *Standard Edition*, vol. 18, 67–143, p. 91.

6. George Boas, "Love," in *Encyclopedia of Philosophy*, ed. Paul Edwards, vol. 5, 89–95, p. 94.

7. F. M. Cornford, "The Doctrine of Eros in Plato's *Symposium*," in *The Unwritten Philosophy*, ed. W. K. C. Guthrie, pp. 71, 78.

8. Gerasimos Santas, *Plato and Freud: Two Theories of Love*, pp. 163–178.

9. A. W. Price, *Times Literary Supplement*, November 4–10, 1988, p. 466.

10. Desmond Lee, in comments on his translation of *The Republic* (Penguin Classics), states that "the literal translation of this well-known phrase is 'and seeing it, establish himself.' The alternative translations commonly given are 'establish himself as its citizen,' or 'establish himself accordingly,' i.e., 'establish it in himself.' The second alternative, here followed, seems to make better sense" (p. 420).

11. Sandel, *Liberalism and the Limits of Justice*, pp. 150–151. John Rawls, A *Theory of Justice*, p. 565.

12. J. Burnet, "The Socratic Doctrine of the Soul," in *Proceedings of the British Academy* (1916): 235–259. David Claus makes this point about Burnet in *Toward the Soul: An Inquiry into the Meaning of Psuche before Plato*, p. 108. Claus is my guide on this topic.

13. E. R. Dodds, *The Greeks and the Irrational*, p. 15.

14. Ibid., pp. 146–147.

15. Ibid., pp. 46–47.

16. Claus, *Toward the Soul*, p. 13. I am transliterating from the Greek.

17. Ibid., p. 101.

18. Ibid., pp. 107–109.

19. Ibid., pp. 153–155.

20. T. M. Robinson, *Plato's Psychology*, supp. vol. 8 of *Phoenix: Journal of the Classical Association of Canada*, p. 8. Robinson is my other guide on this topic.

21. Ibid., p. 50.

22. Santas, *Plato and Freud*, p. 186.

Chapter 4 The Psyche Divided against Itself: *The Republic, Timaeus,* and *Phaedrus*

1. Gary Wills uses this quotation as epigraph to his *Nixon Agonistes*.

2. George Klosko, *The Development of Plato's Political Theory*, p. 66.

3. Allan Bloom, "Interpretive Essay" accompanying his translation of *The Republic*, pp. 380–389. Mary Nichols, *Socrates and the Political Community*, p. 123. Nichols takes a somewhat harder line on this point.

4. Slater, *Glory of Hera*, pp. 75–121.

5. On this point see Alford, *Narcissism*, pp. 75–79.

6. A. W. H. Adkins, *Moral Values and Political Behavior in Ancient Greece*, pp. 70–71, 145–146.

7. Alford, *Narcissism*, pp. 95–97.

8. Or at least the penultimate statement on the *political* self. I assume that the treat-

ment of the self in book 10 has a closer affinity to the cosmological self in *Timaeus* and *Phaedrus*, discussed shortly.

9. Taylor, *Sources of the Self*, p. 143.

10. Kohut, *Restoration of the Self*, p. 177.

11. Robinson, *Plato's Psychology*, pp. 103–106.

12. I have not examined one of the most well-known and striking aspects of the dialogue, Plato's mechanical-cum-geometrical view of the human body, in which its framework is a series of triangles (81b–89e). Although one's impression is of a tremendous alienation from the organic body, it seems more fruitful with Plato to approach his concept of the self via the selfobject transference, and the triangles are not selfobjects (my approach with Hobbes is more direct). Greek thought reaching back to Homer tended to regard the body as a "paratactic aggregate," i.e., a collection of loosely integrated parts. This tradition may be in evidence here, too.

13. Charles Griswold, *Self-Knowledge in Plato's Phaedrus*, p. 101.

14. Robinson, *Plato's Psychology*, p. 117.

15. Ovid, *The Metamorphoses*, trans. Horace Gregory, pp. 464–468.

16. Gregory Vlastos, "The Individual as Object of Love in Plato's Dialogues," in *Platonic Studies*, 2nd ed., pp. 1–34. Quoted in Nussbaum, *Fragility of Goodness*, p. 166.

17. Nussbaum, *Fragility of Goodness*, p. 220.

18. Bernard Knox, "The Theater of Ethics," *New York Review of Books* 33 (December 4, 1986): 51–56.

19. Griswold, *Self-Knowledge in Plato's Phaedrus*, p. 128.

20. See Alford, *Narcissism*, chap. 3, for more examples.

21. Griswold, *Self-Knowledge in Plato's Phaedrus*, pp. 98, 112–114.

22. Ibid., pp. 92–93.

23. Nichols, *Socrates and the Political Community*, p. 137.

24. This is Nichols's position, pp. 153–180.

25. Santas, *Plato and Freud*, pp. 163–178.

26. Kohut, *Seminars*, p. 159.

27. Nichols, *Socrates and the Political Community*, p. 137.

28. Ibid., pp. 48, 63, 78.

29. *Les "Principes de politique" de Benjamin Constant*, ed. Etienne Hofmann, p. 426. Stephen Holmes, *Benjamin Constant and the Making of Modern Liberalism*, p. 95.

Chapter 5 Hobbes and the Archaic Self

1. Laurence Berns, "Thomas Hobbes," in *History of Political Philosophy*, 2nd ed., ed. Leo Strauss and Joseph Cropsey, 370–395, p. 375.

2. Strauss, *Political Philosophy of Hobbes*, pp. vii–viii.

3. C. B. Macpherson, *The Political Theory of Possessive Individualism: Hobbes to Locke*, p. 3.

4. Steven Lukes, *Individualism*, pp. 76–77.

5. Richard Peters, *Hobbes*, p. 226.

6. George Robertson, *Hobbes* (originally published, 1886), p. 57. Cited by David Johnston, *The Rhetoric of Leviathan: Thomas Hobbes and the Politics of Cultural Transformation*, p. xvi. Richard Ashcraft, "Ideology and Class in Hobbes' Political Theory," *Political Theory* 6 (1978): 39, challenges the unity of Hobbes's work from a different direction, focusing on the disjunction between Hobbes's earlier view of history as narrative and his later science of man. Noted by Johnston, *Rhetoric of Leviathan*, p. 4, who in effect rejects Ashcraft's position by focusing on the polemical continuity.

7. Berns, "Thomas Hobbes," p. 379. Hobbes, *Leviathan*, ed. C. B. Macpherson, p. 81.

8. Hobbes, *Leviathan*, p. 81. Sheldon Wolin, *Politics and Vision: Continuity and Innovation in Western Political Thought*, pp. 279–280.

9. *De Corpore* (originally published, 1655), in *The English Works of Thomas Hobbes*, 11 vols., ed. William Molesworth, vol. 1, p. 391.

10. R. S. Peters, "Thomas Hobbes," in *The Encyclopedia of Philosophy*, 8 vols., ed. Paul Edwards, vol. 4, p. 39.

11. Hobbes, *Leviathan*, p. 82.

12. Ibid., p. 83.

13. Albert Somit and Steven Peterson, "Biological Correlates of Political Behavior," in *Political Psychology*, ed. Margaret Hermann, pp. 11–38.

14. Hobbes, "Of the Life and History of Thucydides," introduction to his translation of Thucydides' *History* (originally published, 1629), in *English Works of Thomas Hobbes*, ed. Molesworth, vol. 8, pp. viii, xxi ff. Quoted by Strauss, *Political Philosophy of Hobbes*, p. 109.

15. Kohut, *Restoration of the Self*, pp. 120–125.

16. Johnston, *Rhetoric of Leviathan*, p. 208.

17. Arthur O. Lovejoy, *The Great Chain of Being*, p. 329, quote p. 207. Lovejoy notes that the Great Chain originates in the nonenvy of the god in Plato's *Timaeus* (29e–30d). It is because the god is nonenvious that his goodness overflows into that which is not perfect, starting the Great Chain (p. 315).

18. Ibid., p. 207. Verse attributed to Richardson's *Pamela*.

19. Ibid., chap. 6.

20. Nathan Tarcov, *Locke's Education for Liberty*, pp. 34–35, and nn. 169–170, cites the primary and secondary literature on this topic. The major sources in Hobbes are *The Elements of Law*, *De Cive*, and *Leviathan*. I follow Tarcov closely on Hobbes and the family.

21. Gordon Schochet, *Patriarchalism in Political Thought*, pp. 226, 236–243. Quoted by Tarcov, *Locke's Education*, p. 40.

22. *Philosophical Rudiments concerning Government and Society* (English version of *De Cive*), in *English Works of Thomas Hobbes*, ed. Molesworth, vol. 2, chap. 14, para. 9, pp. 189–190. Tarcov, *Locke's Education*, p. 41.

23. Christopher Lasch, *Haven in a Heartless World*, pp. 162–166.

24. Max Horkheimer, "Authority and the Family," in *Critical Theory*, trans. Matthew J. O'Connell et al., pp. 47–128.

25. Peters, *Hobbes*, p. 185; emphasis mine.

26. Hobbes, *Leviathan*, chap. 10, p. 150.

27. Macpherson, *Political Theory of Possessive Individualism*, pp. 41–46, and Strauss, *Political Philosophy of Hobbes*, pp. 8–12, disagree sharply on this point, Strauss in effect rejecting Macpherson's qualifications regarding power seeking.

28. Hobbes, *Leviathan*, chap. 11, p. 161. This is the key source for Macpherson's position.

29. Strauss, *Political Philosophy of Hobbes*, p. 44.

30. Ibid., and chaps. 4–5 generally.

31. Hobbes, *Leviathan*, chap. 10, pp. 155–156.

32. Jessica Benjamin, *The Bonds of Love*, pp. 51–85.

33. Strauss, *Political Philosophy of Hobbes*, p. 57.

34. Ibid.

35. Hobbes, Introduction to his translation of Thucydides' *History*, in *English Works of Thomas Hobbes*, ed. Molesworth, vol. 8, p. xxviii.

36. Hobbes, *Leviathan*, chap. 10, p. 150.

37. *The Elements of Law: Natural and Politic*, 2nd ed., ed. Ferdinand Tönnies, I.9.6. Quoted in Johnston, *Rhetoric of Leviathan*, p. 50.

38. Hobbes, *Leviathan*, chap. 14, p. 190.

39. Peters, "Thomas Hobbes," in *Encyclopedia of Philosophy*, vol. 4, p. 39. Hobbes's discourse on human nature is in *English Works of Hobbes*, ed. Molesworth, vol. 4, 1–77. See esp. pp. 31–36.

40. Allan Bloom, *The Closing of the American Mind*, p. 174.

41. Hobbes, *Leviathan*, chap. 13, p. 186.

42. Berns, "Thomas Hobbes," p. 389.

43. Max Horkheimer, "Authority and the Family," in *Critical Theory*, p. 101.

44. Hobbes, *Leviathan*, p. 232.

45. Hobbes's qualification that the sovereign may be a self-perpetuating assembly makes no difference. See *Leviathan*, chap. 17, p. 227. It is clear, in any case, that in virtually all his comments on the sovereign, Hobbes is thinking of a single man.

46. Hobbes, *Leviathan*, p. 238.

47. Wolin, *Politics and Vision*, p. 280.

48. Hobbes, *Leviathan*, p. 271.

49. Ibid., p. 272.

50. Wolin, *Politics and Vision*, p. 285.

51. Peters, *Hobbes*, p. 252.

52. Johnston, *Rhetoric of Leviathan*, pp. 71–91, gathers much evidence for the claim that *Leviathan* is aimed at the recently enlarged literate public. Indeed, this is the thesis of Johnston's book.

53. Hobbes, *Leviathan*, chap. 46, p. 698.

54. Johnston, *Rhetoric of Leviathan*, p. 147. Hobbes, *Leviathan*, chap. 38, pp. 483–484, chap. 44, pp. 644–649.

55. Johnston, *Rhetoric of Leviathan*, p. 184.

56. Alan Ryan, "Hobbes and Science," paper presented at the annual meeting of the American Political Science Association, Atlanta, Georgia, September 2, 1989.

57. Strauss, *Political Philosophy of Hobbes*, p. 93.

58. Hobbes, *Leviathan*, chap. 11, p. 166.

59. *Philosophical Rudiments*, in *English Works of Thomas Hobbes*, ed. Molesworth, vol. 2, chap. 3, para. 30, pp. 47–48. Wolin, *Politics and Vision*, p. 257.

60. Thucydides, *History*, bk. 3, para. 82.

61. Wolin, *Politics and Vision*, p. 260.

62. Hobbes, *Leviathan*, chap. 14, p. 191.

63. Macpherson, *Political Theory of Possessive Individualism*, p. 71.

64. Ibid., pp. 72–78.

65. Thomas Nagel, review in *Times Literary Supplement*, July 8–14, 1988, p. 747.

66. Wolin, *Politics and Vision*, p. 266.

67. Ibid.

68. Hobbes, *Leviathan*, p. 81.

69. Hobbes, *Philosophical Rudiments*, chap. 1, para. 3, p. 6.

70. Macpherson, *Political Theory of Possessive Individualism*, p. 68.

Chapter 6 Locke and the Self Held Hostage

1. Bloom, *Closing of the American Mind*, p. 173.

2. Ibid.

3. C. E. Vaughan, *Studies in the History of Political Philosophy Before and After Rousseau*, 2 vols., ed. A. G. Little, vol. 1, pp. 130–204. Willmoore Kendall, *John Locke and the Doctrine of Majority-Rule*, esp. pp. 112–119. Macpherson, *Political Theory of Possessive Individualism*, pp. 194–262. See also Macpherson's "The Social Bearing of Locke's Political Theory," *Western Political Quarterly* 7 (1954): 1–22. Reprinted in *Life, Liberty, and Property: Essays on Locke's Political Ideas*, ed. Gordon Schochet, pp. 60–85 (citations are to the reprint). John Dunn, *The Political Theory of John Locke*. Leo Strauss, *Natural Right and History*, pp. 222–230.

4. Macpherson, "Social Bearing of Locke's Political Theory," p. 76.

5. *Second Treatise of Government*, para. 123. As Peter Laslett points out in his introduction to his collation of Locke's *Two Treatises of Government*, rev. ed., except in his chapter on property or in other cases where material possession is the context, Locke employs the term *property* in its widest sense, referring to the things that are one's own (Laslett, pp. 114–117; on p. 367, note to para. 88, *Second Treatise*, Laslett lists Locke's extended uses of the term). Locke's extended use of the term was not unusual. As Laslett points out, it was not uncommon for men to "talk of the protestant religion established by law as their 'property,' and so forth (p. 116). It is on the basis of considerations like these that Macpherson defines possessive individualism as an attitude of ownership toward oneself (*Political Theory of Possessive Individualism*, p. 3).

The terms *property* and *propriety* both stem from the Latin *proprius*, "one's own." It is this that explains Locke's frequent switching back and forth between the two terms as though they were one—they are. *The Oxford English Dictionary* indicates that *property* and *propriety* were synonyms when Locke wrote. Hobbes also uses the terms as though they were identical (*Leviathan*, chap. 24, pp. 296–297 passim). Although this use is now obscure, it is still seen in the term *proprietary*, as in a *proprietary drug*. By the time Adam Smith wrote *The Theory of Moral Sentiments* (1759), which contains a long section titled "Of the Sense of Propriety," the term was being used in almost its modern sense, to refer to the appropriateness of an emotion or passion. James Glass argues that "in the language of liberalism, the synthesis of what property requires and what society needs came to be known as propriety or appropriateness of sentiment" ("Moral Sentiments and Moral Masochism: Problems in a Psychology of Self," p. 1, unpublished ms.). This fits Smith, about whom Glass is writing. One *wants* to say that it fits Locke, too, that Locke's frequent switching back and forth between the terms *property* and *propriety* shows that he was primarily concerned with our attitude or sentiments toward property, that we not become too greedy, acquisitive, and so forth. In fact, this is what I argue. Mine is not, however, an argument that depends on, or can be sustained by, the relation between these two terms. There is no pattern or meaning to Locke's shifts back and forth (or at least I cannot discern any). Locke is concerned with the appropriateness of one's attitude toward property, but the suggestive play of these two terms is not, in the end, very revealing about his project.

6. Macpherson argues that Locke has a class-based view of the self. There are, in effect, two views of the self in Locke's account (and therefore my focus on a single concept of the self in Locke's work must be misleading), in "Social Bearing of Locke's Political Theory," pp. 79–80. This point is not ignored.

7. Locke, *Second Treatise*, para. 6. (Laslett's collation of Locke's mss. is the basis.)

8. Ibid., para. 27–32.

9. Locke, *An Essay concerning Human Understanding*, ed. Peter Nidditch, 2.27.26.

10. Ibid., 2.27.28.

11. John Yolton, *Locke: An Introduction*, pp. 69–70.

12. Locke, *Some Thoughts concerning Education*, in *The Educational Writings of John Locke*, ed. James Axtell, para. 103–105.

13. Ibid., para. 105.

14. Ibid., para. 110.

15. Ibid.

16. Macpherson, *Political Theory of Possessive Individualism*, p. 237. Tarcov, *Locke's Education for Liberty*, pp. 142–143. *Second Treatise*, para. 34.

17. *Second Treatise*, para. 40–46.

18. *First Treatise*, para. 7.

19. John Yolton, *Locke and the Compass of Human Understanding*, pp. 183–184.

20. Dunn, *Political Theory of John Locke*, pp. 218–222.

21. Janine Chasseguet-Smirgel, *The Ego Ideal*, trans. P. Barrows, pp. 10–25.

22. *Second Treatise*, para. 44. See also para. 27–31.

23. Ibid., para. 88; cf. para. 123.

24. Laslett, *Two Treatises of Government*, pp. 116–117.

25. *Second Treatise*, para. 140.

26. Laslett, *Two Treatises of Government*, p. 118.

27. Norman O. Brown, *Love's Body*, pp. 145–146.

28. Macpherson, "Social Bearing of Locke's Political Theory," pp. 82–83.

29. Tarcov, *Locke's Education for Liberty*, p. 210.

30. Locke, *Essays on the Law of Nature*, ed. W. von Leyden, pp. 147, 123, 133. James Hancey, "John Locke and the Law of Nature," *Political Theory* 4, no. 4 (November 1976): 439–454, pp. 440–442.

31. Dunn, *Political Theory of John Locke*, pp. 187–189.

32. Locke, *The Reasonableness of Christianity*, in *The Works of John Locke*, 12th ed. (1824), vol. 2, pp. 139–140. Cited in Laslett, *Two Treatises of Government*, p. 101, and by Hancey, "John Locke and the Law of Nature," p. 444.

33. *Essay concerning Human Understanding*, 4.19.4.

34. Laslett, *Two Treatises of Government*, p. 106. *Second Treatise*, para. 6.

35. Hancey, "John Locke and the Law of Nature," p. 446.

36. Locke, "Some Thoughts concerning Reading and Study for a Gentleman," in *Educational Writings of John Locke*, ed. Axtell, 498–504, p. 500. *Thoughts concerning Education*, p. 112. Tarcov, *Locke's Education for Liberty*, pp. 1–8.

37. Macpherson, *Political Theory of Possessive Individualism*, p. 25, regarding Hobbes; "Social Bearing of Locke's Political Theory," p. 74.

38. *Thoughts concerning Education*, p. 144, n. 1, by Axtell. Maurice Cranston, *John Locke: A Biography*, p. 371.

39. *Thoughts concerning Education*, para. 33.

40. Cranston, *John Locke*, p. 347.

41. *Thoughts concerning Education*, para. 39, 53.

42. Ibid., para. 58.

43. Axtell, *Educational Writings of Locke*, p. 153.

44. Tarcov, *Locke's Education for Liberty*, p. 89. *Thoughts concerning Education*, para. 35.

45. *Thoughts concerning Education*, para. 42.

46. Adam Smith, *The Theory of Moral Sentiments*, ed. D. D. Raphael and A. L. Macfie, p. 134. Glass points this out in "Moral Sentiments and Moral Masochism."

47. Ibid., p. 137.

48. Strauss, *Natural Right and History*, pp. 222–230.

49. Macpherson, *Political Theory of Possessive Individualism*, pp. 103–106; "Social Bearing of Locke's Political Theory," pp. 74–75.

50. *Thoughts concerning Education*, para. 103–105.

51. Macpherson, "Social Bearing of Locke's Political Theory," pp. 74–75.

52. *Thoughts concerning Education*, para. 58.

53. Tarcov, *Locke's Education for Liberty*, pp. 72–73, quote p. 183.

54. Dunn, *Political Theory of John Locke*, pp. 82–83.

55. *Essay concerning Human Understanding*, 2.27.

56. Bloom, *Closing of the American Mind*, p. 177.

57. *Essay concerning Human Understanding*, 2.27.26.

58. Dunn, *Political Theory of John Locke*, p. 198.

59. John Jenkins, *Understanding Locke*, pp. 21–22.

60. *Essay concerning Human Understanding*, 2.23.5.

61. Christopher Foxe, *Locke and the Scriblerians: Identity and Consciousness in Early Eighteenth-Century Britain*. Quote from a review by John Mullan, "The Lost Soul," *Times Literary Supplement*, August 4–10, 1989, p. 853.

62. *Essay concerning Human Understanding*, 2.27.23.

63. Jenkins, *Understanding Locke*, pp. 117, 123–124. I follow Jenkins closely on this point. *Essay concerning Human Understanding*, 2.27.9, 2.27.21, 2.27.23.

64. *Essay concerning Human Understanding*, 2.27.4.

65. Ibid., 2.27.19.

66. Ibid., 2.27.23.

67. Kohut, *Self Psychology and the Humanities*, p. 236.

68. Jenkins, *Understanding Locke*, pp. 128–129.

69. Freud, "Introductory Lectures on Psychoanalysis," pt. III, in *Standard Edition*, vol. 16, 243–477, p. 434. Quoted by Jeffrey Abramson, *Liberation and Its Limits: The Moral and Political Thought of Freud*, p. 121.

70. Paul Ricoeur, *Freud and Philosophy: An Essay on Interpretation*, trans. D. Savage, p. 280. Quoted by Abramson, *Liberation and Its Limits*, p. 121.

Chapter 7 Rawls: Justice as Fearfulness

1. Taylor, "Concept of a Person," pp. 109–114.

2. John Rawls, "Justice as Fairness: Political, Not Metaphysical," *Philosophy and Public Affairs* 14, no. 3 (1985): 223–251. See also Rawls, "Kantian Constructivism in Moral Philosophy," *Journal of Philosophy* 77 (September 1980): 516–531, for a similar perspective on *A Theory of Justice*.

3. Charles Larmore, *Patterns of Moral Complexity*, p. 107.

4. Rawls, *Theory of Justice*, p. 12.

5. Rawls, "Justice as Fairness," p. 240.

6. Rawls, *Theory of Justice*, p. 440.

7. Sheldon Wolin, *Politics and Vision*, p. 329.

8. Kohut, *Restoration of the Self*, p. 24.

9. Robert Paul Wolff, *Understanding Rawls*, p. 80.

10. Rawls, *Theory of Justice*, pp. 152–153.

11. Ibid., p. 490.

12. Wolff, in *Understanding Rawls*, pp. 129–132, argues that in principle one cannot know the general laws of psychology behind the veil, as knowledge of even general laws of psychology requires intimate knowledge of oneself, such as that gained in the psychoanalytic transference. An insightful objection, it assumes that knowledge gained outside the original position cannot then be rendered abstract and objective and so made available to those behind the veil, an assumption that Wolff does not defend. In any case, Wolff's objection does not apply to the psychological knowledge that fear of loss is the dominant motivation, as Rawls assumes that this fear operates unreflectively in all human beings— i.e., it is not so much knowledge as nature.

13. Norman Frohlich and Joe Oppenheimer, "Principles of Distributive Justice: An

Empirical Approach," draft 1.4 (1989), unpublished ms. George Klosko and Karol Soltan made a number of helpful comments on this point.

14. Rawls, *Theory of Justice*, p. 180.

15. Ibid., p. 176.

16. Ibid., p. 152.

17. Ibid., p. 440.

18. Ibid., pp. 533–534.

19. Freud, "Group Psychology and the Analysis of the Ego," in *Standard Edition*, vol. 18, pp. 119–121.

20. Rawls, *Theory of Justice*, pp. 539–541.

21. Kohut, *Seminars*, pp. 78–79.

22. Rawls, *Theory of Justice*, p. 441.

23. Ibid., p. 464.

24. Ibid., pp. 490–491.

25. Ibid., p. 499.

26. Ibid., p. 445.

27. Ibid., pp. 565, 523.

28. Sandel, *Liberalism and the Limits of Justice*, pp. 147–152.

29. Rawls, *Theory of Justice*, p. 565. Kohut, *Seminars*, p. 159.

30. Hobbes, *Leviathan*, chap. 18, p. 232.

31. Rawls tries to distance himself from Hobbes, stressing that his is the social contract tradition of Locke, Rousseau, and Kant, not Hobbes. But because he never argues or shows *why* Hobbes is outside this tradition, this remains an assertion on Rawls's part. See *Theory of Justice*, pp. 11, 169.

32. Rawls, *Theory of Justice*, p. 561.

33. Ibid., p. 563.

Chapter 8 Rousseau: Political Theory in Defense of Self-Esteem

1. Allan Bloom, in his introduction to his translation of *Emile: or On Education*, p. 20.

2. Robert Nisbet, "Rousseau and Equality," in *Rousseau's Political Writings*, ed. Alan Ritter and Julia C. Bondanella, trans. Bondanella, 244–260, pp. 250–251. Originally published in *Encounter*, February 1974.

3. F. J. C. Hearnshaw, in *The Social and Political Ideas of Some Great French Thinkers of the Age of Reason*, ed. Hearnshaw, p. 172. Quoted by Peter Gay in his introduction to Ernst Cassirer's *The Question of Jean-Jacques Rousseau*, 2nd ed., trans. Gay, p. 15. English Showalter, Jr., "Madame de Graffigny and Rousseau: Between the Two *Discours*," in *Studies on Voltaire and the Eighteenth Century* 175 (1978), p. 89. Quoted in Susan Grayson, "Rousseau and the Text as Self," in *Narcissism and the Text*, ed. Lynne Layton and Barbara Ann Schapiro, 78–96, p. 78.

4. Paul de Man, *Allegories of Reading: Figural Language in Rousseau, Nietzsche, Rilke, and Proust*, pp. 135–136.

5. Emile Faguet, *Dix-huitième siècle*, 43rd ed. (Paris: Société française d'imprimerie et

de librairie, n.d.), p. 345. Quoted and translated by Gay in his Introduction to *Question of Jean-Jacques Rousseau*, p. 6. Ernest Barker, Introduction to *The Social Contract*, p. xxxviii. C. E. Vaughan, *The Political Writings of Jean-Jacques Rousseau*, 2 vols., vol. 1, pp. 80–81.

6. E. H. Wright, *The Meaning of Rousseau*, p. 32. Quoted in Gay, Introduction to *Question of Jean-Jacques Rousseau*, p. 20.

7. Cassirer, *Question of Jean-Jacques Rousseau*, trans. Gay, p. 127.

8. Ibid., p. 120. Rousseau, *Rousseau juge de Jean-Jacques*, and *Dialogues*, in *Oeuvres complètes*, vol. 9, p. 287 (3rd dialogue). Rousseau, *The Confessions*, trans. J. M. Cohen, p. 379 (book 9).

9. *Emile*, trans. Bloom, p. 33. There are frequent references to Locke's *Thoughts concerning Education* throughout *Emile*.

10. *Amour propre* is frequently translated as "vanity" or "pride." *Amour de soi* is the self-love that leads to self-preservation, not the desire to exceed others. Rousseau's most programmatic statement on these terms is found in a note to his *Discourse on the Origin and Foundations of Inequality among Men (Second Discourse)*, in *The First and Second Discourses*, ed. Roger Masters, trans. Roger and Judith Masters, pp. 221–222. In his notes to *Emile*, Bloom nicely distinguishes between amour propre and amour de soi, pp. 483–484, n. 17.

11. *Emile*, p. 68.

12. Bloom, Introduction to *Emile*, p. 10. *Emile*, pp. 64–69.

13. Bloom, Introduction to *Emile*, p. 11.

14. *Emile*, p. 67.

15. Ibid., pp. 223–226.

16. Bloom, Introduction to *Emile*, p. 17.

17. *Emile*, pp. 236–244.

18. Robert Nisbet, "Rousseau and Equality," p. 256.

19. Rousseau, *Discourse on Inequality*, p. 102.

20. Ibid., pp. 104–108.

21. Rousseau, *Dialogues, Rousseau juge de Jean-Jacques*, in *Oeuvres complètes*, vol. 9, p. 287.

22. Bloom, Introduction to *Emile*, p. 22.

23. Giacomo Casanova, *Mémoires (History of My Life)*, quoted from an excerpt in *Rousseau's Political Writings*, ed. Ritter and Bondanella, pp. 203–204. The editors of the Pléiade edition of the *Confessions* refer to Thérèse's baptismal certificate, indicating that she was the daughter of François Le Vasseur. Her last name may have been almost an anagram of Rousseau's own, but the significance is symbolic, not causal, as it were. Thanks are due to Charles Butterworth on this point.

24. *Emile*, p. 334. *Confessions*, books 3, 7. About this use of the term *supplément*, Jean Starobinski writes in *Jean-Jacques Rousseau: Transparency and Obstruction*, trans. Arthur Goldhammer, p. 179: "And Thérèse? She allows Jean-Jacques to stay within himself. She brings him the 'supplement' he needs. Supplement. The word is revealing. It occurs earlier, in the third book of the *Confessions*: 'I learned that dangerous *supplément*, or means of cheating nature (masturbation), which leads in young men of my temperament to various kinds of excesses that eventually imperil their health, their strength, and

sometimes their lives.' The use of this particular word shows us what Rousseau saw in Thérèse: someone he could easily identify with his own flesh and who never raised the problem of the *other*."

25. *Emile*, pp. 162–163. Rousseau tells us that he himself rejected a pension from the king. *Confessions*, pp. 353–354 (bk. 8).

26. *Emile*, p. 49.

27. Cassirer, *Question of Jean-Jacques Rousseau*, p. 62. *The Social Contract, or Principles of Political Right*, rev. trans. by Charles Sherover, para. 56 (bk. 1, chap. 8).

28. *Social Contract*, para. 440–441 (bk. 4, chap. 8).

29. Ibid., para. 54 (bk. 1, chap. 7). Rousseau restates this view of freedom, in which the alternative is not force but dependence, in the "Sixth Walk" of his *The Reveries of the Solitary Walker*, trans. Charles Butterworth, p. 83.

30. Starobinski, *Rousseau: Transparency and Obstruction*, pp. xxii–xxiii (from the introduction by Robert Morrissey, quoting Starobinski).

31. *Social Contract*, para. 54, 63, 86 (bk. 1, chap. 8, 10; bk. 2, chap. 4).

32. Starobinski, *Rousseau: Transparency and Obstruction*, p. xxiii (Introduction by Morrissey).

33. Bloom's Introduction to *Emile*, p. 12.

34. I explore these aspects of narcissism in *Narcissism*, pp. 53–69.

35. Leon Waynberg, "The Illusion of Independence: Narcissistic Aspects of Rousseau's Political Theory" (Ph.D. diss., University of Maryland, College Park, 1988). Although I have not returned to Waynberg's dissertation for several years, I was his chairman, and I know that his basic approach to Rousseau has rubbed off on me. Grayson, "Rousseau and the Text as Self."

36. Starobinski, *Rousseau: Transparency and Obstruction*, p. 179, and n. 147, pp. 394–395.

37. "Great principle": Gustave Lanson, *Histoire de la littérature française*, 8th ed., p. 769. Quoted and translated in Gay, Introduction to Cassirer, *Question of Jean-Jacques Rousseau*, pp. 17–18. "Evil originates outside the self . . .": Starobinski, *Rousseau: Transparency and Obstruction*, p. 17.

38. *Social Contract*, para. 104, 105, 257–258, passim (bk. 2, chap. 6; bk. 3, chap. 10).

39. Nisbet, "Rousseau and Equality," p. 245.

40. James Miller, *Rousseau: Dreamer of Democracy*, p. 119.

41. Ibid., p. 120.

42. Ibid.

43. Gay, Introduction to Cassirer, *Question of Jean-Jacques Rousseau*, pp. 27–28.

44. Miller, *Rousseau: Dreamer of Democracy*, pp. 15–16. As Miller puts it: "In truth, Geneva's government had 'none of the difficulties of democracy' because it was not one. It was a functioning oligarchy. To quote d'Alembert, 'Everything is under the direction of the Syndics, everything emanates from the Small Council for deliberation, and everything returns to it for execution.' By law, common Citizens could neither convene the General Council nor introduce legislation before it. Both powers were privileges of the Small Council."

45. Benjamin Barber, "Political Participation and the Creation of Res Publica," in

Rousseau's Political Writings, ed. Ritter and Bondanella, pp. 292–306. See also Barber's *Strong Democracy*, pp. 128, 200–202, 211–212, passim.

46. Judith N. Shklar, "Jean-Jacques Rousseau and Equality," in *Rousseau's Political Writings*, ed. Ritter and Bondanella, 260–274, p. 270. Originally published in *Daedalus*, Summer 1978. See also on this general point her *Men and Citizens: A Study of Rousseau's Social Theory*, pp. 12–32.

47. Shklar, "Jean-Jacques Rousseau and Equality," p. 271. *Social Contract*, para. 75–78, 140–145 (bk. 2, chap. 3, 12), captures this sense of isolation, though of course Rousseau does not put it this way, preferring to conceptualize isolation as formal community.

48. Shklar, "Jean-Jacques Rousseau and Equality," p. 271. See also on this point *Men and Citizens*, pp. 47–57.

49. James Glass, *Private Terror/Public Life: Psychosis and the Politics of Community*, pp. 94, 96, passim. Whether the political and healing functions of community can ever be combined is unclear to me.

Chapter 9 The Self and Its Discontents

1. Frithjof Bergmann, *On Being Free*, p. 37. Quoted by William Galston, *Justice and the Human Good*, p. 98.

2. Nancy Rosenblum, *Another Liberalism: Romanticism and the Reconstruction of Liberal Thought*, p. 20.

3. Glass, "Moral Sentiments and Moral Masochism," points this out about Smith.

4. Amelie Rorty, "Persons as Rhetorical Categories," p. 67.

5. Freud, *Civilization and Its Discontents*, trans. J. Strachey.

6. Bergmann, *On Being Free*, p. 99.

7. Alan Roland, *In Search of Self in India and Japan: Toward a Cross-Cultural Psychology*.

8. Theodor Adorno, "Sociology and Psychology," pt. 2, *New Left Review* 47 (1968): 79–97, p. 96.

9. Roland, *In Search of Self in India and Japan*, p. 8.

10. Ibid.

11. Ibid., pp. 100–101.

12. Ibid., pp. 226–227, 240.

13. Ibid., p. 240.

14. Ibid., p. 272. Kohut, *Kohut Seminars*, pp. 308–309. Joan Riviere, "Hate, Greed and Aggression," in *Love, Hate and Reparation*, by Riviere and Melanie Klein, p. 50.

15. Roland, *In Search of Self in India and Japan*, pp. 233, 285. See also pp. 226–227, 240.

16. Bruno Bettelheim, *The Children of the Dream*, pp. 171–172, passim. I am bending Bettelheim's interpretation slightly in order to fit Kohut's categories better.

17. A. I. Rabin and Benjamin Beit-Hallahmi, *Twenty Years Later: Kibbutz Children Grown Up*, pp. 55, 139–140, 161–162. This is a follow-up to Rabin's *Growing Up in the*

Kibbutz. Using standardized psychological tests (such as a Hebrew version of the MMPI), as well as a control group in a neighboring agricultural village, the authors find that the kibbutz-raised do not have as many close friendships as the control group; the kibbutz-raised also exhibit more "emotional inhibition." Obviously this does not prove Bettelheim's thesis. See also Stanley Diamond, "Personality Dynamics in an Israeli Collective," *History of Childhood Quarterly* 3 (1975): 1–41.

18. Rosenblum, *Another Liberalism*, pp. 79–80.

19. Ibid., p. 26. Constant, "De la liberté des anciens comparée à celle des modernes," in *Cours de politique constitutionnelle ou collection des ouvrages publiés sur le gouvernement représentatif*, 2 vols., ed. E. Laboulaye, vol. 2, p. 558, passim. Translated by Holmes, *Benjamin Constant and the Making of Modern Liberalism*, pp. 3, 10–20.

20. Rosenblum, *Another Liberalism*, p. 82.

21. Ibid., pp. 147, 151, quote pp. 149–150; emphasis mine.

22. Ann Hartle, *The Modern Self in Rousseau's Confessions: A Reply to St. Augustine*, p. 103.

23. Ibid., p. 151.

24. Rousseau, *Confessions*, p. 348. "Conchyliomania" is Hartle's translation. J. Laplanche and J.-B. Pontalis, *The Language of Psycho-Analysis*, trans. Donald Nicholson-Smith, pp. 296–297 (entry on "Paranoia"). Nietzsche's checking the newspapers immediately after he had a great idea in order to see if it was echoed by some significant world event, such as an earthquake, is exemplary.

25. Hartle, *The Modern Self*, pp. 118–122.

26. Although he does not, of course, use the term *paranoid projection*, Lovejoy emphasizes the assumption of universal connectivity in his essays in *The Great Chain of Being*. Furthermore, because its concepts were themselves so interconnected, the vulnerability of some, such as plenitude and sufficient reason, brought down the whole edifice in the modern era. See pp. 240–243, 315–333. On Augustine and the Great Chain, see pp. 71, 85–86, 159, 330.

27. Stuart Schneiderman, *Jacques Lacan: The Death of an Intellectual Hero*.

28. Nichols, *Socrates and the Political Community*, p. 137.

Works Cited

Classical sources given in the text in the form that is usual in classical studies are not repeated here.

Abramson, Jeffrey. *Liberation and Its Limits: The Social and Political Thought of Freud.* Boston: Beacon Press, 1984.

Adkins, A. W. H. *Moral Values and Political Behavior in Ancient Greece.* New York: W. W. Norton, 1972.

Adorno, Theodor. *Negative Dialectics.* Trans. E. B. Ashton. New York: Seabury Press, 1973.

———. "Sociology and Psychology." Pt. 2. *New Left Review* 47 (1968): 79–97.

Alford, C. Fred. *Melanie Klein and Critical Social Theory: An Account of Politics, Art and Reason Based on Her Psychoanalytic Theory.* New Haven: Yale University Press, 1989.

———. *Narcissism: Socrates, the Frankfurt School, and Psychoanalytic Theory.* New Haven: Yale University Press, 1988.

Ashcraft, Richard. "Ideology and Class in Hobbes' Political Theory." *Political Theory* 6 (1978): 27–62.

Barber, Benjamin. "Political Participation and the Creation of Res Publica." In *Rousseau's Political Writings.* Ed. Alan Ritter and Julia C. Bondanella, 292–306. New York: W. W. Norton, 1988.

———. *Strong Democracy: Participatory Politics for a New Age.* Berkeley and Los Angeles: University of California Press, 1984.

Barker, Ernest. "Introduction." In *The Social Contract.* New York: Oxford University Press, 1948.

Benjamin, Jessica. *The Bonds of Love.* New York: Pantheon Books, 1988.

Benvenuto, Bice, and Kennedy, Roger. *The Works of Jacques Lacan.* New York: St. Martin's Press, 1986.

Bergmann, Frithjof. *On Being Free.* Notre Dame, Ind.: University of Notre Dame Press, 1977.

Berns, Laurence. "Thomas Hobbes." In *History of Political Philosophy.* 2nd ed. Ed. Leo Strauss and Joseph Cropsey, 370–395. Chicago: Rand McNally, 1972.

Bettelheim, Bruno. *The Children of the Dream.* New York: Macmillan, 1969.

Bloom, Allan. *The Closing of the American Mind.* New York: Simon and Schuster, 1987.

———. "Interpretive Essay." In *The Republic.* Trans. Allan Bloom. New York: Basic Books, 1968.

———. "Introduction." In *Emile.* Trans. Allan Bloom. New York: Basic Books, 1979.

Boas, George. "Love." In *Encyclopedia of Philosophy*. Vol. 5. Ed. Paul Edwards. New York: Macmillan, 1967.

Brown, Norman O. *Love's Body*. New York: Vintage Books, 1966.

Burnet, J. "The Socratic Doctrine of the Soul." *Proceedings of the British Academy* (1916): 235–259.

Casanova, Giacomo. "Mémoires" ("History of My Life"). In *Rousseau's Political Writings*. Ed. Alan Ritter and Julia C. Bondanella, 203–204. New York: W. W. Norton, 1988.

Cassirer, Ernst. *The Question of Jean-Jacques Rousseau*. 2nd ed. Ed. and trans. Peter Gay. New Haven: Yale University Press, 1989.

Chasseguet-Smirgel, Janine. *The Ego Ideal*. Trans. Paul Barrows. New York: W. W. Norton, 1984.

Chodorow, Nancy. "Toward a Relational Individualism: The Mediation of Self through Psychoanalysis." In *Reconstructing Individualism: Autonomy, Individuality, and the Self in Western Thought*. Ed. Thomas Heller, Morton Sosna, and David Wellbery, 197–207. Stanford, Calif.: Stanford University Press, 1986.

Claus, David. *Toward the Soul: An Inquiry into the Meaning of Psuche before Plato*. New Haven: Yale University Press, 1981.

Compact Edition of the Oxford English Dictionary. Oxford: Oxford University Press, 1971.

Constant, Benjamin. "De la liberté des anciens comparée à celle des modernes." In *Cours de politique constitutionnelle ou collection des ouvrages publiés sur le gouvernement représentatif*. Vol. 2. Ed. E. Laboulaye. Paris: Guillaumin, 1872.

———. *Les "Principes de politique" de Benjamin Constant*. Ed. Etienne Hofmann. Geneva: Droz, 1980.

Cooley, C. H. *Human Nature and the Social Order*. New York: Scribner's, 1902.

Cornford, F. M. "The Doctrine of Eros in Plato's *Symposium*." In *The Unwritten Philosophy*. Ed. W. K. C. Guthrie, 68–80. Cambridge: Cambridge University Press, 1950.

Cranston, Maurice. *John Locke: A Biography*. London: Longmans, Green, 1957.

de Man, Paul. *Allegories of Reading: Figural Language in Rousseau, Nietzsche, Rilke, and Proust*. New Haven: Yale University Press, 1979.

Devereux, George. "Greek Pseudo-Homosexuality and the 'Greek Miracle.'" *Symbolae Osloenses* 42 (1967): 69–92.

Diamond, Stanley. "Personality Dynamics in an Israeli Collective." *History of Childhood Quarterly* 3 (1975): 1–41.

Dodds, E. R. *The Greeks and the Irrational*. Berkeley and Los Angeles: University of California Press, 1951.

Dunn, John. *The Political Theory of John Locke*. Cambridge: Cambridge University Press, 1969.

Evans, Martha. "Introduction to Jacques Lacan's Lecture: The Neurotic's Individual Myth." *Psychoanalytic Quarterly* 48 (1979): 386–404.

Faguet, Emile. *Dix-huitième siècle*. 43rd. ed. Paris: Société française d'imprimerie et de librairie, n.d.

Foucault, Michel. *Care of the Self: The History of Sexuality.* Vol. 3. Trans. Robert Hurley. New York: Pantheon, 1987.

———. "Technologies of the Self." In *Technologies of the Self: A Seminar with Michel Foucault.* Ed. Luther Martin, Huck Gutman, and Patrick Hutton, 16–49. Amherst: University of Massachusetts Press, 1988.

Foxe, Christopher. *Locke and the Scriblerians: Identity and Consciousness in Early Eighteenth-Century Britain.* Berkeley and Los Angeles: University of California Press, 1989.

Freud, Sigmund. *Civilization and Its Discontents.* Trans. J. Strachey. New York: W. W. Norton, 1961.

———. "Group Psychology and the Analysis of the Ego." In *The Standard Edition of the Complete Psychological Works of Sigmund Freud.* 24 vols. Ed. James Strachey. Vol. 18, 67–143. London: Hogarth Press, 1953–1974.

———. "Introductory Lectures on Psychoanalysis." Pt. III. In *The Standard Edition of the Complete Psychological Works of Sigmund Freud.* 24 vols. Ed. James Strachey. Vol. 16, 243–477. London: Hogarth Press, 1953–1974.

———. "Splitting of the Ego in the Process of Defence." In *The Standard Edition of the Complete Psychological Works of Sigmund Freud.* 24 vols. Ed. James Strachey. Vol. 23, 271–278. London: Hogarth Press, 1953–1974.

———. *Three Essays on the Theory of Sexuality.* 4th ed. Trans. James Strachey. New York: Basic Books, 1962.

———. *Totem and Taboo.* Trans. J. Strachey. New York: W. W. Norton, 1950.

Frohlich, Norman, and Oppenheimer, Joe. "Principles of Distributive Justice: An Empirical Approach," draft 1.4. Unpublished ms.

Gagnebin, Bernard, and Raymond, Marcel. *Confessions.* Vol. 1 of *Oeuvres complètes de Jean-Jacques Rousseau.* Paris: Gallimard, Editions de la Pléiade, 1959.

Galston, William. *Justice and the Human Good.* Chicago: University of Chicago Press, 1980.

Gay, Peter. "Introduction." In *The Question of Jean-Jacques Rousseau,* by Ernst Cassirer. 2nd ed. Ed. and trans. Peter Gay. New Haven: Yale University Press, 1989.

Gill, Emily. "Goods, Virtues, and the Constitution of the Self." In *Liberals on Liberalism.* Ed. Alfonso Damico, 111–128. Totowa, N.J.: Rowman and Littlefield, 1986.

Glass, James. "Moral Sentiments and Moral Masochism: Problems in a Psychology of Self." Unpublished ms.

———. *Private Terror/Public Life: Psychosis and the Politics of Community.* Ithaca, N.Y.: Cornell University Press, 1989.

Goffman, Erving. *The Presentation of Self in Everyday Life.* Garden City, N.Y.: Doubleday, 1957.

Grayson, Susan. "Rousseau and the Text as Self." In *Narcissism and the Text: Studies in the Literature and Psychology of Self.* Ed. Lynne Layton and Barbara Shapiro, 78–96. New York: New York University Press, 1986.

Greenberg, Jay, and Mitchell, Stephen. *Object Relations in Psychoanalytic Theory.* Cambridge, Mass.: Harvard University Press, 1983.

Griswold, Charles. *Self-Knowledge in Plato's Phaedrus.* New Haven: Yale University Press, 1986.

Gutmann, Amy. "Communitarian Critics of Liberalism." *Philosophy and Public Affairs* 14, no. 3 (1985): 308–322.

Hancey, James. "John Locke and the Law of Nature." *Political Theory* 4, no. 4 (November, 1976): 439–454.

Hartle, Ann. *The Modern Self in Rousseau's Confessions: A Reply to St. Augustine.* Notre Dame, Ind.: University of Notre Dame Press, 1983.

Hearnshaw, F. J. C., ed. *The Social and Political Ideas of Some Great French Thinkers of the Age of Reason.* London: Harrap, 1930.

Hobbes, Thomas. *De Corpore.* Vol. 1 of *The English Works of Thomas Hobbes.* Ed. William Molesworth. London: Bohn, 1839.

———. *The Elements of Law, Natural and Politic.* 2nd ed. Ed. Ferdinand Tönnies. London: Frank Cass, 1969.

———. *Leviathan.* Ed. C. B. Macpherson. Harmondsworth, England: Penguin Books, Pelican Classics, 1968.

———. "Of the Life and History of Thucydides." Introduction to his translation of Thucydides' *History.* In *The English Works of Thomas Hobbes.* Vol. 8. Ed. William Molesworth, xii–xxxii. London: Bohn, 1843.

———. *Philosophical Rudiments concerning Government and Society.* English version of *De Cive.* Vol. 2 of *The English Works of Thomas Hobbes.* Ed. William Molesworth. London: Bohn, 1841.

———. "Three Discourses: I. Human Nature; II. De Corpore Politico; III. Of Liberty and Necessity." In *The English Works of Thomas Hobbes.* Vol. 4. Ed. William Molesworth, 1–278. London: Bohn, 1840.

Holmes, Stephen. *Benjamin Constant and the Making of Modern Liberalism.* New Haven: Yale University Press, 1984.

Horkheimer, Max. "Authority and the Family." In *Critical Theory.* Trans. Matthew J. O'Connell et al., 47–128. New York: Seabury Press, 1972.

Hume, David. *A Treatise of Human Nature.* Bks. I and II. 2 vols. Ed. L. A. Selby Bigge. Oxford: Oxford University Press, 1888.

Jenkins, John. *Understanding Locke.* Edinburgh: Edinburgh University Press, 1983.

Johnston, David. *The Rhetoric of Leviathan: Thomas Hobbes and the Politics of Cultural Transformation.* Princeton, N.J.: Princeton University Press, 1986.

Kant, Immanuel. *Critique of Pure Reason.* Trans. N. Kemp Smith. London: Macmillan, 1963.

Kelsen, Hans. "Platonic Love." Trans. George Wilbur. *American Imago* 3 (April 1942): 3–110.

Kendall, Willmoore. *John Locke and the Doctrine of Majority-Rule.* Urbana: University of Illinois Press, 1941.

Kernberg, Otto. *Borderline Conditions and Pathological Narcissism.* New York: Jason Aronson, 1975.

Klosko, George. *The Development of Plato's Political Theory.* New York and London: Methuen, 1986.

Knox, Bernard. "The Theater of Ethics." *New York Review of Books* 33 (December 4, 1986): 51–56.

Kohut, Heinz. *How Does Analysis Cure?* Ed. Arnold Goldberg. Chicago: University of Chicago Press, 1984.

———. *The Kohut Seminars.* Ed. Miriam Elson. New York: W. W. Norton, 1987.

———. *The Restoration of the Self.* New York: International Universities Press, 1977.

———. *Self Psychology and the Humanities.* Ed. Charles Strozier. New York: W. W. Norton, 1985.

———. "Thoughts on Narcissism and Narcissistic Rage." *Psychoanalytic Study of the Child* 27 (1973): 360–400. (Reprinted in *Self Psychology and the Humanities,* 124–160.)

Lacan, Jacques. *Ecrits.* Trans. Alan Sheridan. New York: W. W. Norton, 1977.

———. "The Mirror Stage as Formative of the Function of the I." In *Ecrits.* Trans. Alan Sheridan, 1–7. New York: W. W. Norton, 1977.

———. *Le séminaire de Jacques Lacan.* Ed. Jacques-Alain Miller. Vol. 1. Paris: Editions du Seuil, 1975.

———. "Some Reflections on the Ego." *International Journal of Psycho-Analysis* 34 (1953): 11–17.

———. *Speech and Language in Psychoanalysis.* Translated with notes and commentary by Anthony Wilden. Baltimore: Johns Hopkins University Press, 1968. (Originally published as *The Language of the Self: The Function of Language in Psychoanalysis.*)

Lanson, Gustave. *Histoire de la littérature française.* 8th ed. Paris: Hachette, 1903.

Laplanche, J., and Pontalis, J.-B. *The Language of Psycho-Analysis.* Trans. Donald Nicholson-Smith. New York: W. W. Norton, 1973.

Larmore, Charles. *Patterns of Moral Complexity.* Cambridge: Cambridge University Press, 1987.

Lasch, Christopher. *The Culture of Narcissism.* New York: Warner Books, 1979.

———. *Haven in a Heartless World.* New York: Basic Books, 1979.

Laslett, Peter. Introduction to his collation of Locke's *Two Treatises of Government.* New York: New American Library, Mentor Books, 1963.

Lee, Desmond, trans. *Plato's Republic.* Harmondsworth, England: Penguin Classics, 1955.

Locke, John. *An Essay concerning Human Understanding.* Ed. Peter Nidditch. Oxford: Oxford University Press, Clarendon Press, 1975.

———. *Essays on the Law of Nature.* Ed. W. von Leyden. Oxford: Oxford University Press, Clarendon Press, 1954.

———. *The Reasonableness of Christianity.* Vol. 2 of *The Works of John Locke.* 12th ed. London, 1824.

———. "Some Thoughts concerning Education." In *The Educational Writings of John Locke.* Ed. James Axtell, 111–325. Cambridge: Cambridge University Press, 1968.

———. "Some Thoughts concerning Reading and Study for a Gentleman." In *The Educational Writings of John Locke.* Ed. James Axtell, 498–504. Cambridge: Cambridge University Press, 1968.

Lovejoy, Arthur. *The Great Chain of Being*. Cambridge, Mass.: Harvard University Press, 1957.

Lukes, Steven. *Individualism*. Oxford: Basil Blackwell, 1973.

McCall, George. "The Social Looking Glass: A Sociological Perspective on Self-Development." In *The Self: Psychological and Philosophical Issues*. Ed. Theodore Mischel, 274–287. Oxford: Basil Blackwell, 1977.

MacIntyre, Alasdair. *After Virtue*. Notre Dame, Ind.: University of Notre Dame Press, 1981.

———. "Moral Rationality, Tradition, and Aristotle." *Inquiry* 26, no. 4 (December 1983): 447–466.

———. *Whose Justice? Which Rationality?* Notre Dame, Ind.: University of Notre Dame Press, 1988.

Macpherson, C. B. *The Political Theory of Possessive Individualism: Hobbes to Locke*. Oxford: Oxford University Press, 1962.

———. "The Social Bearing of Locke's Political Theory." *Western Political Quarterly* 7 (1954): 1–22. (Reprinted in *Life, Liberty, and Property: Essays on Locke's Political Ideas*. Ed. Gordon Schochet, 60–85. Belmont, Calif.: Wadsworth Publishing, 1971.)

Miller, James. *Rousseau: Dreamer of Democracy*. New Haven: Yale University Press, 1984.

Mischel, Theodore. "Introduction." In *The Self: Psychological and Philosophical Issues*. Ed. Theodore Mischel, 3–30. Oxford: Basil Blackwell, 1977.

Mullen, John. "The Lost Soul." *Times Literary Supplement*, August 4–10, 1989, 853.

Muller, J. P. "Ego and Subject in Lacan." *Psychoanalytic Review* 69, no. 2 (1982): 234–240.

Nagel, Thomas. "Review of MacIntyre's *Whose Justice? Which Rationality?*" *Times Literary Supplement*, July 8–14, 1988, 747–748.

Nichols, Mary. *Socrates and the Political Community*. Albany: State University of New York Press, 1987.

Nietzsche, Friedrich. *The Will to Power*. Trans. W. Kaufmann and R. J. Hollingdale. New York: Random House, 1967.

Nisbet, Robert. "Rousseau and Equality." In *Rousseau's Political Writings*. Ed. Alan Ritter and Julia C. Bondanella, 244–260. New York: W. W. Norton, 1988. (Originally published in *Encounter*, February 1974.)

Nussbaum, Martha. *The Fragility of Goodness: Luck and Ethics in Greek Tragedy and Philosophy*. Cambridge: Cambridge University Press, 1986.

———. "Review of *Sources of the Self*." *New Republic*, April 4, 1990, 27–34.

Ovid. *The Metamorphoses*. Trans. Horace Gregory. New York: Viking, 1958.

Park, Robert E. "Human Nature and Collective Behavior." *American Journal of Sociology* 32 (1927): 733–741.

Passmore, John. "Review of *The Voice of Liberal Learning: Michael Oakeshott on Education*." *Times Literary Supplement*, May 26–June 1, 1989, 567–568.

Peters, Richard. *Hobbes*. Harmondsworth, England: Penguin Books, 1956.

———. "Thomas Hobbes." In *The Encyclopedia of Philosophy*. Vol. 4. Ed. Paul Edwards. New York: Macmillan, 1967.

Price, A. W. "Review of *Plato and Freud.*" *Times Literary Supplement*, November 4–10, 1988, 466.

Rabin, A. I. *Growing Up in the Kibbutz*. New York: Springer, 1965.

Rabin, A. I., and Beit-Hallahmi, Benjamin. *Twenty Years Later: Kibbutz Children Grown Up*. New York: Springer, 1982.

Rawls, John. "Justice as Fairness: Political, Not Metaphysical." *Philosophy and Public Affairs* 14, no. 3 (1985): 223–251.

———. "Kantian Constructivism in Moral Philosophy." *Journal of Philosophy* 77 (September 1980): 516–531.

———. *A Theory of Justice*. Cambridge, Mass.: Harvard University Press, Belknap Press, 1971.

Ricoeur, Paul. *Freud and Philosophy: An Essay on Interpretation*. Trans. D. Savage. New Haven: Yale University Press, 1970.

Riviere, Joan. "Hate, Greed and Aggression." In *Love, Hate and Reparation*, by Joan Riviere and Melanie Klein, 3–56. New York: W. W. Norton, 1964.

Robertson, George. *Hobbes*. Edinburgh and London: William Blackwood and Sons, 1910.

Robinson, T. M. *Plato's Psychology*. Supp. Vol. 8 of *Phoenix: Journal of the Classical Association of Canada*. (Published by University of Toronto Press.)

Roland, Alan. *In Search of the Self in India and Japan*. Princeton, N.J.: Princeton University Press, 1988.

Rorty, Amelie Oksenberg. "Persons as Rhetorical Categories." *Social Research* 54 (Spring 1987): 55–72.

Rosenblum, Nancy. *Another Liberalism: Romanticism and the Reconstruction of Liberal Thought*. Cambridge, Mass.: Harvard University Press, 1987.

Rousseau, Jean-Jacques. *Confessions*. Trans. J. M. Cohen. Harmondsworth, England: Penguin Books, 1953.

———. "Discourse on the Origin and Foundations of Inequality among Men." ("Second Discourse.") In *The First and Second Discourses*. Trans. R. Masters and J. Masters, 77–228. New York: St. Martin's Press, 1964.

———. *Emile*. Trans. Allan Bloom. New York: Basic Books, 1979.

———. *The Reveries of the Solitary Walker*. Trans. Charles Butterworth. New York: New York University Press, 1979.

———. *Rousseau juge de Jean-Jacques, Dialogues*. Vol. 9 of *Oeuvres complètes*. Paris: Hatchette, 1871–1877.

———. *The Social Contract, or Principles of Political Right*. Trans. Charles Sherover. New York: New American Library. Meridian Books, 1974.

Ryan, Alan. "Hobbes and Science." Paper presented at the annual meeting of the American Political Science Association, Atlanta, Georgia, September 2, 1989.

Sandel, Michael. *Liberalism and the Limits of Justice*. Cambridge: Cambridge University Press, 1982.

Santas, Gerasimos. *Plato and Freud: Two Theories of Love*. Oxford: Basil Blackwell, 1988.

Sass, Louis A. "The Self and Its Vicissitudes: An 'Archaeological' Study of the Psycho-analytic Avant-Garde." *Social Research* 55 (Winter 1988): 551–608.

Schelling, Thomas. *The Strategy of Conflict*. Cambridge, Mass.: Harvard University Press, 1960.

Schneiderman, Stuart. *Jacques Lacan: The Death of an Intellectual Hero*. Cambridge, Mass.: Harvard University Press, 1983.

Schochet, Gordon. *Patriarchalism in Political Thought*. Oxford: Oxford University Press, 1975.

Shklar, Judith. "Jean-Jacques Rousseau and Equality." In *Rousseau's Political Writings*. Ed. Alan Ritter and Julia C. Bondanella, 260–274. New York: W. W. Norton, 1988. (Originally published in *Daedalus*, Summer 1978.)

―――. *Men and Citizens: A Study of Rousseau's Social Theory*. Cambridge: Cambridge University Press, 1969.

Showalter, English. "Madame de Graffigny and Rousseau: Between the Two Discours." *Studies on Voltaire and the Eighteenth Century* 175 (1978): 84–92.

Slater, Philip. *The Glory of Hera: Greek Mythology and the Greek Family*. Boston: Beacon Press, 1968.

Smith, Adam. *The Theory of Moral Sentiments*. Ed. D. D. Raphael and A. L. Macfie. Indianapolis: Liberty Press, 1976.

Somit, Albert, and Peterson, Steven. "Biological Correlates of Political Behavior." In *Political Psychology*. Ed. Margaret Hermann, 11–38. San Francisco: Jossey-Bass, 1986.

Spragens, Thomas, Jr. "Reconstructing Liberal Theory: Reason and Liberal Culture." In *Liberals on Liberalism*. Ed. Alfonso Damico, 34–53. Totowa, N.J.: Rowman and Littlefield, 1986.

Starobinski, Jean. *Jean-Jacques Rousseau: Transparency and Obstruction*. Trans. Arthur Goldhammer. Introduction by Robert Morrissey. Chicago: University of Chicago Press, 1988.

Stern, Daniel. *The Interpersonal World of the Infant: A View from Psychoanalysis and Developmental Psychology*. New York: Basic Books, 1985.

Strauss, Leo. *Natural Right and History*. Chicago: University of Chicago Press, 1953.

―――. *The Political Philosophy of Hobbes*. Trans. Elsa Sinclair. Chicago: University of Chicago Press, Midway Reprint, 1984.

Tallis, Raymond. *Not Saussure: A Critique of Post-Saussurean Literary Theory*. London: Macmillan, 1988.

Tarcov, Nathan. *Locke's Education for Liberty*. Chicago: University of Chicago Press, 1984.

Taylor, Charles. "The Concept of a Person." In *Human Agency and Language, Philosophical Papers*. Vol. 1, 97–114. Cambridge: Cambridge University Press, 1985.

―――. *Sources of the Self: The Making of the Modern Identity*. Cambridge, Mass.: Harvard University Press, 1989.

―――. "What Is Human Agency?" In *Human Agency and Language, Philosophical Papers*. Vol. 1, 15–44. Cambridge: Cambridge University Press, 1985.

Tolpin, Marian. "Discussion of 'Psychoanalytic Developmental Theories of the Self: An Integration.'" In *Advances in Self Psychology*. Ed. Arnold Goldberg, 47–69. New York: International Universities Press, 1980.

Toulmin, Stephen. "Self Knowledge and Knowledge of the 'Self.'" In *The Self: Psychological and Philosophical Issues*. Ed. Theodore Mischel, 291–317. Oxford: Basil Blackwell, 1977.

Unger, Roberto. *Knowledge and Politics*. New York: Free Press, 1975.

Vaughan, C. E. *The Political Writings of Jean-Jacques Rousseau*. 2 vols. Oxford: Basil Blackwell, 1962.

———. *Studies in the History of Political Philosophy Before and After Rousseau*. 2 vols. Ed. A. G. Little. New York: Russell and Russell, 1960.

Vlastos, Gregory. "The Individual as Object of Love in Plato's Dialogues." In *Platonic Studies*. 2nd ed., 1–34. Princeton, N.J.: Princeton University Press, 1981.

Walkup, James. "Introduction." *Social Research* 54 (Spring 1987): 3–9. (Special issue, Reflections on the Self.)

Waynberg, Leon. "The Illusion of Independence: Narcissistic Aspects of Rousseau's Political Theory." Ph.D. diss. University of Maryland, College Park, 1988.

Weber, Max. *The Theory of Social and Economic Organization*. New York: Oxford University Press, 1947.

Wills, Gary. *Nixon Agonistes*. Boston: Houghton Mifflin, 1969.

Wolf, Ernest. "On the Developmental Line of Selfobject Relations." In *Advances in Self Psychology*. Ed. Arnold Goldberg, 117–130. New York: International Universities Press, 1980.

Wolff, Robert Paul. *Understanding Rawls*. Princeton, N.J.: Princeton University Press, 1977.

Wolin, Sheldon. *Politics and Vision: Continuity and Innovation in Western Political Thought*. Boston: Little, Brown, 1960.

Wright, E. H. *The Meaning of Rousseau*. London: Oxford University Press, 1929.

Yolton, John. *Locke and the Compass of Human Understanding*. Cambridge: Cambridge University Press, 1970.

———. *Locke: An Introduction*. London: Basil Blackwell, 1985.

Index

metaphysical selves, 42–43; Plato's polis and, 64, 68–69; and Locke, 113–14; achievement of, 138; and Rawls, 154–55; and autarky, 165–66, 169; myths of, 185–86, 190; illusion of, 188; and noble lie, 190

Values, 175
Vaughan, C. E., 113, 158
Virtue, 94–99, 130–31

Walkup, James, 1
Waynberg, Leon, 208 n35
We-self: and definitional categories, 178;

and separation-individuation process, 179; inner life of, 179–82
Wholeness. *See* Unity of self
Wolf, Ernest, 26, 28–29
Wolff, Robert Paul, 143, 205 n12
Wolin, Sheldon, 86, 173; and Hobbes, 101, 102, 105, 107–08; *Politics and Vision*, 142–43, 144
Women, in ancient Greece, 66–67
World body psyche, in Plato, 71–72, 73
Wright, E. H., 158

Yolton, John, 115–16, 118, 125